Inside the Internet's Resource reSerVation Protocol

Inside the Internet's Resource reSerVation Protocol

Foundations for Quality of Service

David Durham
Raj Yavatkar

Wiley Computer Publishing

John Wiley & Sons, Inc.

NEW YORK · CHICHESTER · WEINHEIM · BRISBANE · SINGAPORE · TORONTO

Publisher: Robert Ipsen
Editor: Carol Long
Managing Editor: Brian Snapp
Text Design & Composition: North Market Street Graphics, Lancaster, PA

This publication is designed to provide accurate and authoritative information in regard to the subject matter covered. It is sold with the understanding that the publisher is not engaged in professional services. If professional advice or other expert assistance is required, the services of a competent professional person should be sought.

Library of Congress Cataloging-in-Publication Data:
Durham, David. 1973–
    Inside the Internet's Resource reSerVation Protocol : foundations
for quality of service / David Durham, Raj Yavatkar.
      p.   cm.
    ISBN 0-471-32214-8 (cloth/website : alk. paper)
    1. Computer network protocols.   2. Telecommunication—Traffic
—Management.   3. Internet (Computer network)   I. Yavatkar, Raj.
II. Title.
TK5105.55.D87   1999
004.67'8—dc21   99-21790
                                              CIP

0-471-32214-8

Printed in the United States of America.

10 9 8 7 6 5 4 3 2 1

CONTENTS

ACKNOWLEDGMENTS

Writing a book is a gargantuan undertaking requiring the contributions and support of a number of individuals. I would like to thank my co-author, Raj Yavatkar, for devoting his time, energy, and great insights to this work. Lenitra Clay was invaluable in helping me research topics for this book as well as editing some of my unreadable first drafts. Pankaj Parmar also helped me configure a test network so I could get the example programs up and running. Finally, I would like to acknowledge Carol Long for teaching us how to write a book and for her amazing patience throughout.

—Dave

First and foremost, I must thank my co-author, David Durham, for his efforts in driving many aspects of this book. Without his drive and repeated cajoling, we would not have finished the book on such a short schedule. I would also like to thank the members of the PC-RSVP team who have been involved in implementation of RSVP, SBM, and traffic control for both Intel routers and Microsoft Windows family of operating systems. My understanding of RSVP and IntServ has benefited greatly from my frequent discussions with the team members. I am also grateful to my friend, Prof. Lixia Zhang, for writing the Foreword for this book despite her busy schedule. As a principal designer of RSVP, Lixia has been one of the main drivers behind the vision of Internet QoS and her endorsement of our efforts means a lot to us. Last but not the least, I am always thankful to my lovely wife, Neeta, and my daughters, Mallika and Manali, for being wonderful.

—Raj

The origin of the RSVP protocol can be traced back to 1991 when I and some other researchers were playing with new packet scheduling algorithms on the DARTNET (DARPA Testbed Network), a network testbed made of dedicated T1 lines and routers. Packet scheduling algorithms simply shuffle the processing order of incoming packets according to some established rates or priorities. To test scheduling algorithms one needs a way to set up state at routers along data flow paths.

In 1991 IP multicast was deployed on the DARTNET, and soon after VAT (Virtual Audio Tool) started being used for weekly teleconferencing over the DARTNET. Due to its sensitivity to delay VAT makes an ideal application for testing scheduling algorithms, yet making resource reservations for VAT requires a multicast-capable state set-up protocol. I was challenged to design a set-up protocol that could support many-to-many multicast applications. My work led to the birth of RSVP.

When the protocol was first conceived, I had no idea that RSVP would grow to become an important piece of the Internet protocol suite. Over the years many people contributed to the success of the protocol through the development, implementation, and deployment process. In particular Bob Braden deserves special credit. Bob and I have co-chaired the IETF RSVP Working Group since 1993 which led the process that moved RSVP from its original design to an Internet Proposed Standard Protocol. As a signaling protocol designed specifically for the Internet, RSVP has a number of novel ideas but getting to those ideas may seem difficult. At first glance the protocol tends to give an impression of being complicated in addition to being a sizable specification.

I am delighted to see the publication of this first book devoted specifically to RSVP. It demystifies RSVP by giving the reader a step-by-step, easy to follow path. It provides complete coverage of the protocol, ranging from the basic concepts to policy control and APIs. The authors, Raj and Dave, are long-time contributors to RSVP development. In this book they share with the reader their first-hand experience from years of implementation and usage.

The effort that started RSVP design is but our first step in developing automatic resource management tools for the Internet. As the Internet moves on, our protocol development effort will necessarily continue to develop new tools for the new needs. I believe, however, that RSVP has addressed the basic concepts and fundamental issues involved in QoS, and because of that premise those who develop a good understanding of RSVP will gain lasting knowledge that extends beyond the protocol itself into daily practical application.

Enjoy your reading.
Lixia Zhang
Professor
UCLA Computer Science Department

A process which led from the amoeba to man appeared to the philosophers to be obviously a progress—though whether the amoeba would agree with this opinion is not known.

—BERTRAND RUSSELL (1872–1970)

Quality of Service, or QoS for short, has become the seemingly unattainable goal of the Internet community for many years now. QoS is the general ability of systems to differentiate between communications traffic in order to provide different levels of service. It represents a fundamental methodology shift from what the Internet has always been, a one-class, best-effort network for all communication.

Given this, it is certainly fair to say QoS is not easy to implement in the context of the Internet. It has repercussions for applications, network devices, network administrators, and end users alike. Nevertheless, QoS is not an uncommon concept in our daily lives. When one wants to mail a package, a number of service options are available. Is that package going to be sent overnight, second-day, or how about just your basic ground rate? If QoS is available though the postal system, then why not through computer data networks? In computer data networks, the question of service is related to the requirements of a particular application: Do you want to make a voice call, or watch a video stream, or perhaps just send an e-mail? These questions are all related to determining what is meant by the timely delivery of a given quality of data.

The questions QoS raises are clear. The solutions can be complex but, as this book will demonstrate, they are real and available today. They are also needed, because without the ability to provide a number of data transfer services, the Internet will remain inadequate for several real-time and interactive network applications that are emerging today.

In this book we will examine a complete set of technologies that work together to actually enable QoS on the Internet. Central to this theme is a protocol that allows applications to describe their requirements to the network so that it can provide the required data transmission service. This is the function of the Resource reSerVation Protocol, or RSVP, and the central topic of this work.

How This Book Is Organized

This book was designed to build on itself, one chapter at a time. It begins by motivating the problem of QoS by examining different types of networking technologies and their properties. The foundational technologies and protocols responsible for the inner workings of the Internet are then reviewed with an eye toward QoS. After a helping of review, you will be given the opportunity to examine newer Internet technologies that allow for efficient multiuser applications of the Internet. The book then takes on the problem of supporting QoS in the Internet—what it means and what its ramifications are. The underlying technologies for supporting QoS are investigated one by one, from protocols to networks and then from mechanisms to administration. We will also provide background for those who are interested in developing applications for QoS-enabled networks. Finally, if you're one of those seeking the tangible, this book includes several sample programs to drive RSVP home.

Chapter 1: Motivation for Quality of Service

This chapter emphasizes the need for QoS in the Internet. It investigates a variety of existing QoS networking technologies in order to uncover their fundamental technical properties. To these, the traditional Internet is compared and contrasted. From this comparison, we proceed to explain the fundamental properties of an integrated network that can provide a variety of services in support of a variety of applications.

Chapter 2: Overview of Internet Technologies

In Chapter 2 you'll dive into the technologies and protocols underlying the Internet—the network of networks. This chapter should be a useful refresher for those already experienced with the details, and it will provide a necessary introduction for those new to the game. It is important to understand what the Internet is before one can understand how it will change. As you review, we will point out how the traditional Internet protocol suites interact with a QoS enabled infrastructure.

Chapter 3: Internet Multicasting

Multipoint communications is one of the most innovative extensions to the Internet today. Internet multicasting raises a host of new possibilities and their corresponding problems for the Internet. In this chapter you'll review the various multicasting technologies, see why they are useful, and examine the kinds of applications they enable. Multipoint communication is an important technological direction for the Internet and one of the driving factors behind the design of RSVP.

Chapter 4: The Internet with Quality of Service: A Conceptual Overview

In Chapter 4 you'll begin to uncover an Internet that can support the integration of a diverse range of services. Here, you'll investigate the kinds of services that a QoS-enabled Internet can support and the applications they enable. Specifically, you'll look at the Integrated Services architecture and its relevant components. This chapter lays the foundation for the design of the RSVP protocol and its necessary supporting technologies.

Chapter 5: Fundamentals of the Resource reSerVation Protocol

RSVP is emerging as the standard protocol for signaling QoS requests to the Internet's infrastructure. It is used by transmitting applications to describe their traffic characteristics, and receiving applications to describe their QoS requirements. RSVP interacts with all capable devices in the network so that the components that actually facilitate QoS understand which resources they need to allocate and for whom. This chapter introduces RSVP as a networking protocol and investigates its properties and functionality.

Chapter 6: Advanced Concepts in RSVP

After RSVP has been introduced in Chapter 6, you'll dive into more advanced topics surrounding the protocol. RSVP is a relatively complex protocol because it can support a variety of services enabling many different kinds of applications. RSVP not only signals the application's traffic characteristics and requirements, but also communicates to the application the network capabilities. Furthermore, RSVP tackles the intricacies of signaling QoS for multicast applications. In this chapter we describe the types of complex problems that RSVP admirably solves.

Chapter 7: Traffic Control

QoS cannot be achieved unless traffic can be controlled. Controlling who sends what and how fast is the job of traffic control, which prevents data communication from one application from negatively impacting the data communications of another. Essentially, traffic control is like the traffic officer who decides who may go and who must stop. Without it the roads and freeways of the Internet would degrade into chaos, from the perspective of QoS. In Chapter 7 we delve into this important component of the QoS architecture.

Chapter 8: Odds and Ends—Differentiated Services and the Last Mile Problem

RSVP is an extensible and flexible protocol applicable to a wide range of networking technologies. In this chapter we discuss some simple extensions to the basic protocol that allow it to be used to reserve resources even over shared network technologies. You'll also learn how RSVP can be mapped onto existing networking technologies that already support QoS functionality. Finally, we will examine the emerging Differentiated Services architecture for providing scalable QoS in the Internet and the applicability of RSVP for delivering quantitative QoS in its model.

Chapter 9: Policy Control and Monitoring for RSVP

Providing different levels of Quality of Service raises important administrative questions. There must be mechanisms for determining who gets what QoS. In a general sense, RSVP usage must be controlled by administratively defined policies. Furthermore, if different services are available, it is useful to know who has reserved which resources. When high-quality service comes at a premium, there needs to be a way to account for its usage. In this chapter we'll review some of the relevant technologies for enabling policy control and monitoring for RSVP.

Chapter 10: QoS-Aware Applications

In Chapter 10 we describe the development of QoS-aware applications. Specifically, we address some of the important issues in the design of real-time applications. You'll also learn about transport mechanisms for applications and their interaction with a QoS-enabled infrastructure. Finally, we'll offer several simple sample programs that make use of popular QoS APIs for RSVP. We leave the reader with the tools to begin experimenting with RSVP and its capabilities.

Who Should Read This Book

This book is for all those who are interested in real technologies for implementing Quality of Service in the Internet today. If you're a network administrator, you will discover the mechanics behind RSVP-enabled networks and the ramifications the technology will have on your network. If you're an application developer, we will show you how to develop real-time applications that are QoS ready. If you're an end user, we can show you what new possibilities QoS-enabled networks may present for you. If you're a technologist, we will show you how RSVP and its QoS components actually work and what they do. Or perhaps, if you're a businessperson looking out for the next big thing in the fast-paced world of internetworking, then just maybe we can help you, too. Finally, if you just want to know what it takes to make QoS actually happen, then please turn the page and begin reading.

PART ONE

Motivation and Background

CHAPTER 1

Motivation for Quality of Service

What Is Quality of Service?

The popularity and widespread use of the World Wide Web (WWW) has caused Internet access to become ubiquitous. However, exponentially increasing traffic and the inability of the Internet infrastructure to cope with the demands have also led to a phenomenon known as the "World Wide Wait." The term *Quality of Service* (QoS) refers to the performance seen by an end user (or an Internet application) across a network or the Internet. This performance can be measured in a variety of ways: time taken to download a Web page, the audio quality of a phone call placed across the Internet (also known as a *voice call* using IP Telephony), or the video quality of a real-time video presentation. In an Internet that offers good QoS, an individual user should be able to ask for and consistently receive a reasonable level of performance irrespective of the amount of other traffic on the Internet. In this chapter, we discuss the term QoS in more detail, describing the underlying technologies and the motivation for introducing new protocols and mechanisms to improve QoS.

Real-Life Analogies to Quality of Service

In some sense, QoS is a rather obvious concept. Have you ever had to wait in the coach line at the airport ticket counter while the first-class line was empty? Remember sitting in traffic during rush hour while vehicles zoomed by in the carpool lane? Or, closer to the computer-networking world, have you ever waited, seemingly forever, for a Web page to be downloaded to your PC? If so, then Quality of Service, or the lack thereof, is an intuitive concept. Another example of QoS from real life is the postal delivery service. Consumers typically have a choice in terms of the kind of QoS they want; a letter mailed via ordinary mail receives an altogether different QoS than the letter mailed using an overnight delivery service. Currently, the Internet does not offer such a choice of differentiated QoS. However, the Internet industry is in the process of deploying new standards that will enable such services. This book describes the standards and mechanisms for implementing end-to-end Quality of Service for computer data networks in general, and the Internet in particular.

In simple terms, Quality of Service in data networks can be measured with respect to the rate at which data can consistently be transmitted across the network. This measurement reflects many important characteristics of the network such as its size (both in terms of the physical distance covered and the number of nodes that must be traversed), and the capacity of its communication links. This measurement should also take into account the delays encountered at various components along the path of the data traffic. Finally, the characteristics of other competing traffic on a network must also be considered. A network's ability to consistently provide some bounds in terms of data transmission rates and delays can roughly determine the Quality of Service offered by the network.

A real-life analogy to the preceding discussion is a car en route from its starting point to its destination. Here the car represents a single piece or unit of data that must travel across a data network. Along its path, the car may have to negotiate several freeways, side roads, and city streets. It may be delayed at stoplights and tollbooths. Finally, the competing traffic, caused by the number of other vehicles, introduces a large degree of unpredictability. These conditions combine to create a commuting environment in which one can roughly estimate the amount of time it takes to travel to a particular destination on a daily basis. Nevertheless, no guarantees can be made, as some variance is expected. Sometimes unforeseen circumstances may cause a large deviation from the rough estimate and such delays may be unacceptable. Showing up late for work may be the implication in the commuting environment. In the case of the Internet, if the delayed traffic belongs to a voice call, users participating in the call may experience unacceptable communication quality characterized by intermittent gaps, awkward interruptions, or cross-talk in the conversation. What is required is a way to regulate traffic so that traffic delays can be avoided altogether.

Application Requirements for QoS

From the perspective of this book, computer networks that lack Quality of Service are more than just occasionally inconvenient, they are a major impediment to implementing certain kinds of applications. Traffic from real-time audio and video applications such as videoconferencing, radio broadcasts, and Internet town hall meetings require predictable service in terms of dedicated bandwidth and bounds on amount of delay experienced by the data being communicated. In addition, mission-critical applications such as enterprise resource planning (ERP) and electronic commerce (e-commerce) need guaranteed QoS to ensure timely response and processing of business transactions. Also, applications that depend on feedback, such as remote control of industrial robots, processes, or instruments (e.g., space telescopes) require guaranteed QoS to ensure correct operation.

Given the size, scope, and utility of the Internet, it can never be expected to meet the individual levels of QoS needed by the diverse set of its consumers and applications. However, the Internet must move beyond its current paradigm of "service for all, but guarantees for none" to a new paradigm that can distinguish among its users and applications to provide a set of differentiated services designed to accommodate the demands of different kinds of traffic. In particular, the Internet's protocols and mechanisms must be extended to a level where it can provide predictable performance. This will result in an integrated network that can enable new types of real-time and interactive applications.

To lay the groundwork for such mechanisms and protocols, we will use the remainder of this chapter to compare and contrast two conceptually different kinds of networks: packet switched data networks such as the Internet, and traditional real-time communications networks such as the public telephone network. The first kind of network is primarily interested in the transmission of digital data, while the second is interested in providing real-time interactive voice communication. We will then explore how services offered by these two styles of networks can be combined into a single integrated network. Such an integrated network forms the theoretical foundation for the remainder of this book and serves as the context from which we will introduce the Resource ReSerVation Protocol (RSVP) for use in the Internet.

Packet Switched Networks

Ever since its inception as a military and academic project, the Internet has been essentially designed to do one thing—transport digital data. Actually, there was a bit more to it than that. This Packet Switched Network was designed to transport data to a varied number of destinations, perhaps even under the Armageddon-like conditions of a third world war . . . at least to the extent that the network could be fault-tolerant in terms of recovery from broken links and lost data.

The U.S. military required a data network to link its computers across multiple bases and institutions around the world. The network had to be highly fault-tolerant so that the data could flow even under circumstances where connectivity could only be provided through an unstable mesh of interconnected computers. This integrated military network was under the Defense Advanced Research Projects Agency (DARPA) program and eventually led to the creation of the National Science Foundation Network (NSFnet) and what is known today as the Internet. Today, however, people send e-mail and surf the Web instead of just performing military simulations or participating in high-energy physics research.

The key to the Internet, since its earliest days, is the concept of the datagram. A datagram is simply a packet of self-addressed data that can be treated independently from all other packets. It describes where it is to go as well as where it came from. As the Internet has grown, it has become a large-scale datagram network or wide area network (WAN). The connotation is obvious in that a datagram on the network is capable of traversing great distances and reaching computers in faraway countries as readily as the computer in the next room. A wide area network can consist of many different types of smaller networks all interconnected on a larger scale. These individual networks are typically called local area networks or LANs. A LAN is generally composed of a single type of network that only needs to serve a relatively small number of computers. LANs can be interconnected by WANs. WANs can be connected to other WANs, and so on until datagrams can traverse the entire globe.

Packet Switched Networks Described

Data is transferred across the Internet in discrete, self-addressed datagrams of information also known as *packets*. These packets have analogies to the U.S. mail system where an envelope encapsulates a letter, which is essentially just information. A single packet in the Internet contains information in the form of source and destination addresses describing where it is going and where it originated. Such addresses are highly akin to the addresses found on an envelope. The addressing information is used to route the packet from its source to its destination. In between its source and destination, the packet is moved from computer to computer, or network to network, exclusively based on its addressing information.

Examining the postal analogy in more detail, the envelope consists of a sender address and a receiver address. A person may write a letter and place it within the envelope. The envelope is then dropped into a mailbox. If all goes well, at some point in the future, the envelope will be delivered to its destination. There, the letter can be read and possibly a response returned to the sender.

Similarly, a computer can generate various forms of digital information. This information can take an endless number of forms such as an e-mail, a data file, or just a single character of text. If the information is destined for a remote location, the computer can encapsulate the data into a packet. This packet will be addressed from the current computer to some remote computer, its final destination. Finally, the packet is released into the network and, if all goes well, will eventually be received at the destination computer.

What happens between the source and destination is termed *routing*, and again there is a postal service analogy. A local postal carrier collects each letter from a mailbox, effectively the source. This letter will be taken to the local post office. Based on the destination address, the letter is sorted for delivery to another regional distributing postal department where it is delivered by truck, train, or plane. At the regional distribution center the letter is again sorted and prepared for delivery to the next distribution center. Some may be accidentally delivered to the wrong distribution center or even the wrong address. As the letter always provides the right addressing information, such anomalies in the delivery process can be rectified. Eventually, the letter will reach a post office near its destination where a local carrier will physically deliver the letter to its final destination.

Likewise, the route over which a packet proceeds basically consists of computers linked together by direct links or shared LANs. One computer will receive a new packet and, based on the address within the packet, will send it to another computer closer to its ultimate destination. This process will continue until the packet reaches the local network where its ultimate destination is located. The receiving host should then receive the packet and verify it was the intended destination for the packet. Finally, the end host can proceed to process the data in the packet. Fortunately, such storing and forwarding of packets of computer data is significantly faster than the physical act of sending a letter.

Best-Effort Quality of Service

It is important to understand that each packet in the Internet is treated independently from all others. This means that a computer that receives a packet decides what is next for that particular packet by examining its particular addressing information. If multiple potential routes exist, one packet may follow a route different from another similarly addressed packet due to their independent treatment. The result is that packets may be delayed, dropped, or even reordered by the network. The packet delivery process is truly best-effort in that no guarantees are made that a packet will ever even reach its intended destination, let alone reach it in any reasonable period of time.

Delay is an important characteristic of the network that needs to be bounded in order to achieve QoS. The amount of time it takes to deliver a packet to its destination depends mainly on three factors: propagation delay, transmission delay, and buffering or queuing delay.

Propagation delay is incurred because the digital data must travel the distance between a packet's source and its destination. Ultimately, the speed of light through a particular medium of transport (e.g., electrons through copper wire) determines the absolute minimum of this delay.

The other two delay factors are a function of how the digital data is transmitted and forwarded. A packet must traverse one or more links before it reaches its destination. Intermediate links are interconnected using routers or packet forwarders. In general, a packet transverses a network by visiting the network's intermediate links and routers one hop at a time. Every time a packet is transmitted over a link, it incurs *transmission delay*. This is the amount of time it takes to transmit the packet over a link. For example, if the link's data rate is 100 bytes per second, it takes one second to transmit a packet containing 100 bytes of data.

Once a packet arrives, a router must process at least some portion of the packet in order to determine the next hop to which the packet is to be forwarded. The time it takes for this operation to complete is dependent on the processing power of the router itself. In addition, the router may buffer the packet for some time if it arrives before the router has completed processing the preceding packet or packets. The total time for this stop-and-go process (called *queuing delay*) is the cumulative processing and buffering time of each routing device along the data path.

This store-and-forward nature of data networks allows packets that must traverse slow or aggregated links to be stored if the link is busy transmitting other data. Obviously, if there were no way to store packets, anytime two packets had to be simultaneously forwarded out the same link, one packet would have to be dropped. Large buffers can be used to store packets from periods of high congestion and send them later when the congestion clears. The result is that the reliability of the network improves at the expense of having to delay some packets in buffers while they wait for link availability.

Fundamentally, data networks tend to be unreliable in that a packet of data is not guaranteed to ever reach its destination. It can be lost anywhere along the path due to misbehaving nodes, congested links, or any other conceivable fault. Anyone who has ever heard the phrase "the check is in the mail" knows that another postal analogy probably can be found as well. An individual package of information set loose in the real world always faces the possibility of getting lost and discarded. In computer data networks, it is up to the communicating end stations to expect the possibility of lost data and take the appropriate measures to send such data again when it has been determined to be lost.

Packet switched data networks do provide a considerable amount of flexibility. They scale very well for data applications and can service a huge number of simultaneous users. When data networks become congested, they simply slow down, they won't turn off or create busy signals. Data can be sent to and received from the network at any time. Nevertheless, the best-effort service that is offered by packet switched networks needs to be revised to support differentiated QoS. Highly delayed, reordered, or even missing data is unacceptable for certain classes of applications. There needs to be guarantees that such applications can receive the service they require. We will begin to investigate networks that deliver well-defined QoS by examining the traditional telephone network.

Telephony Real-Time Networks

A phone network is in some ways similar to a packet switched data network. Primarily the differences are not due to the underlying technology, but rather the high-level service guarantees provided by the network. While it may be acceptable to wait an hour or two for an e-mail message to traverse a computer network, it is not acceptable to say "hello" into the receiver of a phone and wait an hour for the other party to respond. Likewise, although it may be acceptable for a computer to send information multiple times due to lost or damaged packets, a phone conversation over line noise where both parties must constantly repeat themselves is unacceptable.

Phone networks are interested in committing a fixed amount of resources to the parties engaged in a telephone call. The resources allocated are generally based on the amount of information that can consistently be sent over the network or, simply, network bandwidth. It is important that the network be able to send enough data so that the human voice can be easily discerned.

A phone network is also typically interested in providing very specific functionality—that is, the capability for one person to talk to another. Essentially, a connection needs to be set up between the source, or the person initiating the call, and the destination, or the person receiving the call. Additionally, because a phone conversation generally needs to be perceived as continuous, it is necessary to allow the data to continuously flow over the connection. To accomplish this, a fixed amount of resources (whatever amount is required to transmit the human voice) is allocated between the source and the destination for the duration of the connection. The connection itself is established based on the number dialed. The process of dialing the number causes the phone network to set up a path for the data to flow between the two participating phones for the duration of the call.

An example of connection establishment can be taken from the early days of telecommunications. Then a phone connection was established by directly connecting, or switching, copper wires along the path that the voice signal was to take. Phone operators were responsible for actually making the proper connections. Once connected, an analog amplitude modulated signal could be sent from the sender's microphone to the receiver's headset speaker. Essentially, a complete circuit would be set up between two phones.

Digital Telecommunications

Telecommunication networks have evolved a long way from the early days of simple circuits and analog signals. The main improvement was moving from all-analog networks to digital networks. There were two main reasons for going digital. For one, digital signals improved the quality of the networks, reducing noise and cross-talk from other conversations. Second, running large numbers of wires to and from everyone with a phone was becoming a hassle and quite an eyesore in large metropolitan areas. With the advent of the digital age, one wire could be used to communicate multiple voice signals. Specifically, many wires carrying analog signals could be aggregated over a single wire carrying a digital signal. Such aggregation effectively reduced the total number of wires required to communicate the same amount of information simultaneously. Figure 1.1 graphically demonstrates how multiple analog voice circuits can be aggregated over a single digital link.

This process of aggregating a number of connections over a single wire requires the ability to translate the analog signal generated by a telephone into a digital signal. After the digital trunk, the digital signal would be retranslated into an analog signal and sent on to the receiving phone's headset. The result of the analog to digital and digital to analog transformation would be some signal loss, as a finite digital signal can only represent a finite amount of the entire analog spectrum.

Converting an analog signal into a digital signal is accomplished by an analog to digital converter. Such a device is capable of continuously measuring an analog signal over time and producing a digital result. It will typically take some small amount of time to measure, or sample, the analog signal. This measurement can be described as the aptitude of an

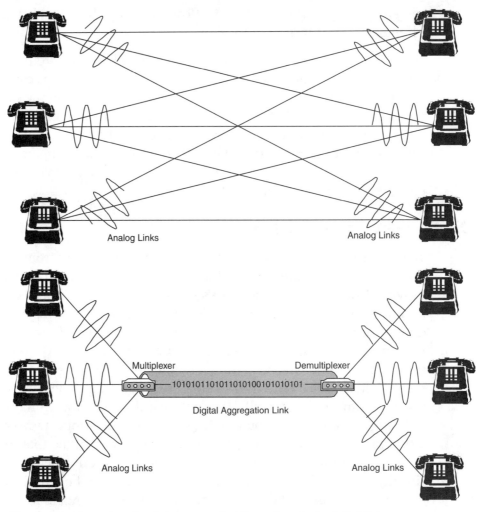

Figure 1.1 Several analog links aggregated through a single digital link.

analog signal for a moment in time. Samples can be taken of an analog signal back-to-back thousands of times per second. Figure 1.2 relates an analog signal to its digital counterpart for a given time interval.

The problem of analog to digital transformation of human speech can be equated in practical terms. For purposes of communicating the human voice, a data rate of 64,000 bits per second is more than sufficient. This is due to the fact that human speech occupies frequencies between 300 and 3300 hertz (or cycles per second). Simply rounding up the higher frequency gives 4000 hertz. The Nyquist criterion [Digital-Systems] requires double the highest analog frequency for the accurate

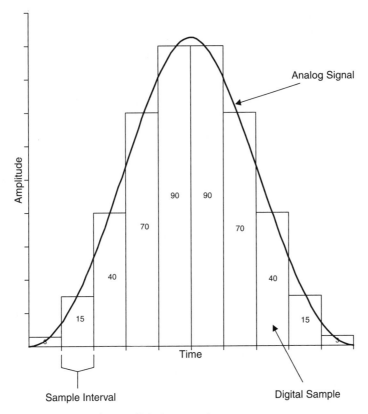

Figure 1.2 Analog to digital conversion.

reconstruction of an analog waveform. Thus, 8000 hertz is an appropriate sampling rate for human speech. Assuming 1 byte per sample we have 8000 samples/second times 8 bits/sample or a data rate of 64,000 bits per second for human speech. In practical terms this data rate sacrifices only the highest audible frequency signals. For example, it is sometimes difficult to properly discern between the sound of the lower frequency f versus the sound of the higher frequency s over a long distance phone connection.

Synchronous Communication Technology

Simply supplying the proper data rate for voice is not enough to produce a phone conversation of acceptable quality. Part of the reason for this is that human perception is readily drawn to discontinuities and even the very occasional negative experience. An infrequent blip or delay will stay in the mind of the user and detract from what might, from a strictly statistical perspective, be considered a nearly flawless connection. Thus, the bandwidth must be consistently available with no interruptions or delay in service for a quality interactive experience.

To provide for the most consistent, predictable, and highest-quality transmission of voice over a digital communications trunk it is logical that the trunk's capacity is divided up evenly and sufficiently for all aggregated signals. One kind of technology that can provide such fairness, consistency, and predictability is called *Time division multiplexing* (TDM). TDM provides a form of synchronous communication over a digital link. Basically TDM allocates a time slice or slot for each aggregated signal. These slots are then ordered in such a way that every signal will receive a time slice at least once per cycle. A cycle or frame can be described as the repeating period that contains every allocated slot.

To better understand how TDM links work and why it is effective in carrying voice traffic, suppose that three voice connections are to be aggregated over a single TDM link. These are the Red, Blue, and Green signals. Each signal comes into the aggregation point's analog-to-digital converter and is converted to a digital signal. As discussed, 64 Kbits/sec is considered a sufficient data rate for voice communication, but for simplicity this example will use 30 Kbits/sec for each connection. Thus, the converter will output a digital signal at the required data rate. Each cycle need only represent each signal's time slice only once. To properly multiplex all three signals, the TDM link must be capable of transmitting data at $30,000 \times 3$ bits per second.

Because a person is able to perceive delays on the order of seconds, the signals need to be multiplexed into cycles on the order of a hundredth of a second. Picking a cycle interval of one hundredth of a second, the amount of data per time slice for each connection would be $30,000/(100 \times 3)$ or 100 bits. Each cycle will contain a total of 300 bits or 100 bits to evenly represent each signal within the cycle. There would then be 100 cycles per second. The order of the connections within a cycle would be Red, then Green, and then Blue.

To properly decode the signals at the other end of the TDM link, the demultiplexer need only count bits. Assuming that both ends know the ordering per cycle is Red, then Green, then Blue, the receiving end need only switch to the next appropriate analog-to-digital converter after every time slice of 100 bits. Thus, the demultiplexer will count 100 bits for Red, then 100 bits for Green, 100 bits for Blue, then another 100 bits for Red, and so on. The resulting data will constantly be fed into the corresponding digital-to-analog converter, and then on to the receiving phone. This simplified illustration of TDM functionality is shown in Figure 1.3.

Avoiding Delay

To avoid unacceptable delay in signal propagation, the data allocated per time slice needs to be kept reasonably small. Queuing up large amounts of data will cause large signal delays. Suppose the data contained within each time slice for the preceding example was increased to 300,000 bits. The result would be a perceived delay of 10 seconds. That is, when one person begins to speak the other will have to wait 10 seconds before hearing anything. Obviously, such an annoying delay would make an interactive conversation rather difficult. At just 100 bits per time slice, the end-to-end delay is limited to just a tiny fraction of a second (1/300) plus the time needed to propagate the signal through the medium and the nodes in between (again, ultimately bounded by the speed of light).

Avoiding Jitter

Jitter is a term used to describe a variation in delay between the source and the destination. If a signal's data is submitted at a constant rate but is not received at the same constant rate, there must be gaps within the signal. These gaps, or pauses in the signal, cause jitter.

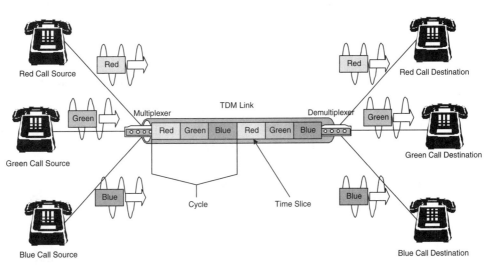

Figure 1.3 Time division multiplexing.

When listening to another person over a phone connection, one would not expect the sound to arbitrarily stop and start. Such a situation would quickly become annoying to the listener. Obviously, TDM must set rigid timing constraints such that a constant data rate will be available and uninterrupted or delayed for acceptable listening. Consistently placing data from one signal into an associated time slice within each cycle will alleviate the issue of jitter as each signal's time slice will appear within evenly spaced intervals.

Efficiency Considerations

The resources available through a TDM channel simulate the resources available though a devoted circuit. They are constant, unvarying, and finite. There are only a finite number of time slices that can be allocated per cycle. When all time slices have been allocated, additional voice connections cannot be established. Effectively, the result of attempting to use a TDM connection at capacity would be a busy signal for any additional users.

The simple fact is it would be uneconomical and illogical to provision the entire telecommunications infrastructure in such a way that everyone could make a call simultaneously. Specifically, if there are 2 million phones on a telecommunications network one would need to provision for 2 million links from each phone to every other phone. The resulting number of links would be the equivalent of 2 million × 2 million, or 4 trillion links! Clearly such a scenario has unacceptable scalability traits. Nevertheless, one phone will typically only be used to call one other phone at a time. Furthermore, there is almost no probability that everyone will attempt a phone call at once. Given these realities, telecommunications companies are able to sufficiently provision their networks so that failed calls due to capacity constraints are minimized.

Nevertheless, synchronous communications technologies such as TDM have some inherent efficiency problems. Specifically, a TDM channel is devoted to supporting a single call for its duration. Even if the call is not transmitting any valuable data, such as during periods of silence, all of the channel's allocated time slices will still be transmitted. It doesn't matter if these slots are carrying useful data or not, they are always transmitted. No other data can be inserted to utilize such unused bandwidth. The result is simply wasted resources. This is one key difference between synchronous communications and packet switched networking. In packet switched networks, a packet containing valuable data can be queued up and sent over a link whenever the link is available.

Integrated Networking

Fundamentally, computer data and voice communications networks are quite similar. Voice can be digitized into binary 1s and 0s, taking the same basic form as an e-mail message or a Web page communicated over the Internet. As was shown in TDM style communication networks, voice data can be divided up and multiplexed over a communications link in discrete units. Likewise, packet switched data networks are composed of discrete packets of information destined for a certain party or parties.

In fact, communication networks originally intended for voice are regularly used to transfer computer data. Most people will use a modem to communicate with their local Internet service provider (ISP). In this case the access communications data network is the local telephone network. So the question is, what will it take for the Internet to carry voice and other real-time interactive media?

Service Characteristics Are Key

The difference between communications networks that primarily carry voice data and computer data networks like the Internet is their service characteristics or, more generally, the Quality of Service they provide. A telephone network must provide highly reliable and deterministic service over a physical or virtual connection. Resources are allocated as complete chunks. When no more chunks can be divvied out, the result is a busy signal for the customer, or no service. Computer data networks, on the other hand, primarily need to be widely accessible and generally available. They are designed to provide for the maximum use of available resources. Ideally, resources are evenly divided between all users. As more customers use the network, a smaller proportion of the bandwidth is available per customer. Nevertheless, data networks will always provide some level of service to the growing number of parities using the network, and thus scale well.

Given the flexibility of a packet switched data network, there is no reason such a network could not also support real-time applications such as voice communications. When considering the similarities of the underlying technologies, the key difference becomes QoS. If different kinds of data traffic could be characterized, and nodes along a route supported all the variables associated with Quality of Service, it would be conceivable that a wide range of services could be supplied within the packet switch methodology.

Generally speaking, what is required is a method by which all entities composing the data path are able to treat data packets differently depending on their service requirements. Since the nodes composing the data path are typically storing a number of packets before forwarding them on toward their destination, the capability exists for treating some data packets better than others. When an outgoing link on a node becomes congested, more and more packets will need to be stored before they can be forwarded, resulting in more delay. Given enough congestion within a period of time, some data packets may even have to be dropped. If all packets were to be treated the same, then every packet would have a random chance of being dropped or delayed due to congestion. But, if some data could be treated differently depending on its service requirements, and all nodes along the data path understood the service requirements of the data they were transmitting, then the story would change.

Again, the lines at an airport ticket counter present an analogy. Typically there are two lines, one for first-class customers, and another for coach customers. The first-class line is typically much shorter than that of coach and has several dedicated attendants. The idea is that the first-class customer will not have to wait long to check into the airline. Obviously, first class-customers are identified by their first class tickets or the system would be abused by those impatient coach travelers who are tired of waiting in line.

Furthermore, there will be a smaller number of first-class passengers than coach passengers since less seats are available in first class. Who gets to be a first-class passenger is generally provisioned beforehand by making a reservation with the airline. When no more first-class seats are available, no more first class reservations will be accepted.

The same is true for packetized data. Some data can be considered as highly important or time sensitive and, thus, first-class data. Nodes along the path should be able to identify data packets having these service requirements. Such packets would be forwarded as quickly as possible and are unlikely to be dropped due to congestion at the expense of data packets belonging to a less constrained class of service.

Thus, to support QoS in a packet switched data network, three steps must be assured. First, the network cannot become overloaded with too many packets requiring high service quality. Second, the individual data sources must inject data entitled to a particular QoS at a consistent and determinate rate or the network must limit how many such packets are admitted. Finally, all routing components comprising the data path must treat QoS entitled packets preferentially. Assuming these three requirements are met, it is possible to define consistent QoS levels for packetized data. Essentially, the packet switched data network is simulating the characteristics of a TDM-style network for some portion of its bandwidth with regard to some portion of the data transmitted. Conceptually, the two methodologies can be merged in this way.

Reasons for Integrated Services Networks

The idea of an integrated network is that of a network that could support a variety of data transmission services, carrying real-time voice, video, and interactive data along with bulk data transfer. Simply put, a single wire could integrate a wide range of services over a common underlying technology.

The single interface to a network providing a variety of services is an attractive concept in itself. Having an integrated phone and Internet network, for example, could allow a person to search online yellow pages for a business or person and then immediately call that individual. If necessary bandwidth were available over the network, home users could order and download movies directly from their TVs. The possibilities are limited only by the performance capabilities of the network infrastructure.

Merging these different kinds of media also enables interesting applications that can run only over an integrated network. Imagine having an audio and visual teleconference with several coworkers while the participants can simultaneously edit an electronic document. Having one integrated communications medium will allow for powerful collaboration capabilities, indeed.

Efficiency is another reason for integrated networks. Since some data is time-critical while other data is not, there is always a potential application for any unused bandwidth resources. E-mail and other bulk media transport such as file transfer could make use of network resources whenever they became available. These are the same applications that have traditionally made use of the Internet, and they are quite capable of working with best effort network service.

Price is yet another advantage of integrated networks. Cost saving is mainly a consequence of the improved efficiency of the network. Network resources can be fully utilized, leaving nothing to waste. Fewer wires and interfaces to install and maintain provide for additional savings. Price also offers an advantage to the network provider, who can sell different services at different prices, making assured bandwidth services a valuable commodity. Additionally, using a single wire and single type of interface also improves efficiency simply by saving space and requiring less maintenance.

Building Integrated Networks

Asynchronous transfer mode (ATM) networks are a kind of integrated services network. ATM was developed to allow voice and data to effectively and efficiently take advantage of the same medium. Like TDM, ATM offers discrete and consistently sized segments of data to be transmitted over a link. In ATM, these discrete units of data are called *cells*. Unlike TDM, where every frame would have had a time slice allocated for it, whether it needs it or not, ATM communication is asynchronous. This asynchronous functionality is due to the fact that every cell contains a small header that describes the route the cell is to take. Essentially, then, a cell of data, just like an Internet-style addressed data packet, can identify itself. This allows the cell, like a packet, to be sent when it is required. If there is no data to be sent, the unused network resources are available for other cells.

ATM Is Connection Oriented

ATM is a connection-oriented technology in the sense that the path data will take from a source to a destination is established ahead of time. Hop-by-hop, each ATM switch along the path will receive the connection setup messages and proceed to allocate resources for the corresponding data. Three bytes in each cell's header are used to correlate the frame with an established connection, or *virtual channel* (VC), and a route, or *virtual path* (VP). Data that identifies itself in this way will then flow over the initialized path. The result is that a virtual circuit can be established end-to-end from a source to a destination. When the source or destination no longer needs the connection, it must be explicitly torn down. The similarities with a telephone network are obvious. A circuit is first established by dialing a number. The circuit can then be used to communicate end-to-end. Finally, the circuit is explicitly torn down by hanging up so that the network's resources will be available for other calls.

Small Data Segments

An important consideration in the design of a network technology is data formats. One must decide if the packets, or cells as the case may be, are variable or fixed in length; how big the headers are; and finally, what size limitations on data segments are required. It is easy to see that if some data segments were small to minimize queuing delay for voice communications, while others were large to minimize network overhead for bulk data, there would be problems in integrating the two for real-time operation. If small segments of data get pushed aside to make way for a large bulk data segment, the constant bit-rate traffic experiences jitter. On the other hand, if the small segments could preempt bulk traffic, the result would be that the bulk-rate traffic would never be transmitted even if bandwidth were available.

A simple example should suffice to illustrate the problems associated with supporting variable cell sizes. First, suppose that voice data segments are small for the same reason discussed in the previous TDM example, and that bulk-data segments are large to improve the efficiency of bulk transport. The voice data should behave just as specified in the TDM example, having regularly spaced segments with 16 bytes of data per segment. The bulk data can be an e-mail message that contains 128 bytes of data. If the link bandwidth was limited to 128 bytes per second, then eight voice data segments could be transmitted in one second, but only four are required for this example, leaving half the bandwidth available for the bulk transport. Still, only one bulk-data segment can be transmitted per second given the bandwidth constraints. The result of mixing the two sizes of segments is that the voice stream of segments may be interrupted for a full second while the bulk-data segment is transmitted. To the user this may be perceived as annoying jitter where the voice conversation has second-long gaps. "Hel-(gap)-lo, Wh-(gap)-at, I-(gap)- did-(gap)-n't hea-(gap)-r you." Figure 1.4 illustrates the problem of trying to fit the small and the large segments on a link simultaneously.

ATM simplified the variable cell size dilemma by keeping all data segments the same size. The trick for the ATM community was to find the

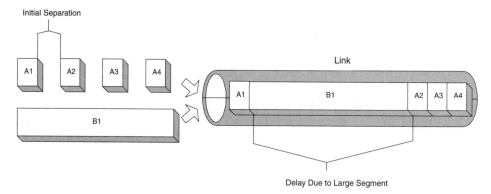

Figure 1.4 Problems with incompatible segment sizes.

optimal cell size, and because ATM was bridging the voice and data network technology, a compromise was needed. ATM uses a fixed-size 53-byte cell, of which 5 bytes are used to used to identify and characterize the cell and the remaining 48 bytes are used to carry data. The fixed size of the frame provides for predictability as well as simplicity. The small size allows the cell to be useful for even time-sensitive voice data.

Different Types of Traffic

ATM basically distinguishes between two types of data: *constant bit rate* (CBR) and *variable bit rate* (VBR) data. CBR data is highly analogous to TDM style data transport. It is data that will consistently appear at regular intervals and requires correspondingly predictable transmission intervals. Voice and other real-time applications usually generate data at a constant rate and require predictable bit rate service from the network infrastructure. Conventional computer data transmissions, on the other hand, usually generate variable bit rate data. Generation of this kind of data is quite unpredictable and tends to be bursty. A much more tolerant form of VBR traffic is called *available bit rate* (ABR) traffic. Because timing is not an issue for ABR traffic, it can take advantage of what network resources are available when they are available.

Providing that a VC can be given priority as long as it is limited to some percentage of the channel's available resources, QoS can be achieved. The most deterministic style of traffic is the CBR traffic. Such traffic can easily be characterized just as in TDM-style networks. Cells will be generated periodically over consistent intervals.

Prioritization, Provisioning, and Policing

Traffic with higher priority can be given precedence by the network over lower-priority traffic. In ATM, priority is granted to traffic that has been allocated resources by the network. This means that cells belonging to an allocated virtual circuit, as identified by their header, will be given preferential treatment. High priority cells will simply have the ability to cut ahead of lower-priority cells. The result is better performance for the high-priority traffic as compared with the lower-priority traffic over the same communications link.

Of course not all traffic can be treated as high priority and yet be guaranteed to achieve high performance. If all traffic has the same priority, the playing field is even and there is no possibility for improvement. The key is to give only a quantifiable amount of traffic high priority. This quantity of traffic should be accurately specified so that the capacity resources required to support the traffic are determined up-front. Obviously, there cannot be more high-priority traffic than there is available capacity to support the traffic. If there were too much high-priority traffic, the performance of the high-priority traffic would still degrade.

Traffic must be characterized and network resources must be explicitly committed to handling a specified amount of traffic through an admission control process. This process is called *provisioning*, since the network resources are being provisioned, or reserved, for a subset of the traffic that is high priority. Provisioning provides a deterministic way to assure that high-priority traffic will receive better, more deterministic performance and thus high QoS.

Provided that the CBR traffic adheres to the provisioned traffic characteristics, QoS can be provided through an ATM network. If the source of the traffic does not adhere to the provisioned traffic description by sending too much traffic, QoS will likely be violated for someone. The implication of provisioning is that the maximum amount of traffic is accurately known ahead of time. If this predetermined maximum traffic load is not accurate, then all bets are off. When a source sends too much high-priority traffic, other high-priority traffic will be affected. If all traffic was voice communication for a number of different calls, some calls might experience jitter or even loss. QoS would be effectively lost for those calls.

So, in order to ensure QoS, there must be a method by which high-priority traffic can be forced to comply with its provisioned characteristics. This process of traffic enforcement is termed *policing.* In ATM, the switches that support provisioning can also perform policing. Thus, the network can ensure that no high-priority traffic is in violation of its pre-determined characteristics. Any traffic that is found violating its specified characteristics can simply be dropped or marked as low-priority traffic.

Overprovisioning and Statistical Multiplexing

If all network resources can be allocated, one may wonder what is the use of best-effort traffic. Despite the ability to provision traffic, one can be reasonably assured that ample network resources will still be available for best-effort traffic at a low cost. The reason for this is the nature of network design.

Overprovisioning is a term used in the networking industry for designing networks that have more than enough resources to handle the amount of traffic they are expected to carry. In telephone networks this means that the network must have sufficient capacity to handle all expected calls. As no one uses the phone all the time, the maximum number of calls expected from any one location to another can be determined to some degree of probability. The network can then be provisioned to handle the maximum number of calls estimated by the statistical analysis. As a result, people can pick up their phones and reliably be able to make a call. Still, a large amount of resources will typically go unused when networks are overprovisioned to support the likely maximum number of calls.

ATM ABR traffic, is not, by definition, able to accurately determine what network resources it requires ahead of time. This traffic, if it doesn't require any special treatment, may simply opt to take advantage of whatever network resources are available. There is no doubt that plenty of resources will not be used by high-priority traffic. CBR and VBR traffic describe an upper bound on the resources that must be provisioned to support the required QoS. This over-provisioning will likely leave some bandwidth unused by the high-priority traffic. The resulting nooks and crannies along a communication channel can be filled with low-priority data traffic. Real-life examples of the least constrained kinds of traffic include e-mail, file downloads, and other non-interactive bulk-data transport. The great advantage of an integrated network is that it can handle a wide variety of applications with a wide variety of data transmission requirements. Ideally, little of the network's available resources will be wasted, and thus the efficiency of the network will be optimal.

As an oversimplified example of ATM in action, consider Figure 1.5. Here, two CBR voice connections and one ABR data connection have been established. The network link illustrated can provision only the two CBR connections with the proper QoS and no more. Excess bandwidth can be used by the ABR data whenever it becomes available. As voice communication is not constant, there are pauses in speech and periods of silence, some network resources will occasionally become available. The ABR data cells can be transmitted whenever a provisioned CBR cell does not arrive from its source. The result is a fully utilized network link.

RSVP and the Internet

Although ATM is an excellent example of an integrated networking technology, ATM is not the Internet. ATM is but a single networking technology. QoS can only be achieved within the confines of its technology. The Internet, on the other hand, is a network of networks, and likewise is comprised of a heterogeneous variety of networking technologies. Ethernet, FDDI, and Token Ring are just a few examples of the kinds of networks that comprise the Internet. Even ATM networks are regularly used in the Internet.

The Internet trancends these underlying network technologies to create a user-level experience of a single homogeneous network. Computers in Texas on an Ethernet network can communicate with computers in France on a Token Ring network as easily as if they were in the same room. This capability is due to the overlying Internet protocol suite that can be mapped to a wide variety of network technologies. Figure 1.6 shows how the Internet bridges networks and unites varied technologies.

So, to provide QoS in the ubiquitous network that is the Internet, protocols and standards have to be developed that can work across the different networking technologies that compose the Internet. Much can be learned from specific instances of integrated networks such as ATM. The key components for QoS can be described as *traffic prioritization, provisioning,* and *policing.* Assuming that these three components can be properly implemented by the various networking technologies that compose the Internet, there must be a common way to signal QoS requirements throughout the Internet. The Internet's Resource ReSer-

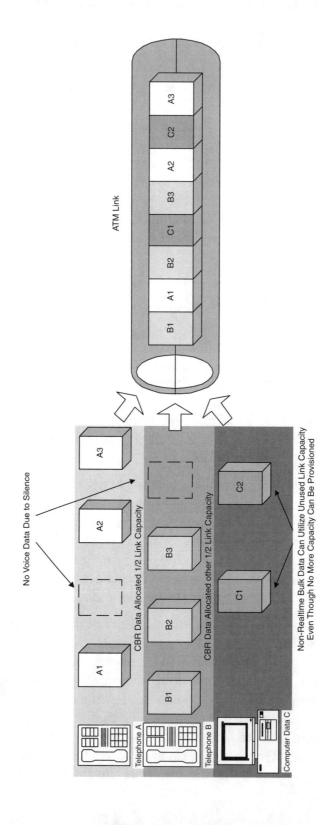

Figure 1.5 ATM handling allocated CBR traffic and unallocated ABR traffic.

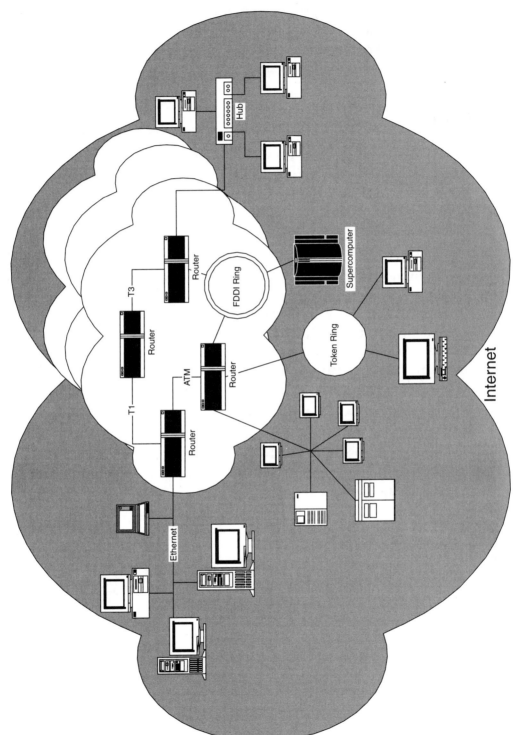

Figure 1.6 The Internet, a network of networks.

Vation Protocol (RSVP) was developed to be the standard mechanism to precisely signal QoS requirements to the wide area network's infrastructure. The remainder of this book will describe RSVP and its mechanisms for supporting QoS in the Internet.

Summary

This chapter briefly described traditional computer data networks, telecommunications networks, and integrated networks that combine the best properties of both styles of networking. These different styles of networks were examined so that the concept of Quality of Service for computer data networks could be better understood.

QoS was defined in terms of the predictability of data transport through a communications network. Predictability was discussed in terms of available bandwidth, delays in data transmission, and congestion avoidance. Assuming that these network capabilities are sufficient and consistent for properly provisioned traffic, entire classes of new real-time applications can be developed to take advantage of the Internet's infrastructure. Eventually, the Internet may evolve into a ubiquitous integrated network able to handle all forms of media communications.

The next two chapters will review the Internet in greater detail. They will investigate the protocols, standards, and technologies that are fundamental to the operation of this network of networks. An understanding of these fundamentals will clarify the mechanisms for implementing QoS in the Internet domain.

CHAPTER 2

Overview of Internet Technologies

The purpose of this chapter is to introduce wide area networking in general, and the fundamental Internet protocols in particular. Additionally, this chapter will examine the core Internet technologies from the perspective of Quality of Service. It is important to understand that the traditional Internet was not based on an infrastructure designed to support different qualities of service. Rather, the Internet and its underlying technologies were designed for a network that, in general, supported only an unreliable best effort service. Protocols were developed to take advantage of the best-effort service and provide the Internet with a mechanism that allowed it to degrade gracefully under load. This capability made the Internet a successful medium for transporting data at a rate complementary to the current network conditions. This chapter will investigate the relevant core Internet protocols and technologies and explore how they can interact within a QoS networking methodology.

Wide Area Networking Overview

Wide area computer data networking is the evolution of networks from isolated islands of connected computers to connected networks. Although this evolution may at first seem elementary, the reality is that isolated networks are diverse in that they implement a widely varying number of technologies and protocols. Addressing schemes must be developed so that all entities on a network can be uniquely identified and located in a scalable manner. To integrate networks on a grand scale requires a homogeneous set of technologies and standardized protocols.

A standardized set of protocols allows otherwise incompatible network technologies to communicate. This is possible simply because even unrelated technologies can provide mappings to a standard. The standard acts as a common, or shared, third party, alleviating the need for diverse network technologies to know how to communicate with each other directly. With a common protocol suite, networks can simply communicate with one another via the standard. Meanwhile, individual networks directly take advantage of their specific protocols and underlying physical technologies internally. These underlying technologies facilitate the act of communicating with the networked nodes within their scope.

Wide-scale addressing defines the ability of each communicating entity or node in the wide area network to identify itself. Each identity must be unique, but must share a common address format. Additionally, the approach to addressing must be scalable, because a wide area network will likely encompass a huge number of nodes.

Integrating Diverse Physical Networks

As has been stated, wide area networking requires that networks be able to communicate. Thus, the goal of internetworking is to provide a bridge between a diverse set of computer networking technologies by using a standard protocol suite. The issue then becomes how the standard set of protocols are integrated with, or mapped onto, the underlying communications mechanism. This mapping is facilitated by layering the various network protocols and functionality.

Encapsulation makes the goal of internetworking practical to implement. Basically, the underlying network protocols encapsulate the standard protocol suite within their data. Gateways to other networks and end nodes can then work with both the underlying networking technology and the standard protocol suite. The proprietary networking protocols and hardware interactions can be viewed as encapsulating and transporting the standard protocol set. Abstractly speaking, these interactions can be viewed as *protocol layering*. Figure 2.1 demonstrates the way in which protocols can be encapsulated within one another.

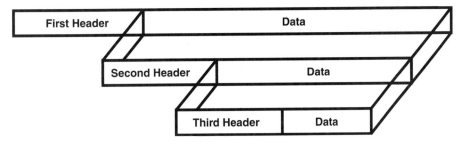

Figure 2.1 Protocol encapsulation.

Protocol Layering

Protocol layering simply refers to the reuse and isolation of communication protocols and their functionality. Each layer serves a specific task, and builds on the layers below it. Ideally, well-defined and static interfaces exist between the layers. The lowest layers directly provide individual nodes with the ability to communicate. The standard protocols are then built on this base. A common interface between the layers provides the mapping. An implementation of a layered protocol can be described as a *protocol stack.*

Protocol layering, by segmenting functionality, also simplifies implementation. Each protocol and the corresponding functionality of its layer in the protocol stack can be developed and verified independently of the higher layers. The result is a robust set of layered technologies with the lower layers providing basic functionality enhanced by the higher layers.

The OSI Model

The ISO-OSI reference model is the International Standards Organization's Open System Interconnection architecture. Although the corresponding protocol suite lost favor to the Internet's protocol suite, the resulting layering model is still used as a benchmark for comparison with other protocol stacks. There are seven layers in the OSI reference model: the Physical, Data Link, Network, Transport, Session, Presentation, and Application layers. Figure 2.2 illustrates these OSI-defined layers.

The Physical Layer, as the name implies, maps to the physical wires and interface hardware that physically connect two or more systems together. It also represents the mechanism that can put data onto a wire or other medium. Likewise, this layer represents the corresponding mechanism that can receive the digital data at the other end of the medium.

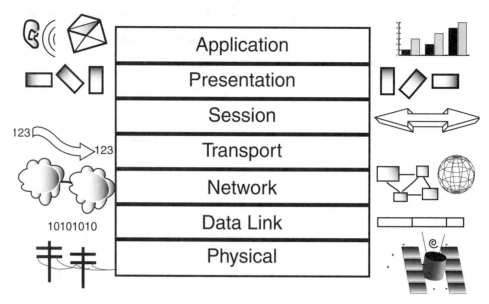

Figure 2.2 The OSI architecture.

The Data Link Layer represents the functionality that translates the basic bits and raw data in the physical layer into useful packets and flows. Thus, a stream of binary 1s and 0s can be partitioned into useful data blocks. Additionally, in shared and switched physical media, the data link layer can provide an addressing scheme for the local components. In some cases this layer can also facilitate the retransmission of data damaged after being transmitted in the physical medium.

The Network Layer is the layer that facilitates wide area networking. This layer is the translation layer that allows diverse physical networks to communicate with one another. It enables virtual end-to-end connectivity between hosts within disparate networks. Typically, this layer will have its own wide-scale addressing mechanism, and is concerned with scalability for the potentially huge number of network nodes.

The Transport Layer provides error control and flow control for the Network Layer. It provides an abstraction that, to higher-layer protocols, makes the end-to-end communications channel look reliable. It can also be responsible for sensing network conditions and throttling back when the network appears to be overloaded. When all communicating entities apply this functionality, the network can provide better scalability in that congestion will only cause a fair degradation in quality for all, as opposed to complete network lockout for some.

The Session Layer offers a further abstraction on the Transport Layer by providing virtual duplex connectivity and prioritized flow control. Duplex connectivity means that bidirectional communication is supported. Prioritized flow control allows critical messages from multiplexed flows to proceed before the lower-priority messages within the session layer queue.

The Presentation Layer presents the communicated data in a form compatible with the native computer architecture. As with written languages, some computers prefer to read their data left to right, while others prefer to read right to left. When systems from these differing representations communicate, the presentation layer will translate the data into the receiving system's native format.

Finally, the Application Layer represents the applications that need to communicate. These may be e-mail applications, Web browsers, video/audio applications, or whatever other application a programmer has invented or will invent. The underlying layers have greatly simplified the redundant functionality required for two computers to communicate. Thus, an application can simply reuse this functionality instead of reinventing the communications wheel.

The TCP/IP Model

As this book is primarily interested in the Internet and its supporting technologies, the remainder of this chapter will introduce the core Internet protocols. These are the protocols that supply the basic communications facilities for the Internet and its applications. This set of protocols is known as the Transmission Control Protocol/Internet Protocol (TCP/IP) suite. The TCP/IP model can be compared to the OSI reference model described previously. When compared to the OSI architecture, TCP/IP supplies the equivalent of the network layer, transport and session layers. Any number of communications technologies and networking protocols can then comprise the physical and data link layers, so long as they can encapsulate the TCP/IP protocol suite and its functionality. Thus, TCP/IP represents the standard protocol suite for the Internet.

QoS Considerations

We have now shown how wide area networking can be achieved in heterogeneous networks. *Internetworking* implies the integration of diverse networking technologies. This integration obviously has implications for the underlying service characteristics of the wide-scale network. Diverse networks inherently imply diverse QoS. Differing physical networks have different characteristics in terms of latency, reliability, and jitter. End-to-end service quality over a wide area network cannot be greater than that offered on the intermediate network with the lowest effective service quality. The obvious analogy is that of a chain which is no stronger than its weakest link. Thus, it is important to remember that the lowest common denominator determines the end-to-end QoS in an internet paradigm.

An additional caveat in applying QoS functionality to an existing protocol stack is related to the very concept of protocol layering. Protocol layering fundamentally implies that higher layers abstract the functionality of the underlying layers. Thus, a degree of layer independence is achieved which has the benefits of faster development time and more finely tuned implementations. Unfortunately, rigid layering may also hide information that needs to be exposed for proper integration into a QoS framework if the layering architecture was not designed with QoS in mind.

The application layer will probably require a mechanism for communicating QoS requirements, because it is the applications that best know their own requirements. An e-mail application may be perfectly usable with a best-effort and relatively slow QoS while a real-time video application would need to specify a very precisely constrained and fast QoS. The underlying layers must have the ability to conform to the application's requirements to achieve a desirable result for the user.

The remainder of this chapter will examine the Internet core protocols and technologies with QoS considerations in mind.

Addressing: Domains and Subnets

Just as in the postal service analogy, the TCP/IP model of internetworking requires a method for identifying the computers connected to the Internet. This is accomplished by associating a unique address with each host connected to the network. Internet addresses are distributed by a central authority to ensure uniqueness. Beyond supplying addresses, however, the central authority cannot control how, or even know if, these addresses are used once they are given out.

The Internet Address Format

Every node actively communicating on the Internet can be represented by an address that uniquely identifies the node. This address is a scalar 32-bit number which allows for a total of 4,294,967,296 unique addresses. Typically, an Internet address is represented in four blocks separated by periods. Each block can contain a number ranging from 0 to 255, or 1 byte of address data. In this format, Internet addresses range from "0.0.0.0" to "255.255.255.255". Thus, "128.23.134.15" and "139.132.2.239" are both examples of Internet addresses.

Domain Categorization

Since the TCP/IP protocol suite is designed for wide area networking, it is important that the addressing scheme also be scalable. In the Internet, this scalability is achieved by interpreting Internet addresses hierarchically. An address hierarchy is important because without it every Internet address would be interpreted merely as a single scalar value. Under such a scenario, every node on the Internet would then have to know the precise location of every other node in order to communicate. Considering that there are over 4 billion possible addresses, this clearly would not be a scalable solution.

The Internet addressing scheme is fundamentally divided into a two-level hierarchy. The first level identifies individual networks, each with its own number, while the second level identifies the physical hosts within the network. There are three classes of addresses for network enumeration: A, B, and C. The type of addressing scheme is determined by the first zero bit in the Internet address. If the most significant bit is set to zero, then the addressing structure is that of a class A address; if the second bit is zero and the first bit is one, it is a class B structure; and if the third bit is zero and the first two bits are one, it is a class C structure. There are 128 class A networks with 16,777,216 possible hosts in each network, 16,384 class B networks with 65,536 possible hosts each, and 4,194,304 class C networks each theoretically allowing 256 possible hosts.

This addressing scheme simplifies the task of those nodes that must route packets through the Internet. Instead of having to know the location of each and every host on the entire Internet, it is often sufficient to know the location of the host's corresponding network. Only when the packet reaches its intended network need the host number be considered. Likewise, in a postal service analogy, it is sufficient to consider the state to which a letter is destined when it is being delivered across the country. Only when the letter reaches its intended state will the city and street information need to be considered.

Subnet Categorization

Unfortunately, the simple two-level class-based hierarchy originally developed for hierarchical addressing in the Internet proved insufficient. To allow for further hierarchical categorization of the Internet address space, the concept of subnetting was developed. Subnets further extend the addressing hierarchy into a three-level model. The subnets allow for networks and hosts to be more flexibly determined. To support subnetting of Internet addresses, a variably sized subnet field was added after the network field. This subnet field can be used to further break up the addressing space. Organizations typically determine the size of the subnet field by applying a subnet mask to the overall Internet address. This mask is used to distinguish the bits in the Internet address that identify the hosts from the bits that identify the subnet. Figure 2.3 illustrates the network address formats for classes A, B, and C networks together with the subnet and host numbers.

Reliability Considerations

Reliability is another important aspect in determining service quality. Reliability in a packet switched network mainly implies the ability of the network to successfully transmit a packet of data end to end. The fewer packets that can run the gauntlet of the network, the less reliable the network. Obviously, if the data is not reliably reaching its destination, service quality will be negatively affected.

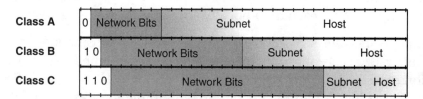

Figure 2.3 The Internet's addressing scheme.

Unreliable by Design

The very concept of internetworking suggests reliability is never assured. This is due to the fact that internetworking implies the integration of diverse networking technologies. Obviously, some networking technologies are unavoidably unreliable. As the lowest common denominator will determine the overall reliability of the network, the Internet cannot make any guarantees.

In the Internet, nodes can fail, links can break, and errors in routing are always possible. Even more fundamentally, because every node and link in the network has limited capacity, congestion provides little recourse other than the premature discard of packets. When a packet is injected into the Internet, one can only assume a best-effort attempt will be made by the network to deliver the packet to its destination. Although packets may be lost, the network does have the ability to send failure messages in the case of packets dropped due to congestion and other operational circumstances. Even these messages can be lost, however. In the end, the network cannot be counted upon to determine whether or not a packet has successfully been delivered. This is the task of the participating end systems.

Congestion is the most typical reason for the unreliable nature of the Internet. When nodes become overloaded with traffic, their limited capacity will force them to discard overflowing packets. Over-engineering networks, however, can circumvent congestion so that capacity is not a limiting factor. Strictly controlling traffic is another method of alleviating congestion. In the case of QoS, network traffic must be tightly regulated to assure competing traffic will not degrade service quality. Ideally, a mechanism needs to exist whereby bandwidth resources can be set aside in general so that particularly important or sensitive data flows can avoid congestion altogether.

Protocol Requirements for Reliability

Reliability in the Internet can be regulated either directly by the end applications or by specific transport level Internet protocols. This dual approach is actually quite flexible, as some applications are more impacted by reliability considerations than others. A real-time audio application, for example, may be tolerant of mild data loss. For such applications, data loss would simply be translated into a brief degradation in audio quality. Other applications, such as data file transfers, do require highly reliable data transport. It is obviously unacceptable for an important file to become corrupted in transport.

To combat unreliability when required, end stations must be able to communicate not only the information being sent, but also an acknowledgment for the information successfully received. If the recipient does not acknowledge a sent packet, it will have to be retransmitted. Excessive retransmissions, however, can lead to a highly inefficient use of network resources and can potentially lead to ever-escalating network traffic. Thus, it is equally important that retransmission protocols be sensitive to network conditions and adapt their data rates so as not to further overload the network.

Internet Topologies

The Internet is a very diverse computer data network interconnecting a widely varying array of communications technologies. The Internet is also a highly heterogeneous network in terms of organizational structure and control. No single organization owns the Internet. Rather, the Internet is composed of a conglomeration of networks operated by governments, companies, and a variety of other organizations. These networks make up the Internet in that they comply with the standards and provide connectivity to other networks.

Multiple Paths, Connected Networks

Due to the nature of internetworking, there are usually multiple routes through which a data packet may travel. The path a packet takes though the Internet is quite similar to the path a motorist may take on a cross-country journey. Depending on road conditions, weather, or just plain preference, a motorist will not always follow the same route journey to journey. Similarly, packets from end station to end station may not always follow the same path though the Internet. The path is determined by routing policies, link status, and perhaps someday, even by dynamic network conditions such as congestion.

From the perspective of the end user, the Internet appears as a holistic, interconnected system despite its reality. When interconnecting networks on such a large scale, it is useful to have each network act autonomously. In the Internet, such networks are called *autonomous sys-*

tems (AS). Within the borders of each AS, a collection of networks is engineered and managed to meet the needs of its users or customers. These individual ASs can then be connected to one another to supply global connectivity. Between these independent networks, well-defined relationships exist and network connectivity information is exchanged via standard protocols.

Intranets

Intranet is a term typically applied to internal Internet-compliant networks within a corporation or other organization. The organization controls and likely owns the internal network. An internal information services department within the organization typically manages its Intranet. Limited connectivity to other organizations or the external Internet as a whole is usually provided through a small number of secure gateways.

For purposes of enabling QoS on computer data networks, intranets provide several clear advantages. For one, they are internally controlled and maintained. This allows the relevant nodes and systems to more easily be updated with the technologies and software necessary to precisely control resources. Additionally, since the network is used exclusively by the organization, QoS capabilities can be clearly applied to specific critical applications or individuals. Real-time distance learning applications, for example, can be given the appropriate service qualities required for multimedia presentations. The additional headache of usage billing may also be inapplicable for intranets since the use is restricted to known internal users.

Internet Service Provider Model

Internet service providers (ISPs) are companies and organizations that provide Internet connectivity and related services to others. ISPs will typically control and manage their networks. Customers pay ISPs for this Internet access. Also, some ISPs will offer additional services to companies that wish to outsource their networking requirements altogether. In these cases, ISPs will manage and maintain the client company's networks as well as provide controlled Internet access.

QoS capabilities have a wide range of implications for ISPs. Without QoS-enabled networks, ISPs are forced to physically engineer networks to meet their customers' service requirements. The less expensive alternative of simply sharing common network resources creates the potential for congestion. The ability to precisely provision network resources gains one ISP the advantage over another in that congestion can be controlled while still maintaining the network at its greatest efficiency.

Another important point is that ISPs must often maintain relationships with other ISPs, simply because of connectivity requirements. Because information inevitably flows across different organizational boundaries, it is important that proper QoS levels be universally maintained. It is not sufficient for a single ISP to offer QoS capabilities if the end-to-end communication channel ranges over multiple service providers. Thus, to offer nearly universal QoS capabilities, ISPs must be able to provide compatible signaling and control mechanisms.

The Core Protocols

This section will investigate the underlying Internet protocols in some detail. These are the protocols that compose the TCP/IP protocol suite. They provide basic end-to-end transport, connectivity and flow control. The specific protocols that comprise the TCP/IP protocol suite are the Internet Protocol versions 4 and 6, the User Datagram Protocol, and the Transmission Control Protocol.

As QoS in general and RSVP in particular are the topics of this book, it is important to be well grounded in the realities of the Internet. QoS relates to the way data is handled when transported by the network, and transporting data is what the core Internet protocols are all about.

The Internet Protocol

The Internet Protocol represents the Network Layer Protocol of the TCP/IP protocol suite. Currently, the most widely deployed version of this protocol is IPv4. It is, in fact, the protocol the Internet was founded upon. This is the version of the protocol that we will discuss first.

Internet Protocol Header

The IP datagram consists of a header followed by the data being transported. The protocol's header is comprised of the information required to effectively transport the data portion end-to-end across the Internet.

This includes the Internet addresses of both the source and destination, as well as various control and management fields. In total, the protocol header is a minimum of 20 bytes long. Figure 2.4 illustrates the IP header format.

The first several fields of the IP header are devoted to protocol-version-number handling characteristics, and the size of the packet. The version field is used to identify the version of the protocol header format. In this case it is 4. The Internet Header Length (IHL) field represents the length of the header as a number of 32 bit chunks. This value is used to determine the offset to the data portion of the packet. The Type of Service field is used to describe the handling characteristics for the packet overall. The Total Length field is the overall size of the packet as measured in bytes. Based on this field, the maximum IP packet size is limited to 65,535 bytes.

The next three fields in the IP header are committed to fragment management. This includes fragment identification, handling requirements, and location. The subject of fragmentation will be addressed in more detail later.

The Time to Live, Protocol, and Checksum fields provide additional control- and error-detection facilities. The Time to Live number is used to control the lifetime of the packet in the network. The Protocol field identifies the next layer protocol encapsulated in the data portion of the

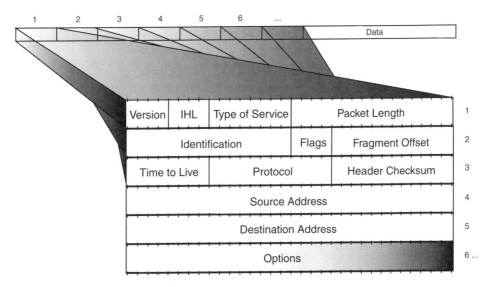

Figure 2.4 The IP header.

packet. The Checksum is simply used to provide a method for detecting if the packet's header has been corrupted during transport.

The source and destination fields contain the IP address of the packet's origination and the prescribed receiver, respectively. Finally, the variable-length options field is available for communicating with network layer devices in the Internet.

ICMP

An IP packet may directly transport the Internet Control Message Protocol (ICMP) in its data field. This protocol provides error-reporting capabilities with respect to the handling of IP packets by network nodes. When a packet is discarded for any of a number of reasons, the discarding node will generally generate an appropriate ICMP message and relay it to the packet's source. This message will contain the reasons for the delivery failure, which the packet's source may then employ to avoid future errors. Other ICMP capabilities include relaying various control messages and configuration information back to a host. Since the ICMP information is relevant to the handling of IP packets by other network layer elements, it is considered part of the network layer in the TCP/IP protocol suite.

Of course, there is no guarantee that ICMP messages will not themselves be discarded. As with any packet sent into the wide area medium, data loss, corruption, and even replication are always possible. Thus, end stations should not count on the network reporting error conditions for every erroneous packet.

Fragmentation

Fragmentation is an interesting subject for QoS consideration. Fragmentation happens when the size of an IP packet is too big for the underlying physical network to handle. Indeed, physical networks have a wide range of packet size limitations. When a network is encountered that cannot provision for the IP packet size all at once, the packet can be fragmented into a number of smaller packets that will fit. The maximum packet size a network can transmit is called the *maximum transmission unit* (MTU) of the network.

It has already been shown how packet size also plays an important role in providing consistent QoS for multiplexing links. Low-priority, large-sized packets may never be transported in the midst of a large number of high-priority, small packets with a requirement for tight delay bounds. There is simply no way to stuff the large packet between the regularly timed smaller packets without skewing their timing.

One unfortunate side effect of fragmentation is that packet fragments can always be lost or corrupted. When any fragment is lost, the entire packet will have to be discarded. This is highly undesirable if the reliability of the network is of the same order as the size of the original packet. For example, consider a network that allows for a maximum packet size of only 120 bytes. Now suppose an IP packet 1020 bytes long must be sent over this network. The packet 1020 bytes long will have to be fragmented into 100 packets 120 bytes each (20 bytes for the IP header). Further suppose there is a probability that 1 out of every 10 packets will be corrupted or lost. Likewise, if any of the fragmented packets are lost the entire IP packet is lost. Clearly this is not leading to an acceptable situation. Even though 90 percent of the packet fragments are correctly transported, the end result is that almost every complete IP packet will be discarded. Because most of the IP packets will be missing fragments, most of the IP packets will be discarded. In the end, very little is actually being communicated end-to-end.

Due to the reliability issues imposed by various network technologies it is useful to determine the overall MTU size end-to-end. This can be accomplished by setting the Fragmentation Flags field in the IP header so as to not allow fragmentation. When a packet that cannot be fragmented reaches a network with an MTU size smaller than the packet's size, the packet will simply be discarded. A node that drops an IP packet due to its MTU size should also send an ICMP packet back to the sending host. The ICMP message is used to report the error condition that a packet was dropped due to its MTU size. For reasonably constant network technologies it is sufficient to simply send packets of decreasing size that cannot be fragmented. By knowing the size of the largest packet that either successfully reached its destination or did not trigger an ICMP error, the MTU size of the data path can be reasonably determined.

Time to Live

The Time to Live (TTL) field in the IP header is used to control the amount of time a packet can exist on the network. It is officially measured as the number of seconds a packet may live on the network but is effectively measured as the number of hops from one node to another an IP packet can traverse through the network. Typically the TTL is set to a value representative of the maximum number of hops required for the packet to successfully reach its destination. This is because each node in the Internet that processes the IP header must decrement the TTL value by at least 1. When the TTL value reaches 0, the packet is to be discarded.

The existence of the TTL field prevents packets from being routed infinitely, never reaching their destination. If a loop exists in the data path, then a packet could simply be routed cyclically from node to node. If each node deducts from the TTL field, then a packet caught in such a loop will eventually be discarded.

Additionally, the TTL field can be used to scope a packet's range. This is useful when the number of hops a packet should take is known. If the TTL is set to a corresponding value, packets will be less likely to go out of these bounds. Also, in QoS applications where latency is a prime consideration, the number of possible hops can be set to a value corresponding to the maximum acceptable latency. Taking such actions will prevent a packet that would surely be discarded from continuing its ill-fated journey through the Internet.

Protocol Options

The IP header's Protocol Options field can provide a range of management and debugging services. Nevertheless, as the name option implies, defined options may not be widely deployed. Initially, they provided source routing capabilities for IP packets as well as security handling labels. Route recording was another defined option. However, the very limited size of the options field proved inadequate for the purposes for which it was intended. There are simply too many possible routing hops in the Internet today. Most of the options defined for IPv4 have simply outlived their usefulness and are not typically supported.

Precedence and Service Types

The Type of Service (TOS) field of the IP header is used to provide information related to the service characteristics preferred by the packet. This value can reflect the required delay and priority aspects of the packet. Higher-priority packets can preempt lower-priority packets when being forwarded on some devices. Specifying delay sensitivities will also allow for the prompt delivery of the packet in some devices.

Under precisely controlled circumstances, the TOS field can provide a simple method for providing differentiated services on the Internet. No additional protocols are required to communicate the service requirements to network layer nodes in the network infrastructure; the required information is simply carried in the TOS field. This is feasible if there is a common mapping of the TOS values into corresponding service characteristics. If all nodes in the Internet can provide the same service characteristics for the same TOS settings, then end-to-end QoS can be achieved. Nevertheless, the TOS field must be set and verified by trusted entities in the network. If all that was required for an individual to receive the highest Quality of Service at the expense of all others was to set the TOS bits appropriately, everyone would attempt to set this field to the best value. Obviously, the end result would be the same homogeneous best-effort service on which the Internet was built. The concept of enabling differentiated services in the Internet using the TOS field in the IP header will be examined closely in Chapter 8.

User Datagram Protocol

The User Datagram Protocol (UDP) is a simple Transport Layer protocol in the TCP/IP protocol suite. It is useful for no-frills data transport over the Internet. The UDP header and its data are encapsulated within an IP packet. This means the UDP header will immediately follow the IP header as part of the whole IP packet.

UDP Header

The User Datagram Protocol consists of a simple header followed by the data being transported by the datagram. The protocol's header is comprised of the virtual source and destination port of the data as well as the total length of the datagram. The length field includes the length of the UDP header and is expressed in bytes. A checksum is also provided to detect corrupted data if necessary. In total the UDP header is 8 bytes long. Figure 2.5 illustrates the UDP header format.

The size of a UDP packet is determined by the IP header. As was previously shown, the IP header provides a 16-bit field for specifying the size

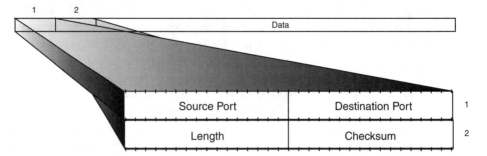

Figure 2.5 The UDP header.

of the packet. This size limits the packet size to 65,535 bytes including the IP and UDP headers with a combined minimum size of 28 bytes.

Ports

The source and destination port fields in the UDP header are useful for coordinating data delivery on an end station. In effect, ports allow for the multiplexing of transported data from specific applications available on a computer. Just as the many hosts that are connected to the Internet must be able to uniquely identify themselves via an Internet address, applications running on a host must likewise be able to distinguish themselves. Ports identify different types of applications that may be running on a computer system. In total, 65,535 different ports can be represented on a single host. Server applications are provided well-known port numbers to which clients can specifically direct their messages. In the end, the port number allows datagrams to be delivered to their corresponding applications, thus avoiding any confusion as to which application the data was actually intended for.

Connectionless Transport

Datagram transport in the Internet is equivalent to a form of connectionless transport. A datagram can be sent just like a letter would be through the U.S. Postal Service. It is enough to fill in the addressing information, include the data, and set it free into the Internet. No additional setup is required.

If all goes well, a UDP packet will eventually reach its intended destination. If the packet is lost, however, UDP will not alert the sending application of the loss. No guarantees are provided that a sent packet will ever reach its destination. Thus, it is up to the UDP-based applications to handle lost packets. For an application sending a UDP packet to know if the data was received by the destination, the destination will have to acknowledge its receipt of the packet by sending a message back to the sender. No additional flow control or retransmission facilities are provided by the UDP protocol.

UDP is useful for real-time multimedia applications tolerant of data loss but intolerant of excessive delays. Since such applications require that packets arrive in a timely fashion, the delays created by redundantly transmitting lost packets would be unacceptable. Such delayed packets would simply be discarded by the application anyway. Thus, a datagram must be successfully transmitted on the first attempt to be useful for such applications. When network conditions cause high packet loss rates, a real-time application will likely have no other recourse than to degrade in terms of audio or video quality.

Transmission Control Protocol

The Transmission Control Protocol (TCP) provides Transport Layer and some Session Layer functionality for the TCP/IP protocol suite. It is much more advanced than UDP and provides a number of sophisticated connection-oriented data communication services. TCP provides end-to-end virtual connectivity, reliable transport, and flow control over the Internet.

Virtual Connectivity

Virtual connectivity between two hosts can be obtained though the use of the Transmission Control Protocol. Connectivity implies that a logical connection exists between two hosts on the Internet. From the perspective of an application, the virtual connection functions like a highly reliable direct link to another system. All information will seem to reach its destination in order, nonreplicated, and uncorrupted, once a connection can be established.

TCP data is encapsulated within an IP packet just like the User Datagram Protocol. The difference is that TCP provides the additional services that simulate a connection on behalf of an application. In fact, no real connection exists—TCP data is transported across the Internet with the same best-effort reliability offered to all IP derived packets. It is the software on the end stations that handles all the problems associated with network congestion, packet replication, and data loss.

Just like a phone connection, a virtual TCP connection must first be established between two participating end points. Once a connection request is accepted by the second party, data may be transmitted. Also like a phone connection, a virtual TCP connection must be disconnected when connectivity between the two parties is no longer required. A connection can also be lost due to negative network conditions.

From the perspective of the application using TCP services, data is sent and received in the form of a continuous stream. This means that the size of the data to be transported is irrelevant. Data of any size can be sent or received over the connection at any time. There is no need for the application to packetize its data into discrete chunks for transport as is the case for UDP.

TCP Header

The Transmission Control Protocol consists of a header followed by any data being transported. The protocol's header is comprised of the information required to reliably reconstruct a data stream back into its original form at an end station. Also included is port information which is used for multiplexing streams to applications within a host system, akin to the port number used by UDP. In total, the TCP header is a minimum of 20 bytes long. Figure 2.6 illustrates the TCP header format.

The first two fields in the TCP header identify the source and destination ports. The Destination Port field represents a registered application on the end station. For an end station to accept a TCP connection request for a specific port, the end station must have an application listening on that port. If no application is available for the specified port, a connection simply cannot be established.

The next two fields uniquely identify a specific TCP packet. For a sent packet, the Sequence Number field identifies the current sent packet. This 32-bit number is sufficiently large to uniquely identify an individual packet within the stream of TCP packets. Sequence numbers, once synchronized, are incremented by one for each new TCP data-byte generated by an end station. The Acknowledgment Number field is used to acknowledge the receipt of TCP data-bytes. It is set to the next sequence number that the receiver is expecting to receive. By providing space for

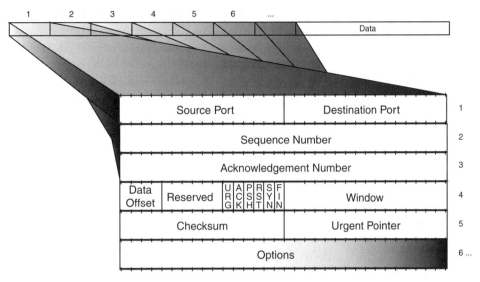

Figure 2.6 The TCP header.

both a sequence number and acknowledgement number in the TCP header, newly generated TCP packets can also acknowledge the receipt of TCP data bytes previously received by the end station.

The next field in the TCP header is a data offset value. This number represents the number of 32-bit chunks in the TCP header, and thus is effectively a pointer into the data portion of a TCP message.

Six control bit values make up the flag field in the TCP header. The control bits are effectively flags that, when set, specify different control parameters for the current TCP packet. These flags include the Urgent Pointer Field significant flag (URG) which is set when the data in the Urgent Pointer Field is valid. The Acknowledgement Field significant flag (ACK) is set to represent that the Acknowledgement Number Field is valid. The Push Function flag (PSH), when set, implies the data contained in the TCP packet must be pushed to the receiving application. When the Reset Connection flag (RST) is set, the connection is to be reset. The Synchronize Sequence numbers flag (SYN), when set, means that the sequence number state is to be reset to that specified in the Sequence Number field. Finally, the No More Sender Data flag is used to flush the data stream on the receiving end station.

The Window field is crucial to the flow control properties of TCP. The window advertises the maximum amount of data, in terms of bytes, the originator of the TCP packet is willing to accept. This window provides an end station with a mechanism to control the upper bound on data rate of the flow.

Rounding out the TCP header are the Checksum field, the Urgent Pointer field, and the optional Options field. The checksum is used to detect corrupted TCP packets including damaged data. The Urgent Pointer can be used to identify urgent data within the data stream. Finally, the Option field provides for a number of options that are primarily used for testing purposes.

TCP Functionality

To begin a TCP session, the two communicating hosts must establish a connection. The side that initiates the connection process is called the active side, while the side that accepts and acknowledges the connection is called the passive side. The connection process begins when the active side sends a TCP header with the Synchronize (SYN) flag set and the active side's initial sequence number. The passive side will then acknowledge the connection request by returning a TCP header with the Synchronize and Acknowledge flags set. The acknowledgement will specify the passive side's initial sequence number in the Sequence Number field and the acknowledgement to the active side's sequence number in the Acknowledgment Number field. The connection is established once the active side acknowledges this passive side's synchronized response. The result of this procedure is a virtual duplex connection between the two hosts.

Once the duplex connection is established, data may flow in either direction. When a TCP packet containing data is received at either end of the connection, the recipient must acknowledge that the data has been received. If no acknowledgment is received before a time-out period, the packet will be retransmitted. For TCP, the timeout period is based on the estimated round-trip time, which is the observed time it takes for a sent packet to be acknowledged. It is important to note that every TCP packet does not need to be acknowledged by a receiver. Rather, for bulk-data transfer, multiple packets can effectively be acknowledged by the receiver by simply acknowledging the last TCP packet of the continuous sequence.

The fact that TCP communication is always full duplex has implications for QoS support. Even if the data is flowing in one direction exclusively, acknowledgments will have to continuously arrive from the other direction. If the acknowledgments are lost, retransmission will occur. Thus, it is useful to apply equivalent QoS in both directions for TCP. If no TCP packets are being acknowledged due to congestion, the sender will slow down and retransmit, effectively nullifying any QoS provisions for the simplex data path. It is also useful to note that it is possible that each half of the duplex data path may follow different routes through the Internet. That is, the acknowledgments may follow a different route than the data being acknowledged.

When a TCP connection is no longer needed, the participating systems can close the connection. Since the connection is duplex, it must be closed once for both directions. Typically, the active side will initiate the termination of a TCP connection. This is accomplished by sending a TCP packet with the FIN flag set. The passive side will then acknowledge the close message, effectively closing the corresponding direction of the connection. When the passive side is ready to close its side of the connection, it will likewise send a TCP packet with the FIN flag set. When the active side acknowledges this packet, the connection is formally closed in both directions. If the passive side initiates the close, the process is simply reversed. Successive lost packets due to a broken link or severe network congestion will also effectively close the TCP connection.

Flow Control

TCP also provides mechanisms by which the flow of data over the virtual connection can be controlled. TCP flow control comes in two primary flavors: ability for the receiver to control the sender's data rate, and the sender's ability to adaptively adjust its data rate based on the network's estimated capacity.

The receiver is able to control the sender's data rate via the use of the Window field in the TCP header. When acknowledging TCP packets, the receiver can advertise a window size. The window tells the sender how much data it can send to the receiver before an acknowledgment is received. The value of the window is based on the amount of buffer space on the receiver available for holding incoming data. The algorithm is fairly simple; the sender can send data up to the window size advertised by the receiver before it must wait for an acknowledgment. Once an acknowledgment is received, the sender may continue sending data up to the amount expressed in the new window size. By this process, the receiver can control how much data is sent to it. This process prevents a fast sender from overpowering a slow receiver during bulk-data transfers.

The sender is able to gauge and adapt to network conditions by observing the rate at which sent packets are being acknowledged. Through this method, a sender will attempt to discover the available capacity of the network. Since network routes can change and since congestion can arise, it is important that the sender be able to continuously adapt its data rate. When packets are dropped, retransmissions must occur. A retransmission is clearly a waste of network resources, and progressive retransmissions by a large number of hosts can potentially lock up a network's capacity.

To discover the capacity of the data path, a TCP sender will utilize the slow-start algorithm. This algorithm determines how many packets a TCP sender can send before waiting for an acknowledgment from the receiver. Initially, only one packet can be sent before an acknowledgment is received. Every time an acknowledgment for a sent packet is received, the number of unacknowledged packets that may be sent increases by one. Thus, the number of packets that may be sent before an acknowledgment is received increases exponentially.

This process is illustrated in Figure 2.7. Here, TCP packets are represented as boxes being delivered from their source to their destination. The network is represented as a slotted wheel which pulls packets from one end to the other. The top of the wheel represents the forward data path, while the bottom half of the wheel represents the backward data path. The speed at which the wheel turns corresponds to the speed of the network, and the number of slots in the wheel represents the available capacity of the network.

At first, one packet is transported by the wheel, and one acknowledgment is eventually received. Now two packets may be sent. After both of the acknowledgments for these packets have been received, four packets may be sent. Since the capacity of the wheel is two packets, the rate of the data packets corresponds to the rate of the acknowledgments, and a steady state is obtained.

When lost packets are discovered due to a timeout or multiple acknowledgments, a threshold is set to be half the number of packets last transmitted. If a timeout occurs, the number of packets that may be sent are reset to just one. The process repeats until the number of packets being

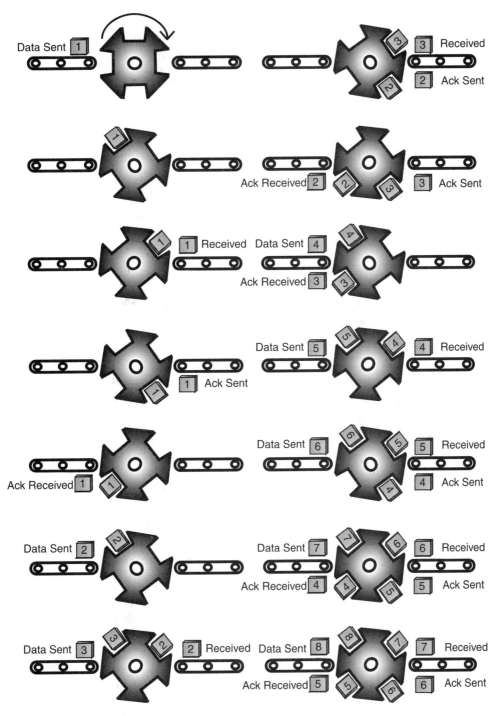

Figure 2.7 TCP network gear analogy.

sent reaches the threshold. Above the threshold, the number of packets that can be sent will only increase by one per round-trip time period. This is the TCP congestion avoidance algorithm.

The adaptive flow control characteristics of TCP are also important in understanding how TCP will react in a QoS environment. Since, as has been illustrated, TCP automatically controls its data rate, any allowances granted by the network can be discovered by TCP. If a TCP data stream is granted access to a well-defined service level that effectively slices out a chunk of the network's resources for the stream, TCP will, at a minimum, adapt its data rate to match perceived capacity. Basically, TCP will probe the network for the maximum transmission rate it can usefully obtain, and will continue to transmit at least at this rate.

MTU Discovery

TCP will also attempt to gauge the MTU size of the data path to prevent fragmentation. This is accomplished by progressively sending TCP/IP packets of decreasing size with the Don't Fragment flag set. The MTU size of the largest packet to be acknowledged by the receiver that does not prompt an ICMP error message from the network will reflect the MTU size for the current data path. All TCP packets for the flow will then be sent with this MTU size. As paths may always change in the Internet, TCP will continue to watch for ICMP errors, and will occasionally increase the MTU size in an attempt to probe the network.

Since TCP is generally used for the bulk transport of data, it is logical to use the biggest packets possible. This is because the greatest data-to-header size ratio makes for the most efficient use of network resources. As a worst-case illustration, if the MTU size was set to 41 bytes for TCP transport, there would only be room for, at most, 1 byte of data in each TCP packet. Meanwhile, 40 header bytes would be transmitted for each of the TCP packets. Effectively, 97.5% of the network's capacity would be transmitting the redundant header information. Obviously, it is better to try to use as much of the network's resources as possible for data transport, not header information.

Next-Generation Internet Protocol

The Internet represents an evolving technology. As more and more systems become connected to the Internet, and as newer and more powerful physical networks arise, the underlying Internet protocol suite will have to change as well. The Internet's protocol suite must accommodate an ever growing number of users and uses. Additionally, given the huge investment and the pervasiveness of Internet Protocol version 4, backward compatibility is a must. Internet Protocol version 6 (IPv6) was developed to solve internetworking issues of the future.

The Need for Expanded Addressing

In the IPv4 header, addresses are expressed as 32-bit values. This provides for a total of 4,294,967,296 unique Internet addresses. With the tremendous growth of the Internet, it is obvious that this limit is not satisfactory. There are many more people in the world than there are Internet addresses. Furthermore, due to the hierarchical addressing schemes used in the classical Internet, every Internet address cannot be effectively utilized. This situation limits the available Internet addresses even more.

Due to this obvious problem, IPv6 was developed to accommodate a far larger pool of addresses. The IPv6 address is 128 bits in size. This allows for an incredible number of unique addresses. Certainly, it is safe to say, 2^{128} (or $4,294,967,296^4$) addresses is far more than sufficient for the foreseeable future. One advantage of this vast address space is that it allows for hosts to automate their configuration and eliminates the need for a central authority to delegate every Internet address.

IPv6 Header

IP version 6 consists of a header followed by the data being transported. The protocol's header is made up of the information required to effectively transport the data portion end-to-end across the Internet. This includes the 128-bit Internet addresses of both the source and destination as well as various class, flow, and management fields. In total the new Internet Protocol header is 40 bytes long. Unlike the IPv4 header, the IPv6 header is not of variable size (a convenience allowing for simplified processing). Figure 2.8 illustrates the new IPv6 header format.

As in IPv4, the version appears as the first field in the IPv6 header. Obviously, the version is set to 6 for IPv6. This is followed by the Class field, which fulfills a similar role to the ToS field in the IPv4 header. The Class field is used to classify a specific service level or priority for use by QoS-enabled devices. Such a priority is used to signify the relative importance of a particular packet compared to others.

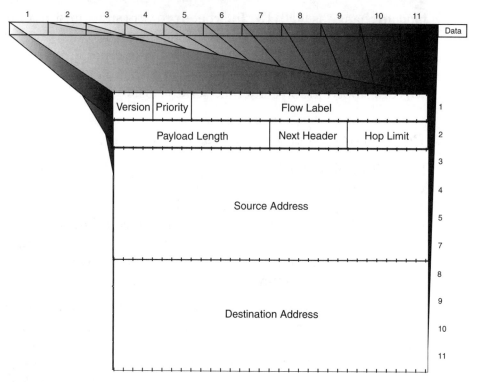

Figure 2.8 The IPv6 header.

The Flow Label field allows the packet to be associated with a particular virtual flow. It provides a method for easily identifying IPv6 packets from the same source to the same destination for special handling. The Length field identifies the total size of the IP packet, including its data. Again, the maximum packet size is 65,535 bytes, just as in IPv4.

The Next Header field identifies the next level header following the IPv6 header. This provides IPv6 with the ability to chain a number of headers together to implement higher level management, routing, or transport layer encapsulation. This ability to chain headers removes the need for the Options field found in the IPv4 header and greatly simplifies the IPv6 header while allowing for extensible functionality.

The IPv6 Hop Limit field is effectively equivalent to the IPv4 TTL field, only in IPv6, the hop limit does not misleadingly measure itself in units of time; it simply represents the number of hops though which the IPv6 packet may pass. Finally, the 128-bit source and destination address round out the IPv6 header.

One interesting field in the IPv4 header that is absent from IPv6 header is the checksum field for the header. This is because the data link layer in most modern networks already contains a method for verifying the integrity of the data it is transporting. Also, the higher-layer data transport protocols such as UDP and TCP contain their own checksums. This being the general case, an additional integrity check would be redundant. Not having to calculate and verify a checksum at every node along a data path also represents an obvious performance gain.

Internet Routing

Simply speaking, routing is the mechanism that enables a packet to be correctly guided through a network from its source to its ultimate destination. The Internet essentially consists of a number of connected computers or nodes. Each of these nodes may have one or more interfaces that connect it to other nodes. The interconnection of nodes via links to other nodes creates paths over which IP packets may flow. These paths may be based on multiple links through multiple hops. Thus, if a complete interconnected path exists between the pertinent end stations, a packet can be successfully delivered from its source to its destination.

The nodes that are actively involved in routing data packets are called *routers*. A router is a node that has multiple interfaces, each of which has links that connect to other nodes in the network. When a router with several interfaces receives an IP packet on an interface, it essentially has to decide to which of its other interfaces the received packet is to be forwarded. Routers are aware of the physical, data link, and network layers. They actually perform routing based on information corresponding to the network layer. In the Internet, this means routers specifically look at the information in the IP header and determine which of its interfaces is the best for forwarding the corresponding IP packet to its destination.

A simple analogy to packet routing is a motorist traveling on vacation. Network links are similar to roads. Roads are interconnected and provide a way for a motorist to reach his or her destination. The car and driver traveling on a road are analogous to an IP packet traveling along a link. Gas stations, then, often act as routers. A motorist can stop at the gas station to get directions; based on this information the motorist will get on the road that best leads to his or her destination. However, in the

Internet, there is a router at every intersection, and every encountered router determines which of its intersecting links a particular IP packet is to follow.

RIP

The Routing Information Protocol (RIP) is a simple routing protocol useful in small intranets. RIP is essentially a distance vector protocol providing distance information from a node to all other nodes in the network. Every router in the network will broadcast messages about its connectivity to other nodes on the network. Routers receiving these messages will add this connectivity information to their local distance vector table. This table collects the shortest observed distances from the local router to all other known nodes and networks. The table will also specify the various local interfaces to which the corresponding remote nodes and networks are connected for the distance described. The distances can be calculated in terms of a number of hops between the local router and the remote router in question, or the cumulative cost of all intermediate links.

To illustrate the basic functionality of a distance vector routing protocol such as RIP, consider a network consisting of five nodes connected by five links. Such a simple network is illustrated in Figure 2.9. In this network, node A is directly connected to nodes B and C through links 3 and 1. Node B is also directly connected to node D through link 5. Node C is directly connected to the nodes A, D, and E though links 1, 4, and 2, respectively.

At the start, all the nodes have a table that is composed of one entry—the distance vector to themselves. This is zero distance and the link is

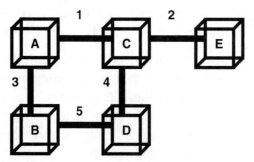

Figure 2.9 A simple network topology.

local to the node. As a next step, all nodes will broadcast this information over all their local links to their neighbor nodes. As the broadcasted distance messages arrive on the nodes' various links, the incoming distance value is incremented to account for the link just traversed. These new distances to the other nodes are then compared to those same distances known in the local routing tables for different links. If there is no shorter distance via a different link to a node in the routing tables, the new distance and the link on which the data was received is added to the routing table. If there is already a recorded distance to a node for the same link, this value will be updated to the most recently reported distance for that link.

To observe this process, consider node A. Initially, node A has the following routing table containing only local data. It will broadcast this information over its two links, 1 and 3.

FROM A TO	OVER LINK	HAS DISTANCE
A	Local	0

Soon, messages arrive from nodes B and C reporting their known routing data. First, node A receives the message from B over link 3 that states node B's distance to itself is 0 hops. Then, node A receives the message from node C over link 1 that states node C's distance to itself is 0 hops. Both of these distances will be incremented to represent the distance from these two nodes to node A. Since there are no entries for the nodes B and C, node A will update its routing table with this information:

FROM A TO	OVER LINK	HAS DISTANCE
A	Local	0
B	3	1
C	1	1

Node A proceeds to forward this new information out the appropriate links. The appropriate links in this case are all node A's links, since the idea is to broadcast, except the node on which a message was originally received. This is because sending the same message out the link on which it was received would be redundant. Thus, a message noting the distance from A to B is 1 hop is sent to node C via link 1. Likewise, a message noting the distance from A to C is 1 hop is sent to node B via link 3.

Following this logic, node A will eventually receive another message from node B over the link 3 stating that the distance from it to node D is one hop. Node A will increment this value, and add it to its routing table. Since this is a new or changed entry, the information will be broadcast over link 1, which is opposite to the link on which the message was originally received.

FROM A TO	OVER LINK	HAS DISTANCE
A	Local	0
B	3	1
C	1	1
D	3	2

Similarly, node C will likely send node A the distance from it to node D via the link 1. Again, this distance will be reported as 1 hop. Again node A will increment this distance and check its routing table. This time, however, node A will notice that it already has an entry for D in its table for a distance that is less than or equal to the distance reported by node C. Thus, nothing is done and no message is broadcast.

Eventually node A may receive a message from node B over link 3 reporting that the distance from node B to node E is 3 hops. After incrementing this value, node A will add this information to its routing table since it did not have an entry for node E. This message will then be broadcast over link 1. Node A's routing table would look as follows:

FROM A TO	OVER LINK	HAS DISTANCE
A	Local	0
B	3	1
C	1	1
D	3	2
E	3	4

It is expected that node C will eventually notify node A over link 1 that the distance from node C to node E is only 1 hop. When node A increments this value, it will observe that this is a shorter distance to node E than the distance in its routing table. Thus, node A will update its table with this new information and will broadcast a message over the link 3.

By this point, the routing algorithm will have stabilized, with no new routing messages to generate so long as the topology does not change. Only the occasional refresh messages will be observed, causing no fluctuation in the routing table. The convergent table would then look like the following:

FROM A TO	OVER LINK	HAS DISTANCE
A	Local	0
B	3	1
C	1	1
D	3	2
E	1	2

Of course, reliability is clearly an issue in the Internet. In large networks, there will be failures and routing must be able to adapt so that connectivity can be maintained. Suppose the link 5 between the nodes B and D fails. This will cause node B and node D to send new messages that specify this condition by reporting an infinite distance between them. Eventually, such a message from B will be received by A, causing it to update its table:

FROM A TO	OVER LINK	HAS DISTANCE
A	Local	0
B	3	1
C	1	1
D	3	Infinite
E	1	2

As soon as node C receives the message from node A that the distance to node D is infinite, node C will consult its table and see that there is a shorter distance to node D available through the link 4. Node C will then send a message back to node A over link 1, specifying its distance to node D as one hop. Node A will increment this value and, since two hops is certainly less than infinity, will update its table. Node A will then broadcast this information through link 3, whereby node B will be notified of the updated connectivity information to node D. Node A's resulting table shown below is convergent and the connectivity failure has been averted through the use of the redundant link.

FROM A TO	OVER LINK	HAS DISTANCE
A	Local	0
B	3	1
C	1	1
D	1	2
E	1	2

This example illustrates some of the functionality of a simple distance vector protocol and has shown a number of interesting capabilities. First, it was shown that routing nodes on a network can cooperate to discover the connectivity of the network. Second, the shortest current distance between any routing node and any other node on the network can be discovered in a distributed fashion. Finally, fault tolerance and recovery is possible, creating a robust routing infrastructure for the network.

Although RIP is a relatively simple routing protocol, it is neither secure nor efficient. The protocol is relatively distributed, but this only means that RIP creates a large number of messages that must be broadcast throughout the network. This results in a protocol with poor scaling properties. The routing algorithm is also relatively inefficient in terms of the time it takes for the routing tables on all routers in the network to completely converge. Due to RIP's apparent inefficiencies, more sophisticated routing protocols have been developed.

OSPF

The Open Shortest Path First (OSPF) routing protocol is at once more powerful than RIP and somewhat more complex. Instead of every router keeping a table listing distances from the local router to all other known nodes or networks, OSPF routers will keep a local network map. This map lists all the direct connections between all known nodes or networks. From this table, the router can calculate the shortest path from itself to any other node on the network. Given that the table describes the connectivity information or link state information about the network, OSPF is considered to be a link state protocol.

It is the job of the OSPF routing protocol to relay information about the network topology. Each router on the network will broadcast messages about its direct connectivity. This information includes the router, its links, and the other nodes that its links directly connect. As this information is flooded throughout the network, each router can build a local table that describes the overall network topology. A link state table describing the topology previously discussed might appear as follows:

FROM	TO	OVER LINK	HAS DISTANCE/COST
A	B	3	1
A	C	1	1
B	A	3	1
B	D	5	1
C	A	1	1
C	D	4	1
C	E	2	1
D	B	5	1
D	C	4	1
E	C	2	1

The messages that relay the connectivity information are defined in the standards space. Thus, the 'O' for Open in OSPF. The 'SPF' describes the second half of OSPF's routing functionality, the local calculations required to determine optimal routes.

Once routers have a complete map of the network connectivity, they still must make consistent routing decisions. Essentially, every router can use the connectivity information to locally calculate the shortest path to any destination node on the network. It is important that the metrics of this algorithm are consistent so that differing routing behaviors will not develop between different router implementations. Having every router figure its own route, inconsistent with other routers' calculations, may lead to routing loops and other undesirable outcomes.

The algorithm that is expected to be applied to calculate the routes in OSPF is E. W. Dijkstra's Shortest Path First (SPF) algorithm. This algorithm is ideal for efficiently finding the shortest distance between two nodes in a graph, or a network for purposes of routing.

OSPF is by far a superior routing protocol to RIP. First of all, with all calculations efficient and local, a router is able to quickly converge on the appropriate table of distances. Second, by allowing for local processing of the network topology map, a router has great flexibility in deciding how to route packets. Such flexibility allows a router to take into account the metrics of the data it is routing to determine the most compatible route. Additionally, a router using OSPF can even take advantage of parallel paths if they are roughly equivalent. Parallel paths can be utilized by sending traffic over all of the available paths instead of just one path. Taking advantage of parallel paths will likely improve throughput by distributing the network traffic. Of course, a flow of packets taking multiple paths might cause out-of-order packets at the destination, but the TCP/IP protocol suite was designed to handle such issues.

Other Routing Mechanisms

RIP and OSPF are far from the only mechanisms for implementing routing on the Internet. We haven't discussed policy-based routing, nor the mechanisms for exchanging routing information between autonomous networks. Additionally, it is likely that many of the routing protocols that exist today are going to be updated and improved. Many other forms of distance and link state protocols have come and gone on the Internet. Some networking vendors have even developed their own proprietary routing protocols.

Additionally, in the next chapter, multicasting and multicast routing will be investigated. Multicasting presents yet another set of routing technologies where more than one source and destination may be contributing to a common flow. It is important because multicasting presents a host of issues when combined with QoS, and RSVP has been carefully designed with multicast in mind.

The purpose of this section on routing was to point out that there is more than one way to route a packet. The issue for QoS is how much involvement in the routing mechanism is required to achieve the desired service characteristics. In general, the idea of separating the concepts of routing and signaling is useful if QoS is to become persuasive on the Internet. This is not to diminish the role routing plays in providing end-to-end QoS, but rather to make the development and deployment of mechanisms for supporting QoS practical.

QoS Routing Considerations

In the preceding sections, routing technologies in the Internet have been briefly introduced. As described so far, none of the routing mechanisms directly take into account dynamic aspects of affecting QoS when routing. The implications that routing has on service characteristics still need to be considered. In both RIP and OSPF, routes can, and often do, change. The path a data flow may take will likely vary over large enough periods. Still, the path data takes is all too crucial to many of the parameters defined by QoS. If a high-speed fiber suddenly fails and a router begins diverting real-time packets to a slower link, the result might lead to unacceptable quality. Other factors such as delay, jitter, and latency are also likely to be affected. In short, when routes change, it is important that any defined QoS service characteristics be maintained for the new data path.

It is practical enough to calculate routes based on static distance or cost metrics. Even additional link characteristics such as capacity and delay bounds can be considered when calculating routes using OSPF. Nevertheless, the Internet presents a moving target for determining ideal routes. There is a wide range of dynamic aspects useful for QoS-based route determination as well.

The usage of a link is just such a dynamic metric. The level of congestion experienced by a node is always changing as traffic comes and goes. If parallel paths exist on which a packet may travel, the current usage of each of the paths would be a useful metric for determining the ideal route. This implies some form of feedback mechanism whereby the network can monitor and report its current operating capacity for all possible paths.

Feedback mechanisms, however, don't tend to scale well, and may not be timely enough to be useful. If nodes in a network rapidly switch between being congested to underutilized and back, it would be difficult for other nodes in the network to synchronize with each other's current conditions. Any feedback mechanism would have to be very responsive, if not predictive, to the traffic behaviors. As it is likely that traffic patterns are going to be random at the finer time scales, it is impractical to address congestion networkwide in real time.

Nevertheless, nodes can observe the traffic behaviors they experience over wide time scales and average the results. Such coarse grain information might be useful for establishing the general load experienced by nodes in the network. As this information will not change rapidly, it is possible for all nodes on a network to advertise the average amount of load they are experiencing. Other nodes in the network can then update their link state databases with this information and use it to make the appropriate routing decisions.

QoS must ultimately be provided end-to-end across a network to be useful. It is not enough for a routing device to consider its own parameters or the next hop's parameters when dealing with a QoS flow. Rather, it is important that every node has some knowledge about the entire data path and its own role in the data path. To some level of granularity, QoS aware routing can provide a picture of the characteristics of a data path. Still, this picture is flawed. There must be a way for the network to accurately allocate specified QoS parameters end-to-end, so that all participating hops may deterministically allocate their resources in support of particular data flows.

The purpose of this book is to formally present the mechanisms by which the QoS requirements of a data flow may accurately be described and relayed to the network. This is the information a QoS routing procedure will ultimately require to choose the best path for a data flow requiring special service, and RSVP can be used to signal this information.

Summary

This chapter has reviewed the concepts, protocols, and technologies behind the vast data communications network known as the Internet. The Internet is a conglomeration of physical layer communications technologies bounded together by the common Internet TCP/IP protocol suite. This suite of protocols provides end-to-end communications and connectivity throughout the Internet. Additionally, TCP provides adaptive capabilities that have allowed the Internet to maintain a ever growing number of users and their associated data traffic. This is what the Internet was, and is: an international network perfectly suited to the transport of packetized data.

A number of issues concerning the introduction of QoS into the Internet paradigm have been investigated. The integration of so many diverse networking technologies presents some interesting questions for QoS deployment. It is always the weakest technology encountered by a data flow along its path that will determine the overall quality of that data flow. Furthermore, reliability has never been a given in the Internet. QoS capabilities change the classical model of the Internet in many subtle ways. Nevertheless, the Internet is able to evolve, and its core technologies can adapt. Today, the Internet is growing to support applications and services never before possible; the remainder of this book will investigate how these changes are being accomplished.

CHAPTER 3

Internet Multicasting

The Internet is a flexible communications infrastructure that can support a wide range of functionalities. The programmable components comprising the Internet are capable of doing more than just blindly forwarding data from a single source to a single destination, or setting up point-to-point communication channels between devices. This chapter focuses on one extension of the basic communications model that allows a single flow of data to be simultaneously sent to a selectable range of destinations. This is the concept of *multicasting*. Multicasting contrasts with the previously discussed model where data is transmitted as a simple unicast stream from a single source host to a single destination. Rather, a multicast session represents a composite data stream generated by potentially many sources and received by potentially many destinations. Furthermore, Internet multicasting is highly efficient in terms of the resources it consumes on the network. That is, when communicating a single stream of data to multiple distributed components, data need not be replicated unnecessarily anywhere in the network.

Multipoint Communications Overview

Before jumping into the technologies behind multipoint communication on the Internet, it is useful to review the need for such a capability. Presentations, conferencing, mass news distribution, and program distribution need to send the same data to many parties at the same time.

Suppose the CEO of a large corporation needs to perform an interactive multimedia presentation for all the corporate employees worldwide. What is a CEO to do? Should the corporation coordinate with a global range of broadcast companies to use their satellite and other broadcast communications components? This would be extremely difficult, but possible, as long as the corporation is willing to pay significant costs for even the shortest of presentations.

What if, instead, the corporation could make use of its own computer data network to achieve the same result? Most corporations today are already connected to the Internet. Their branch offices and plants are, thus, already connected together, at least for data communications purposes. If the bandwidth and multimedia applications were available, it would indeed be possible to use this data communications medium to do corporation-wide presentations.

As another illustration, consider that most phone companies provide technology that allows people to have multiperson conversations. Many people know how to perform a three-way call. But why stop at three end points? Why not a four- or fifty-way call? To accomplish such things using the telephone network, multiple parties must call into a single point, called a bridge, that then acts to bind the multiple calls into a single shared call. Such technologies are essential for teleconferencing. Nevertheless, bridges are often expensive to use and require third-party support. Additionally, if it were a broadly distributed or even international teleconference, every location would potentially have to make an individual long-distance call into the central bridge. Again, the Plain Old Telephone System (POTS) presents an expensive and potentially inefficient option.

With new technologies such as Internet telephony as well as a suite of audio and video applications, it's possible to do the phone conference without the phone, or at least the classical phone network. Since the Internet is so flexible, it is possible to make the act of conferencing much more efficient and feature-rich than could be achieved with just a telephone.

To illustrate another example of multipoint communication, consider cable television. The cable brings into the home a wide range of channels broadcast from the central cable station. Not everyone receiving the cable signal is watching every channel simultaneously. Nevertheless, all these channels are continuously consuming much of the cable's bandwidth at all times. One might imagine that if only the signal for the currently used channel was sent over the cable, the rest of the cable's bandwidth would be available for other purposes.

This is not to suggest that a computer will replace the cable box on top of a television anytime soon, but times are changing. In the Internet there is the potential for millions of channels. Each of these channels can be targeted to a receiver only when required, freeing up the communications medium for other data. Perhaps someday there will be just a single cable used for everything, including telephony, data communications, and, yes, even Internet-broadcast television. Again, multipoint communication plays an integral role in such a vision.

The preceding examples indicate the need for efficient multipoint communications in the Internet. In general, the ability to communicate with multiple parties simultaneously is an important capability. The Internet provides an integrated communications medium that makes efficient multipoint communication possible. The rest of this chapter will investigate the underlying technologies emerging in the Internet to make such multipoint communication a reality.

Unicast Communication

Unicast communication is the ability for one endpoint to communicate with another endpoint across a network. This is often described as point-to-point communication. The core Internet protocols and routing technologies were designed to support such unicast communication. That is, they were designed so that a packet of data could be transported from its single source to its single destination. The Internet Protocol contains the addressing and control information for unicast packet transport, as was shown in Chapter 2.

Indeed, much can be achieved through unicast communication on the Internet. E-mail is sent from one party to another. To view a Web page, a connection is established with a Web server and then the text or graphics may be downloaded. When accessing a computer data file from a remote location, a unicast connection is established with the file server where the file resides. Through this connection, the file may then be downloaded. Essentially, any time one node needs to communicate with another, unicast communication is all that is required.

Additionally, unicast-style communication is relatively easy to achieve on the Internet. As long as the location of the destination host or at least

the destination host's network is known, it is a straightforward procedure to route a packet from its source to its destination. It has already
been shown how this can be achieved using the hierarchical and unique
addressing scheme employed in the Internet, much like mailing a letter
through the postal system. Furthermore, since hosts don't move around
frequently, it is possible to keep a relatively static database containing
their locations.

Nevertheless, there are some deficiencies in the simple unicast scheme.
These deficiencies are apparent when a single host must send the same
data to multiple destinations simultaneously. If unicasting were the
only possibility, a packet would have to be replicated at the host
machine for every destination for which it was intended. The sending
host would also have to know the ultimate destination of each of the
packets it generates. Furthermore, all this replicated information would
be an inefficient use of network bandwidth. Consider Figure 3.1.

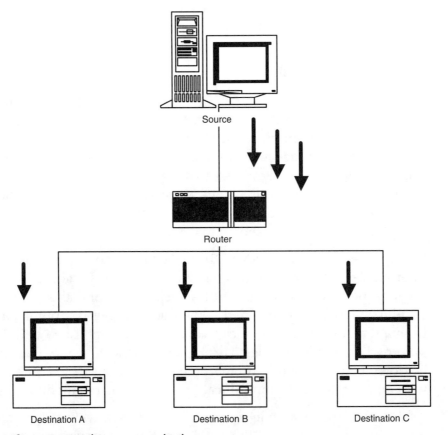

Figure 3.1 Unicast communications.

In this illustration, a host is shown sending the same data to three different locations. These three remote destinations are located on the same subnetwork. Since there is a single link between the sender and the subnetwork, three times the bandwidth is required on this link to communicate the same information three times. This situation quickly becomes unusable if there are many intended destinations for the same data. Clearly, unicast communications is not sufficient for communicating the same information to a large number of parties simultaneously.

Broadcast Communication

Broadcasting is the simplest way to achieve multipoint communications. Radio and television are examples of broadcast media. In these cases, a common shared medium is used to communicate a finite number of signals to multiple destinations. Thus, millions of people can watch their favorite television program at the same time.

It is also possible to broadcast information via the Internet. The previous chapter has already mentioned broadcasting as a mechanism by which routing protocols flood topological information throughout a network. For a router to broadcast a packet, it only needs to send the same packet out all interfaces other than the one on which it was received. In this case, a single packet can be multiplied into many packets as it is broadcast from router to router.

Some of the underlying networking technologies that comprise the Internet are already based on broadcast techniques. The shared-segment Ethernet-style networks, for example, broadcast every packet to every host connected to the local area network. In such networks, broadcasting is inherent for all communicated data. A sender will simply release the data addressed for a specific host into the network. The network will then broadcast the data to all the hosts connected to the medium. Then, all the receiving hosts merely filter out the data that was not specifically addressed to them. Special broadcast addresses can also be used, where every host on the network would receive the appropriately addressed data. In this case, only one packet would need to be created and transmitted, yet all the connected hosts would be able to receive and interpret it.

However, broadcasting has deficiencies of its own. Obviously, not every host on a network is going to be interested in every piece of data being communicated. Some information is simply private between two parties. Flooding data everywhere is also a highly inefficient use of network resources, particularly if the data is only intended for a select few parties. Furthermore, broadcasting information throughout a network is quite insecure, as anyone can listen in on potentially private conversations. There needs to be a middle ground wherein a packet can be sent to a select subset of interested destinations.

Multicast Communication

Multicasting lies somewhere between the extremes of unicast and broadcast communications. Multicasting allows for the communication of the same information to a select number of destinations in an efficient manner. It is also a more flexible way to achieve multipoint communication within the Internet in general.

To multicast a packet, a host only needs to determine the appropriate multicast address and send its data to this address. A range of Internet addresses are dedicated multicast addresses. Once the source host sends a packet, the first hop router will detect this multicast packet. Provided it knows what destinations are interested in the multicast packet, the router will forward copies of the packet out all interfaces that eventually connect to the interested destinations. The destinations interested in the multicast data are known as the *members* of the multicast group.

It is important to note that multicast communication via the Internet is receiver-based. This means that the interested receivers of multicast data will register to express interest in the corresponding multicast group address. The data sent to the specified multicast address will then be forwarded to the registered destinations. By letting the destinations announce their interest in a particular multicast session, multicast data will not have to be broadcast to uninterested hosts. By registering for a multicast group, a host effectively makes itself a member of that multicast group.

Optimizations Achieved through Multicast

When a router receives a multicast packet, it will forward the packet out its interfaces that eventually connect to the ultimate destinations for the packet. Only the interfaces that eventually lead to the selected destinations will forward the multicast packet. If there is no interested receiver for the packet connected to a particular interface, the multicast packet will not be sent out that interface. This is the key to why multicast communication makes the most efficient use of available bandwidth in the network.

Compare and contrast Figures 3.2, 3.3, and 3.4. They demonstrate the unicast, broadcast, and multicast ways of sending the same data to multiple destinations. In Figure 3.2 it is clear that a large amount of packet replication must take place at the source to unicast its data to multiple destinations. On the other hand, Figure 3.3 shows that broadcast traffic will simply flood everywhere, even to hosts that have no reason to receive the data. Figure 3.4 shows the ideal multicast case, where a packet is replicated only when necessary as it is routed throughout the network on its way to the appropriate destinations. In the multicast case, only one copy of the data appears on any given link en route to an interested destination.

Uses of Multicast

A large number of potential applications already exist for multicast technology. Real-time audio and video applications are the most common uses of multicast-style communication. Audio and video applications

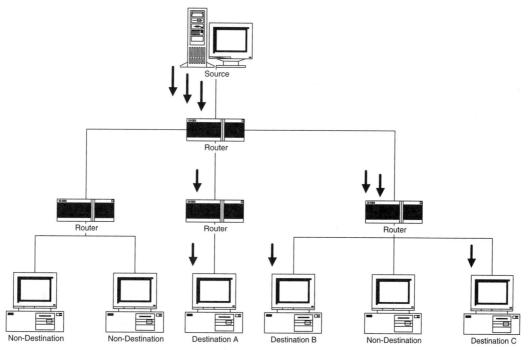

Figure 3.2 Unicast multipoint communication.

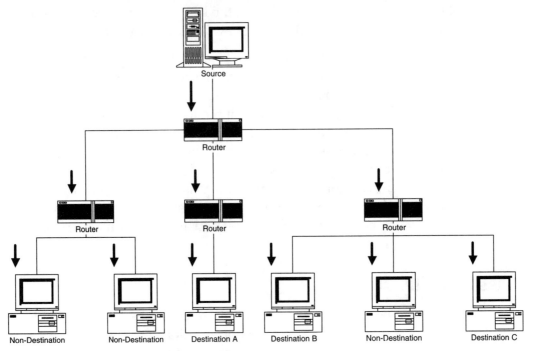

Figure 3.3 Broadcast multipoint communication.

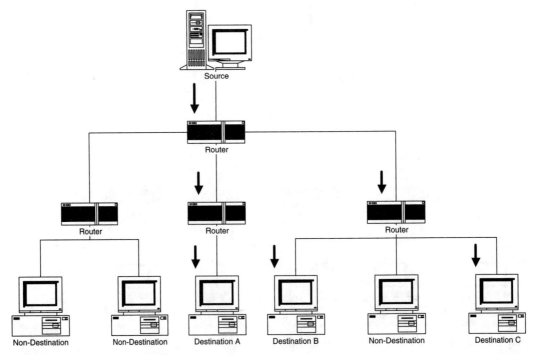

Figure 3.4 Multicast multipoint communication.

enable distance learning, group conferencing, and presentations. Collaboration applications are another potential use of multicast technology. Collaboration applications allow for the simultaneous multiparty editing of documents, presentations, or other material. Such applications allow physically remote individuals to collaborate on the same project at the same time. Of course, there are also the much-ballyhooed push applications. These applications follow the push model, where content is pushed to the interested remote hosts without requiring the hosts to individually query about the data. Contrast the push model to the pull model, where the hosts must specifically query a remote server about its current content.

Multicasting is also applicable to distance learning applications. Suppose that a university has several campuses distributed across a state. A central classroom might host a lecture. The other distributed classrooms may then receive the presentation. Since everything is in real time, the remote sites could send questions back to the presenter and other classrooms. In all, the experience appears like an interactive audio and video presentation to all locations. Figure 3.5 shows just such a multicast scenario for distance learning.

Figure 3.5 Illustration of distance learning.

Another example of collaborative work might be engineers working on the design of a new car. Physically remote engineers can make use of a specialized computer-aided design package that would use multicast technology to allow all the engineers to interact with the design in real time. As one engineer might change an attribute of the car's design, the others would be able to see the results and then make modifications of their own.

One can also imagine services that push the latest stock ticker information using multicast technology to a number of interested parties. Similarly, breaking news, business reports, or just about any other information could be pushed simultaneously to the appropriate networked machines. Such is a far more efficient use of network resources than allowing potentially millions of hosts to constantly poll a news server for the latest information on a breaking story. Indeed, applications that can make good use of multicast technology are limited only by the imagination.

Multicasting and QoS

Of course, any communications technology dealing with real-time interaction, or audio and video applications, must take Quality of Service into consideration. Multicasting is no exception. Since multicasting allows information to be simultaneously distributed to a number of destinations, it is important that the appropriate QoS be achieved for every destination receiving the multicast. If, due to network congestion, some destinations received low-quality multicasts, the technology would clearly prove inadequate and possibly unusable for some of the most obvious applications.

Additionally, in terms of the push model for the simultaneous delivery of content, QoS plays another role. Given that the Internet is inherently unreliable, some of the multicast content will probably be lost. If the multicast is truly widespread, the probability for loss increases significantly. Obviously, if all the content must be received by all the destinations, it is important that some degree of reliable delivery be achieved. Again, by giving multicast traffic a higher Quality of Service, dropped packets due to congestion can potentially be avoided.

In general, QoS plays a significant role in determining the applicability of multicast technology in the Internet. QoS technology simply must take the multicast model into account, because it is likely to become pervasive on the Internet. This is particularly true because multicasting will probably be used for real-time and interactive applications that require a high level of QoS to be effective.

IP Multicast

Now that the concepts behind multicast communications have been examined, it is time to investigate the underlying technologies that make multicasting possible on the Internet. First, we'll look at the method for addressing multicast packets within the Internet addressing scheme and the Internet Protocol. Next, the techniques for accessing multicast groups will be investigated. Finally, the methods for routing multicast packets throughout a network will be described.

IP Unicast Classes

The point-to-point addressing model used in the Internet has already been described. There are three classes of addresses (A, B, and C) that allow a hierarchical interpretation of the Internet's address space in terms of networks and hosts. Subnets further group host addresses together so that a single subnet represents a group of hosts on the same local network. By making the address space hierarchical, routing devices typically need only consider networks and subnetworks when routing, not the exact location of every device in the entire network. This greatly reduces the amount of information that must exist on a routing device to correctly transport a packet to the next hop closer to its ultimate destination.

For a packet being unicast from its source to its destination, a device routing the packet will first examine the network address portion of the destination address. The router can then select the interface that will best transport the packet to the required network. If the routing device is already within the network described by the destination address, then the routing device will consider the subnet to which the address corresponds. If the subnet information is still insufficient, the router will finally consider the destination host's address to properly route the packet out one of its interfaces. By following this simple procedure, a single packet can be forwarded, hop-by-hop, from its source to its destination in a highly scalable manner.

Of course, the unicast scenario is obvious. Every host on the Internet has a unique IP address by which it can be identified. Sending a packet to a host only requires that the sender have knowledge of the destination host's address. The question now is how this model can be extended to support the concept of multiple destinations receiving identical data from the same sender.

IP Broadcast Addresses

Broadcast has been described as a simple form of multisender to multi-receiver communication. When a message is broadcast, multiple hosts can receive the message. Just as with a radio or television broadcast, anyone within range can receive the broadcast signal; likewise, anyone within a common network can receive a broadcast packet.

Broadcasting is supported via special Internet addresses. When these addresses are used in the destination field of a packet, it is assumed the packet is for everyone within a network, as the packet is directed to the broadcast address. Of course, it would not be efficient to broadcast messages over the entire Internet, so broadcast messages can be confined to specified networks.

Internet broadcast addresses are represented by setting the entire set of host number bits in the Internet address to 1. This represents the network scope of the broadcast. Such a broadcast is relative to the network class portion of the IP address and, thus, is supposed to be broadcast throughout the network. As an example, if the network portion of the IP address is 128.34, then a packet to be broadcast throughout such a network would be addressed as 128.34.255.255. In this case, the network is a Class B network and the host number of the address is set to all 1s (where the decimal number 255 equals the binary number 11111111).

IP Class D Addresses

Now that the Internet's addressing scheme has been examined for both the unicast and broadcast cases, it is time to examine how multicast addressing is achieved. First, it is important to remember that multicast is a scoped form of broadcast where only a select number of hosts will receive the messages. Furthermore, multicast addressing must provide for a large number of possible multicast sessions or channels. Just allowing one address, as with broadcasting, is simply insufficient for multicasting. Thus, to meet these requirements, multicast addresses are represented as a new class of IP addresses.

This address class for multicast addresses is akin to the Class A, B, and C addresses previously discussed. The multicast class is called the Class D address. It is distinguished via the same mechanism that is used to distinguish between Class A, B, and C addresses. If the most significant zero bit in the IP header is in the fourth bit position, then the address is considered to be a Class D, or multicast, address.

The 28 bits of the Class D address provide 268,435,456 possible multi-cast addresses for IPv4-style addresses (Figure 3.6). Nevertheless, only 8,388,608 multicast addresses are generally applicable due to the map-ping constraints imposed by certain data-link layer multicast ad-dressing schemes. Specifically, the ever-popular Ethernet-style local area network's addressing scheme only specifies 23 bits for use as mul-ticast addresses. Thus, only the low-order 23 bits of the IPv4 multicast address are mapped into the Ethernet multicast address, leaving the rest unused. Still, millions of multicast addresses provide plenty of channels for multipoint communication throughout the Internet. Imag-ine a television that could tune into over 8 million channels!

IPv6 also supports multicast addresses and, as always, many more than IPv4 due to its significantly increased address range. Specifically, there are 112 bits available to specify a multicast group in the IPv6-style address. Eight additional bits are used for flags and for specifying the scope of the multicast group. The scope of the multicast address deter-mines how far the multicast traffic is to travel within a network. Such traffic can be confined to a link, site, organization, or allowed to reach globally.

IPv4 can also scope multicast traffic by simply limiting the TTL in the IP packets sent by the source. Once the TTL for a multicast packet expires, the packet will simply be discarded just as described in Chapter 2. Effectively, this will limit the number of hops a multicast IPv4 packet may travel.

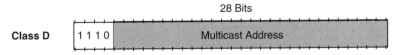

Figure 3.6 Illustration of Class D address.

Receiver-based Model

IP Multicast employs a receiver-based model. That is, the potential receivers decide what multicast traffic they want and when to send a request to join the group. This technique is advantageous in terms of scalability. The source does not need to know what all the potential destinations are. It only needs to appropriately address its multicast packets so that they may be transmitted to the correct multicast group. Hosts that wish to receive the multicast can then register for the multicast group by sending the appropriate message to their closest router.

In the receiver-based model, only the closest routing devices to the destination need to be aware of a destination's interest in the multicast group. Such routers will then either forward any multicast traffic they receive for the group to this destination, or will make a request to another routing device closer to the source to receive the multicast traffic. The end result will be a scalable solution that enables potentially millions of hosts to receive traffic sent to the same multicast group.

Compare this solution to the alternative where the source needs to know who all the potential receivers are. This is called the *sender-based* model. In this case, it would be difficult for the single source to keep track of potentially millions of destination hosts. Furthermore, there would need to be millions of addresses specified, one for each destination. Even the data would need to be replicated, once for each destination. Clearly, the sender-based model is fundamentally flawed in terms of scalability. It is much better for the receivers to selectively and explicitly join a single multicast group and distribute the whole process throughout the network. Of course, the act of joining a multicast group requires an underlying protocol for communicating the join request.

IGMP

The Internet Group Management Protocol (IGMP) is the protocol that allows a host to request to join a multicast group. Clearly, this protocol was built to support the receiver-based model for multicasting. A host that wishes to receive multicast data will send an IGMP message specifying the corresponding multicast group address. The packet format for the original version of the IGMP message is shown in Figure 3.7.

The first field of the IGMP message contains the four-bit version of the protocol. In this case, the protocol's version is 1. The second field

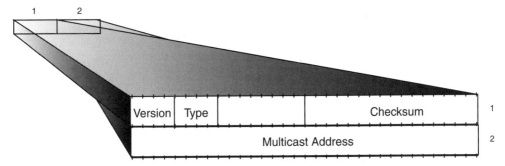

Version	Type				Checksum	1
		Multicast Address				2

Figure 3.7 IGMP packet format.

specifies the four-bit IGMP type. Following this, the checksum field is useful for detecting whether or not the IGMP message has been corrupted, and, therefore, should be ignored. Finally, the Class D multicast group address is contained in the last field of the IGMP message.

Hosts that want to join a multicast group issue IGMP requests. When a host is ready to receive multicast traffic for a specific multicast group, it will prepare an IGMP message with the corresponding multicast address. The message is sent to a specially reserved multicast address so that a router elected to field the membership requests will receive this message. This same router will also periodically query all devices connected to it about their multicast group membership. These queries will result in IGMP messages for every multicast group that still has interested receivers on the network. Basically, a host will receive the router's query, and will then resend an IGMP message for each multicast group from which the host is still interested in receiving data. If the host has already observed an IGMP message from another host expressing interest in the same multicast group, it will not reissue a redundant IGMP request for that group. This last step avoids flooding the network with too many IGMP messages.

When the elected router receives an IGMP request from a connected host, the router will note the multicast group of interest. The router will then proceed to send the IGMP up a hierarchy of routers composing a branch of a multicast session. If a router receives other IGMP requests on different interfaces, it will proceed to send the appropriate multicast traffic to those interfaces as well. Only one IGMP message per router need be sent upstream to other routers on the multicast tree, however. This procedure is illustrated in Figure 3.8.

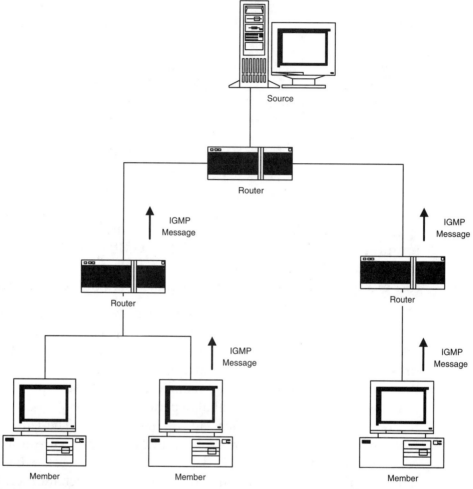

Figure 3.8 IGMP message forwarding.

Models for Multicasting

Now that the concept of multicasting has been defined and described, it is time to investigate how multicasting might effectively be carried out on a network. Indeed, multicasting is a fundamentally different concept from unicasting. The issues of scalability and routing are also different for multicasting. The fact is, in a receiver-based model for multicast traffic, receivers may come and go at will. This dynamic functionality is inherent to multicasting. Furthermore, multicast traffic must be carefully handled so as not to go awry within a network, potentially causing storms of replicated traffic. To understand how multicast communication should best be treated within a network, it is first important to understand what underlying assumptions can be made about the multicast topology. Different multicast techniques can then be developed to cater to each contrasting assumption.

Dense-mode Multicast

One assumption that can be made about multicast topologies is that there is typically dense membership for a particular multicast group. In a dense multicast topology, receivers interested in a particular multicast session are likely to be grouped together. This means they will probably share the same subnetwork. In general, dense multicast topologies will have clusters of interested destinations while the rest of a network will remain relatively devoid of interested receivers.

A dense topology can be accurately assumed for many multicast examples. Consider the distance learning example where a university multicasts a course to several distributed classrooms. In this situation, most of the destinations will be on the university network concentrated in the subnetworks associated with the various classrooms. Usually the multicast group membership is primarily within the classrooms interested in the multicast session.

In cases of dense multicast topologies, broadcasting small amounts of the multicast session would probably be fine. Since most of the receiving parties are close together, a simple model could be developed so that the multicast traffic would be concentrated within a few subnetworks, with the source of the multicast relatively close.

Sparse-mode Multicast

The converse of dense multicast topologies is sparse multicast topologies. The assumption here is that the density of the receivers is rather sparse—that is, there are relatively few members interested in any particular subset of the multicast traffic within any one specific part of a network. The membership is not specifically localized to some subset of the network; rather, the interested destinations are spread frugally throughout the network.

In such multicast topologies, it is crucial that the multicast delivery model used scales appropriately over large networking regions. The assumption is that the number of hosts interested in receiving a multicast session within any one region is relatively few. Thus, there should not be a lot of unnecessary traffic relayed over large spans of networks that are, for the most part, uninterested in any particular multicast session. Very simply, any technique that involves broadcasting group information is probably a poor candidate for sparse multicast topologies.

Spanning Trees

A spanning-tree-like topology is one of the simplest means by which nonredundant multicasting can be achieved. A *spanning tree* can be considered a virtual network topology that removes all redundant paths. In a physical network topology, there are typically multiple routes throughout. Many of these routes present redundant paths that data may take en route from its source to its destination. This is no different than the fact that most people have several potential routes they can take from their home to their place of work.

The spanning tree is a snapshot of a network topology that picks only one path to route data and simply doesn't use redundant paths. At the same time, the spanning tree results in a fully connected network where a data path still exists between every pair of nodes on the network. The result is a tree where a root node can be selected from which all other nodes can be considered children of the root node. Figure 3.9 demonstrates the metamorphosis of a fully interconnected network into one that is interconnected by a spanning tree. In this illustration, only the links that are associated with the spanning tree are ever used to transmit data.

The advantage of the spanning tree is that it removes the potential for loops though which data might be cycled indefinitely. In the case of multicasting, the spanning tree provides one map by which data can be effectively moved from its source to all its potential destinations. If all routing devices in a network are aware of the spanning tree, they will know who their one parent node is. All requests for multicast membership will then

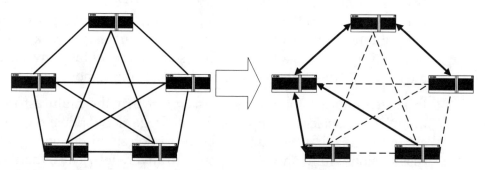

Figure 3.9 An example of a virtual spanning tree for a fully interconnected network.

be forwarded up the spanning tree from child to parent. Similarly, multicast traffic can be sent down the spanning tree from parent to child. Eventually, the multicast request will reach a parent node that has access to the multicast session. This node can then forward the multicast traffic out the interface on which a multicast request was received.

Reverse Path Forwarding

Reverse Path Forwarding (RPF) is a distributed approach to constructing a multicast tree. The objective is to find the shortest path from a multicast destination back to a multicast data source. This technique assumes the underlying topology of the network is such that a single, consistent shortest route can be determined from a destination back to a source.

In RPF, multicast traffic from every source is periodically allowed to flood into the network. This traffic is used to announce the existence of a multicast data source. The RPF technique is based on the shortest known route back to the multicast source, or parent. Every router will probably know the shortest route to a multicast data source within the network. Thus, when multicast traffic arrives at a router from a multicast source, the router will discard the traffic if it came from another router that was not on the shortest path back to the multicast source. Furthermore, given sufficient knowledge of the network's topology, a router can avoid forwarding multicast from a specific source to any other downstream routers that do not consider this router to be the shortest path back to the multicast source. The result is that multicast traffic from a specific source will follow a nonredundant spanning tree path through the rest of the network.

In general, multicast traffic is only continuously forwarded out a router's link if there is a known member for the multicast session downstream from the link in question. This membership must be explicitly announced through a mechanism such as IGMP. Additionally, when all downstream membership for a multicast session is gone, the multicast tree should be pruned so that there is no unused traffic flooding the associated links. This graft-and-prune mechanism allows for dynamic group membership in the RPF technique.

Shared Trees

A shared tree topology is one of the simplest ways to cater to a sparse topology scenario for multicast traffic. Effectively, the shared tree is a common spanning tree for an entire multicast group. The reason spanning tree topologies are well-suited to sparse mode multicast is that there is just one link by which a multicast session may be received or sent. This spanning tree topology is known up front. Thus, there is no doubt where a multicast join request needs to be sent—it is always sent to the parent node in the tree. There is just one parent node for every device on the network. Furthermore, given the predefined topology, it is not necessary to announce a multicast group by flooding the entire network with unwanted traffic. Multicast traffic is simply forwarded to the root of the shared tree.

Shared-tree multicast routing techniques can construct a spanning-tree-like topology for each multicast group. Such trees are constant regardless of the membership of the multicast group. It is inconsequential whether a member is a sender or a receiver; the multicast group tree remains constant. Thus, routers only need to keep a single shared tree for each multicast group, and not for every source group pair. This fact makes shared trees advantageous over source-based tree techniques such as RPF from the perspective of scalability.

Multicast Routing Protocols

Multicast routing is key to supporting multicast in the Internet. This is because multicast must be supported by the components comprising the infrastructure of the network. The problem of routing for multicast moves from forwarding a packet from its source to a single destination, to the model where a packet is to be replicated and forwarded to potentially many destinations located throughout the network. To accomplish this unique routing functionality, a variety of multicast routing protocols have been developed.

RIP to DVMRP

The Distance Vector Multicast Routing Protocol (DVMRP) was the first popular implementation of a multicast routing protocol. It implements a RPF-style multicast routing scheme that works with RIP. Thus, like any RPF-style protocol, DVMRP is interested in the source address and multicast group information to calculate routes.

Basically, DVMRP must determine how to forward a multicast packet based on its source and group information as well as on knowledge about what interfaces connect to group members. When a DVMRP router receives a multicast packet, it will first examine the packet to see if it came in on a link that represents the shortest path back to the source. If it does, the packet is accepted, and then is forwarded out all remaining links that connect to devices for which this router represents the shortest route back to the source. If downstream routers are not interested in the multicast traffic because they are not aware of any members, they will send a prune message for the corresponding multicast group. On receipt of the prune message, the upstream router will stop sending the associated multicast traffic. If a router that has sent a prune message decides it now wants the multicast traffic, it can send a graft message that effectively cancels the effects of the previous prune message. The router can then receive the multicast traffic.

Because multicast senders will come and go, it is important that even pruned states are periodically refreshed. A prune message will only stop the multicast traffic for a short period of time. When this period expires, the multicast traffic will again be forwarded, and the prune messages will have to be repeated. This process avoids complicated state management for the highly dynamic multicast sessions.

To see how DVMRP operates, consider the example topology illustrated in Figure 3.10. Here, there is a single source (S1) sending multicast data and three potential members (M1, M2, and M3) for the multicast group. All the nodes are connected via routers R1, R2, and R3.

To see how things work, suppose S1 is initially not sending any traffic but M1 has issued an IGMP join request for the multicast group. The router R2 will first receive this join request and will remember the request. Eventually, S1 will begin sending traffic to the multicast group. In this case the router R1 connected to S1 will receive the multicast traffic from the source. The router will then proceed to flood the multicast traffic out its two interfaces to routers R2 and R3. It does this because it knows that R2 and R3 consider it to be on the shortest path back to the source. When router R3 receives the traffic, it will not forward it to R2 because R3 is not in the shortest path from R2 to the source. Since R3 has no members for the multicast traffic, it will send a prune message back to R1 to stop receiving the multicast. When router R2 receives the multicast packet from R1, it will notice that R1 is its shortest path back to the source. Since R2 has an outstanding IGMP request from M1 for the multicast group, R2 will not send a prune message to R1. Thus, R2 will continue to receive the multicast traffic from R1 and will forward it onto M1.

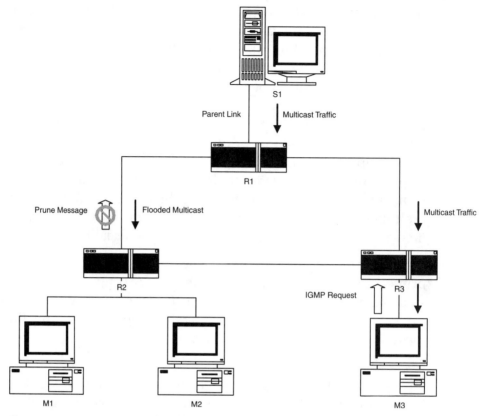

Figure 3.10 DVMRP example topology.

If M3 eventually issues an IGMP request to join the group, R3 will send a graft message to R1 stating its newfound interest in the multicast group. R1 will then cancel the outstanding prune state for R3 and will proceed to forward the multicast traffic to R3.

Finally, suppose M1 departs the multicast group. When it does, it will stop responding to R2's periodic IGMP queries for that multicast group. When R2 no longer receives any response to its queries, it will send a prune message to R1. As a result of this message, R1 will stop forwarding the multicast traffic to R2.

Like RIP, DVMRP is a simple and effective routing protocol. Also like RIP, DVMRP has its share of deficiencies. DVMRP's tendency to flood the entire network with multicast traffic until it is explicitly pruned back has some serious scalability issues. Its dependency on RIP means it also suffers from RIP's slow convergence characteristics as described in Chapter 2. Fortunately, DVMRP is not the only multicast routing protocol available.

MOSPF

DVMRP may work fine for networks that rely on the RIP routing protocol, but what about OSPF networks? It was shown in Chapter 2 that OSPF has advantages over RIP in terms of performance and flexibility, and that OSPF routing is increasingly deployed in the Internet. Thus, Multicast Extensions to OSPF (MOSPF) have been defined to support OSPF networks.

Like DVMRP, MOSPF is an RPF-style multicast routing protocol. It must calculate the shortest path back to a multicast source. MOSPF, however, is able to use the OSPF link-state database records to specify group membership on a link-by-link basis. These records can then be broadcast to all participating MOSPF routers. This results in every router knowing not only the network topology, but the group membership throughout the topology as well. Thus, there is no need for the multicast flooding prevalent in DVMRP. Hosts seeking to be members of a multicast group will simply notify their elected MOSPF router via an IGMP message. This router will then prepare a link-state record and broadcast this group membership information to all MOSPF routers in the network. The appropriate routers along the shortest path to the source will then proceed to forward the multicast traffic to the new member.

CBT

Core-Based Trees (CBT) were developed to cater to the sparse multicast topologies. In fact, the philosophy behind CBT multicasting is that sparse multicast topologies are the likely rule in the Internet.

Inherent to CBT is the concept of an established core node for multicast groups. This core node corresponds to a routing device at the root of a multicast tree for an entire multicast group. So, in CBT, a spanning tree exists for just the multicast group, not every traffic source within the multicast group. Not having to explicitly keep track of every source allows CBT to scale better than RPF-style multicast routing protocols.

Since a single spanning tree exists for every group, all devices that want to become members or contributors to the group must talk through the core node. Figure 3.11 illustrates a CBT multicast topology. Here all of a group's multicast traffic is first forwarded through the core node and then finally on to the members.

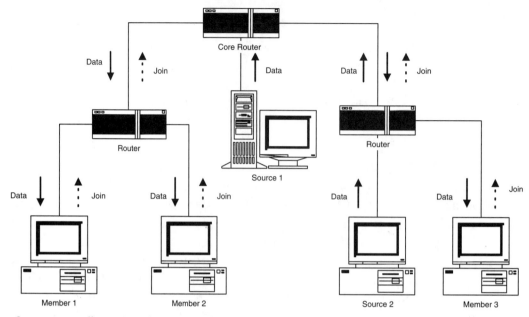

Figure 3.11 Illustration of Core-Based Tree multicast topology.

CBT also defines more sophisticated signaling between multicast routing devices. When a multicast router receives an IGMP request to join a particular multicast group, the router will attempt to join the group by sending a join request to the next router one hop closer to the core router. This router will then send a join request to the next closest router to the core router until a join message finally reaches the core, or a router that has already seen another join request for the same multicast group. When the core router receives a new join request, it will issue an explicit acknowledgment. These acknowledgments are then forwarded hop-by-hop back to the device making the initial request.

PIM

Protocol-Independent Multicast (PIM) is another multicast routing protocol that is not directly associated with a particular unicast routing protocol. PIM strictly provides the protocols and functionality for multicast routing, and works independently of the underlying routing functionality of the router. Since PIM was developed for the specific purpose of multicasting, it provides support for both sparse and dense multicast topologies via two essentially distinct mechanisms.

PIM for dense multicast topologies (or PIM dense mode) is somewhat akin to DVMRP. It works by periodically flooding multicast traffic from its source throughout the network. Prune messages are then used to remove the unused branches from the multicast tree. Unlike DVMRP, PIM dense mode is not dependent on the underlying device supporting RIP.

PIM for sparse multicast topologies (or *PIM sparse mode*) is akin to the Core-Based Trees approach to multicast routing. The difference here is that PIM sparse mode uses the concept of rendezvous points instead of core devices. Nevertheless, the functionality of the two is essentially the same. Multicast sources forwarded their data to the rendezvous point, and group members will then communicate with this centralized location to obtain the respective multicast traffic.

PIM has advantages in that it is not specifically tied to a single underlying unicast routing implementation. PIM also provides a number of options and supports several different multicast topologies. Nevertheless, all this flexibility comes at a cost with respect to complexity. PIM is more complex than the previously discussed multicast routing methods. It also forces routing devices to implement dual routing protocols, one for unicast and another for multicast. The routers must then maintain separate routing tables for each protocol in turn.

QoS Considerations

From the perspective of QoS, multicast creates a number of conundrums. The simple concept of point-to-point connections regularly seen in telephone networks must give way to the concept of multipoint communication. Fundamentally, multicast elevates the role of the receiver to keep things scalable. Instead of having the sender decide which devices in a network should receive traffic for a particular multicast session, the potential receivers ask for the multicast traffic. Thus, potentially millions of hosts throughout a large network can participate in a single multicast session on a need-to-receive basis.

The concept of a receiver-based methodology is, indeed, key. Receivers specifically ask to become members of a multicast group. Furthermore, different receivers may have different requirements as far as service quality is concerned. Some may be perfectly content with best-effort Quality of Service while others may want the highest quality possible. Ultimately, it is the receivers that know their requirements and it is the responsibility of the QoS signaling protocol to communicate the receivers' needs. The concept of a receiver-based model will provide a precedent for definition of a QoS signaling protocol for the Internet as described in the next chapter.

Additionally, just as with unicast, multicast provides a number of different methods for routing packets throughout a network, as shown in this chapter. Thus, it is important that QoS signaling mechanisms do not become particularly tied to a specific implementation. Rather, the QoS signaling mechanism should be as routing-protocol-independent as possible.

Summary

Multicast provides a new model for the mass distribution of content over the Internet. Multicasting allows a single flow of data to be efficiently sent to a select number of destinations. IP multicast delivery is also a scalable solution because it is up to the receivers to explicitly join multicast groups, thus allowing for potentially millions of receivers to participate in the same multicast session. This receiver-based model for content distribution is a key concept for consideration when applying QoS signaling to multicast.

In the next chapter, the methodology behind QoS within the Internet will be examined with an eye toward the Internet Resource ReSerVation Protocol (RSVP). The point to keep in mind is that multicasting has an impact on the design of protocols that can signal and describe QoS in terms of data transport. Multicasting is another way to transport data and deserves special consideration in its own right, especially since the likely applications for multicasting include real-time audio and video broadcasting.

PART TWO

QoS in the Internet

CHAPTER 4

The Internet with Quality of Service: A Conceptual Overview

Traditionally, the Internet has only supported a best-effort Quality of Service. Ideally, any packet injected into the Internet is treated as any other. Such fairness works for simple data transport because of protocols such as TCP that act politely and give way when congestion arises. Nevertheless, what is good for one type of application is potentially unacceptable for another. This chapter will investigate what it means to extend the basic best-effort model in the Internet. It will cover the basic concepts, issues, and implications of an Internet that can support a wide range of service qualities to meet the needs of a vast array of applications and uses.

Best-Effort to Differentiated Service Quality on the Internet

The classic best-effort model long assumed in the Internet has a great advantage in terms of simplicity. Almost all data being transported can be transported in the same way. Essentially, this model is analogous to vehicles traveling down a single-lane road where passing is not allowed.

This simple model has continued to work over the years as the Internet grew exponentially in size. The reason for this is that the communicating nodes within the Internet's domain are relatively well-behaved. Protocols like TCP act politely when conditions deteriorate and congestion arises. In this scenario, an e-mail might simply take a few extra minutes to be delivered or a Web page might take a few extra seconds to download. Thus, applications simply see a graceful degradation in service as opposed to a complete blackout. This model has worked well for applications like e-mail, file transfer, and Web browsing that can slow down yet continue to function properly.

Nevertheless, such bulk-data applications represent only a fraction of all classes of applications. Certainly, any communications application such as IP Telephony that involves real-time user interaction or multimedia depends on the constant availability of sufficient network resources. When congestion occurs, such applications will likely become unusable. Additionally, under some conditions, extensive degradation of service quality can affect even bulk-data applications. In the case of mission-critical applications, their access to the network should not be impeded by frivolous uses of the network. When business suffers, money is lost, and the best-effort model of networking is to be blamed.

Finite Network Resources

Obviously, no network can offer limitless resources. A telephone network, for example, is limited to a finite number of possible simultaneous connections. If there are more attempted calls than connections supported by the network, some calls simply will not go through. The Internet has capacity limitations as well, as it is limited by how much bandwidth can be used. In the Internet, bandwidth resources are not allocated in whole chunks as is done with connections over telephone networks. Rather, bandwidth is consumed when data packets are present. When there are too many packets that need to be communicated, leading to congestion, some packets will probably be delayed or even dropped. The result is simply that data is lost.

One can think of packet switched networks as functioning like sifting sand through a funnel, as shown in Figure 4.1. Each grain of sand can be thought of as a data packet to be communicated over a link. The neck of the funnel represents the communications link through which the data, or sand in this analogy, must eventually pass. Finally, the body of the funnel represents the memory or queuing capacity of a network device connected to the link. The capacity of the funnel's neck at any moment in time is finite, the principle behind the basic egg timer. The capacity of the funnel body, although greater, is also finite. The bandwidth of the funnel's neck can be thought of as the rate at which sand can be sifted through the neck. This could be measured in the number of grains of sand moved through the funnel neck per second. Now, when one starts dumping sand into the funnel, the body will fill and the sand will be sifted out through the neck at a constant rate. If the rate of sand being dumped into the funnel exceeds the rate at which it can be sifted out the neck, the sand will eventually overflow the body and, for argument's sake, will be lost.

Similarly, in packet switched networks, devices can get overloaded with too much data. In the most basic case, this overload can happen if a high-capacity link feeds into a low-capacity link. Just as when too much sand is dumped into the funnel, something has to give. The routing device supporting the two links will only be able to store a finite amount of information before it is forced to start throwing packets away. Likewise, even if all links have the same capacity, congestion can still result. When multiple links feed into a single link, the aggregation of the combined traffic from the multiple links will quickly overwhelm the shared link, again resulting in lost data. Figure 4.2 illustrates the potential for packet loss due to aggregating too much traffic onto a single link.

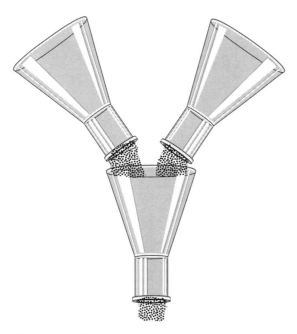

Figure 4.1 Funnel overflow analogy.

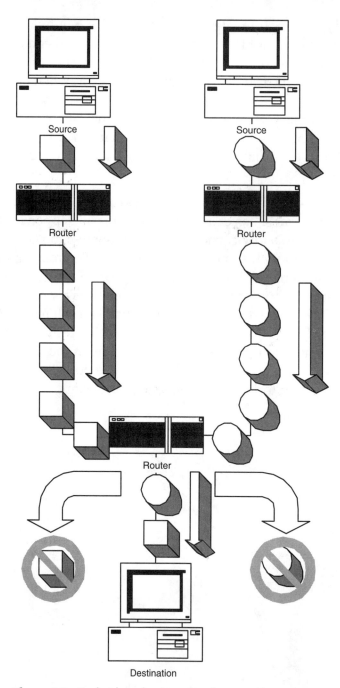

Figure 4.2 Packet loss due to network congestion.

Real-Time Traffic Requirements

Even if queuing capacity were infinite, just getting the data end-to-end eventually would not always be sufficient. Real-time applications such as videoconferencing need to have their data communicated promptly, and in a consistent manner. Such data must arrive at its destination on schedule or it will be useless.

Consider, for example, a simple uncompressed video stream that displays a sequence of pictures in a black-and-white frame with 10 rows and 10 columns of pixels. For the picture to appear to move smoothly, a frame would probably have to be updated every tenth of a second. Supposing that every frame corresponds roughly to a data packet, and there is no buffering of the frames, it is necessary that a data packet arrive at the receiving host every tenth of a second. If a frame is delayed and arrives out of order, it is useless to display it because it missed its appropriate place in the sequence of frames.

Of course, the need for timely delivery is not limited to video and other real-time applications; it is also necessary for even the classical bulk-data applications. A user downloading a Web page would likely find excessively slow loads unacceptable. Similarly, it would be unacceptable for a scheduled nightly backup of files at a remote office to take days to complete simply because of excessive congestion on the required links.

The previous simple examples illustrate the point that there is more to communicating data than just eventually transmitting it from its source to its destination. Some data is time-sensitive and must be delivered in a correspondingly timely fashion. Quality of Service for such applications must not only take into consideration reliable transfer, but other delivery characteristics as well.

Engineering Networks

Large networks are typically built up over time by a committed staff of network technicians. These individuals have the job of creating networks that allow an organization to effectively conduct its business. The people who build networks are involved in far more than just running around in back rooms connecting wires and cables to hubs, switches, and routers. They must carefully consider the current and projected use of the network's resources and design the network to satisfy these usage requirements. As data communications technology plays a more and more significant role in the operations of organizations, it is crucial that the networks stay functional, or significant losses in productivity and business may result.

The simplest method of dealing with the capacity provisioning dilemma is to provide more than sufficient resources for everyone. This is often referred to as overengineering networks, and it can temporarily solve capacity issues. Overengineering takes into consideration the maximum projected usage of a network's resources, and designs a network that can meet or surpass this maximum required capacity. Considering the funnel analogy again, an overengineered funnel would have a neck that is wide enough to move sand at a rate greater than sand can be entered into the funnel's body. In networks, this means the links and the devices connecting the links will have capacity as great or greater than the cumulative data sources feeding the links require. Thus, instead of inventing a new paradigm for data communications, one can simply supply more of the same technology to solve potential capacity problems.

Overengineering networks within organizations is possible because an organization controls its internal networks and typically has the financial resources to buy the latest and greatest gear. Since networks are evolving very rapidly in terms of capacity or bandwidth, there is always technology available to overengineer a network. When congestion is seen to occur, the links and devices in contention can simply be upgraded to a capacity that solves the problem, albeit perhaps only temporarily.

Nevertheless, overengineering is a far from optimal solution to contention for network resources. Constantly upgrading to the latest and fastest technology is an expensive fix. First of all, it involves buying new and expensive equipment. Next, technically savvy individuals must actually integrate the new technologies into the existing infrastructure. People who operate the networks must then learn about the new hardware and software now comprising major portions of the network. Finally, this process seems to have no end. There is always going to be a greater need for network resources than there will ever be network resources. Computers keep getting faster and the applications that they run demand more and more networking resources. This trend is not likely to stop anytime soon.

Overengineering is also an inefficient solution. It implies that throwing sufficient bandwidth at a resource capacity problem will provide a solution. This might indeed be the case, but it means that there will likely be a significant proportion of bandwidth that goes completely unused much of the time. If the target is enough capacity for the maximum projected usage, and networks typically operate with only average usage, the extra capacity is simply wasted.

Finally, overengineering is not going to achieve guaranteed success. There are always unforeseen resource contention issues. Real-time applications that are overly sensitive to any interruption in service, no matter how occasional, will visibly suffer. Failing to adequately deliver content for such applications will inevitably diminish the degree to which Internet data communications technology can effectively be employed for these applications. The probable use of such applications over the entire scope of the Internet leads to further doubts about the extent to which wide area networks (WANs) can be properly and economically overengineered. Overengineering simply will not scale to support the needs of the whole of the Internet.

Because simply throwing more of the same technology at capacity problems is not a likely solution, it is important to consider an entirely new approach to the capacity dilemma. To determine what form such an approach should take, one must consider what really needs to be achieved in data communications today. The proper engineering of networks to meet the needs of business will always be an important objective. There simply needs to be a way to deterministically control how the network resources are used.

Priorities and Application Requirements

Fundamentally, networks provide communications services for applications. How these communications resources are to be used depends on what applications are using them. Some applications are inherently more important than others. Additionally, the choice as to which applications are the most important depends on their usefulness to an organization, or even to the individual user. Finally, some applications have well-defined communications requirements that must be met to function appropriately, regardless of their relative usefulness or priority.

Categorizing and prioritizing application traffic ensures that when network resources are in short supply, the most important applications will outrank less important applications. Thus, the most important applications will have the first rights to the network's resources, and the remaining capacity will be available for the less important applications.

Determining which applications are critical and which are not is a custom decision. It will probably vary from organization to organization. For example, a corporation would not want to see the vast majority of its network resources consumed by those who merely want to play networked games. Rather, mission-critical applications or the most essential work-related applications must take precedence. It would be extremely useful to be able to sort out all the traffic competing for network resources and give preference to those that are most deserving.

When too much high-priority traffic exists, it is likely that the same network resources will once again be in contention. Thus, it is important that a balance be struck between what is important and less important, and that sufficient capacity exists to meet the typical needs of all traffic. If networks are engineered properly, traffic prioritization will allow for the most intelligent use of the resources available.

Nevertheless, simple prioritization of traffic does not satisfy all requirements an application might have. As has been shown, some applications still require specific performance behavior from the network. This specific description of required performance would be difficult to represent with a simple priority value. Rather, an application must be able to describe its desired behavior accurately end-to-end. Somehow, every network element in the data path must be aware of an application's performance requirements. Each node must then do its part to see that such fine-grain requirements are met so the application may perform optimally.

Once network traffic can be prioritized and the network successfully meets all the requirements of high-priority applications, there will probably be plenty of bandwidth left over. This remaining bandwidth is available for the best-effort delivery of data that is not of a time-critical nature, such as e-mail, World Wide Web browsing, Internet news, or file downloads. This list could be summarized as all traffic generated by the classical best-effort-oriented applications that have always been part of the Internet's landscape. Table 4.1 represents examples of applications and their most likely traffic classifications.

Mechanisms for Achieving QoS in the Internet

Fundamentally, enabling the Internet to support QoS requires that several new technologies exist and be implemented in the Internet. These

Table 4.1   Traffic Classifications for Popular Applications

BEST EFFORT	REAL-TIME	MISSION-CRITICAL
E-mail	IP telephony	E-commerce
Web Browsing	Video	Database
Internet News	Collaboration	Accounting/Billing

technologies provide the mechanisms by which QoS may be achieved. They have implications for every application that must be QoS-enabled, as well as every device comprising the network's infrastructure.

End-to-End Considerations

When considering the end-to-end interactions for data communications, one finds a host acting as a sender and another acting as a receiver. The sender generates data, which, if all goes well, is eventually received by the destination. In this scenario, there are at least two instances of a particular application communicating with another application over the network.

Each side of the communication must know how best to communicate with the other. The sending application will likely send data at some known rate. The receiver at the other end should ideally be able to receive the data at the same average rate. The underlying software and components on the two end systems should not cause the interruption of service for the given applications. Obviously, QoS must begin and end with the endpoints themselves. A poorly designed software architecture and/or inadequate hardware will prevent a quality experience no matter what the capabilities of the network infrastructure.

Network Involvement

It is the network that must have the bandwidth resources necessary to provide the right QoS. This means the network must be involved in order to support various levels of QoS. The devices comprising the networking infrastructure are the points at which bandwidth resources can be effectively monitored and controlled. These points must be aware of the kinds of traffic they support, be able to identify high-priority and specialized traffic, and handle the traffic appropriately.

Additionally, the network must provide a consistent model for handling traffic requiring QoS. That is, since networks are composed of a variety of devices by a variety of vendors, all these devices must provide a common mapping to consistently express QoS requirements. The standard for consistently interpreting the QoS requirements and handling network traffic is defined by the Internet Engineering Task Force's (IETF) Integrated Services specifications. See the Bibliography for a listing of the relevant Integrated Services documents.

Signaling Application Requirements

Given that the network infrastructure must be capable of providing QoS, how does the network determine which traffic requires what specific QoS? Obviously, there must be some means for an application to signal its QoS requirements to the network. The application is likely the only piece in the puzzle that truly knows what is needed to achieve an acceptable result for a user of the application.

Once the application determines what QoS it requires from the network, this information must be relayed to the network. Again, the network is the piece of the puzzle that can actually deliver, or not deliver, as the case may be, the requested QoS. This signaling must be performed in a standard way so that a heterogeneous mix of network components can all properly interpret the QoS request and then handle the corresponding traffic appropriately. A standard signaling mechanism implies a standard protocol.

In the Internet today, the standard QoS signaling protocol is the Resource ReSerVation Protocol (RSVP)—the main focus of this book. Simply speaking, RSVP provides a way for an application to signal its service requirements to all devices in the network that will handle the associated traffic, end-to-end. If all devices in the network support RSVP, it is possible for the network to transfer the traffic associated with an application in a deterministic and consistent manner, suitable to the application's needs.

Queuing Concepts

In packet switched networks, queuing is the process of holding packets in a temporary store at a router before they are forwarded. Reconsidering the funnel analogy, a queue represents the body of the funnel. When the link capacity is not sufficient to transfer all the converging packets, a device will simply store the excess packets in some form of a queue. Eventually, queued packets will be forwarded out the link under contention.

A very basic form of a queue is the first-in, first-out (*FIFO*) queue. In such a queue, the first packet to be queued is the first to be forwarded. A FIFO queue is analogous to a simple, single-file line, such as a line of cars waiting at a stop sign. Preference is given to the packets first to arrive. If the rate at which packets arrive at a FIFO queue is consistently greater than the rate at which a corresponding link can transfer the packets, the FIFO queue will continue to grow. Eventually, the queue will exceed its finite capacity and excess packets will be lost. Which packets are lost is just a matter of chance. A single FIFO queue does not give preference to one packet over another. A simple FIFO queue is illustrated in Figure 4.3.

Multiple FIFO queues can be applied to the same link. The extra queues can be used to provide a simple form of priority-based queuing, where higher-priority traffic is given first access to the link. As an illustration, consider two FIFO queues servicing a single link. Suppose one queue was given preferential access to the link, while the other was only given access to the link if the first were empty. That is, if any packets were in the first queue, they would all have to be dequeued and forwarded out the link before the second queue would get a chance to forward its packets. If higher-priority traffic was sent to the first queue, and lower-priority packets were sent to the second queue, a higher level of service could be achieved for the higher-priority packets. This basic implementation of priority-based queuing is illustrated in Figure 4.4.

Chapter 7 will investigate a number of queuing methods that can be used to implement QoS in the Internet. Chapter 7 will also include details about how queuing can be properly employed in network devices to provide the required level of service.

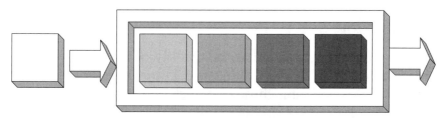

Figure 4.3 FIFO queue.

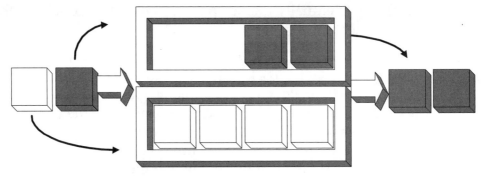

Figure 4.4 Priority-based queuing.

Concept of a QoS Flow in the Internet

Packets traveling end-to-end from the sending host's application to the receiving host's application over the Internet loosely resemble a data flow. Just as water flows through streams and sand flows through a funnel, data flows through a network. For a flow to receive QoS in the Internet, sometimes it is preferable that the packets that comprise the flow consistently follow the same path through the network from the source to the destination. In Chapter 2, we demonstrated that a consistent route can be established for data traveling end-to-end through the Internet. It has also been shown that data could be scattered across multiple redundant links between its source and destination if, for instance, routing protocols such as OSPF are employed. Nevertheless, this kind of scattering packets into the wind does not yield an adequate data flow. This is because packet-forwarding characteristics of the different paths will likely be dissimilar. To achieve a consistent flow of data end-to-end over a network it is important that all packets of data from the same source to the same destination follow the same route through the network.

Hop-by-Hop Flow Setup

It is important to realize that the Quality of Service a flow receives is determined by the cumulative data-forwarding properties of each and every device and link through which the flow proceeds. Again the weakest-link-in-the-chain property applies. That is, the end-to-end Quality of Service of a flow can be no better than that offered by the device or link along the data path that provides the lowest Quality of Service. A data flow must be able to signal its requirements to each and every device along its path if there is to be any guarantee that the desired QoS can be provisioned end-to-end.

The task of provisioning can be simplified if data consistently follows the same path through the network. Given this simplification, the cumulative requirements of a flow can be serially communicated from one device, or *hop,* to the next on a flow-by-flow basis. There is a one-to-one relationship between neighboring nodes along a data path. Every data packet for a provisioned flow will be consistently given to the same next hop along the same data path. The hop-by-hop setup of a data flow is illustrated in Figure 4.5.

Flow Identification and Classification

Now that the concept of a data flow has been established, it is necessary to understand what a routing device needs to do to identify a flow. A *flow* can be described as data packets traveling hop-by-hop through the network from the originating application on a specific host to a receiving application at the destination host or hosts. The TCP/IP protocol suite that includes the IP, TCP, and UDP protocols was introduced in Chapter 2. Typically, routing devices must access the IP header in the data packet to know where to route a packet. These same devices can also look at the UDP or TCP header to determine the destination port on the receiving host to which the packet is targeted. This port corresponds to a particular application. The set of information about where the packet originated, where it is going, and to which application it corresponds provides one mechanism by which packets related to a specific flow can be distinguished from those related to other flows. Thus, it is a relatively simple task for a routing device to identify a particular packet as belonging to a particular flow.

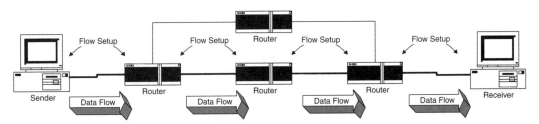

Figure 4.5 Hop-by-hop flow setup.

Once a flow and its data can be associated, a flow's data packets can be classified as requiring a specific Quality of Service. The routing devices along the path of a flow can take the appropriate actions to achieve the required Quality of Service on behalf of the flow. To do this, all the devices along the path must first be aware of the specific QoS requirements of the flows they service. They must then be able to provision the necessary level of quality based on their packet-forwarding capabilities. If the flow's requirements can be provisioned, then the flow's packets will be treated in accordance with their requirements and hop-by-hop quality of service will be achieved.

Homogeneous and Heterogeneous Flows

A homogeneous data flow is comprised of a number of packets traveling from the same source to the same destination, or multiple destinations, that have the same QoS requirements. In a unicast case, there will only be one flow, from a single source to a single destination. A unicast flow is inherently homogeneous. In a multicast case, homogeneous flows are not the only option.

In Chapter 3 we showed that multicast traffic routing is largely receiver-based. A potential multicast receiver will elect to become a member of a multicast group and, thus, receive the associated multicast traffic. If the multicast receiver-based model is extended to account for the QoS requirements of the receiving applications, each receiver should be able to select an associated Quality of Service.

If all multicast group members have the same QoS requirements, all the corresponding flows can be considered homogeneous. In such a case, the sender can simply select a Quality of Service that corresponds to the characteristics of the flow it generates. All receivers will then abide by the sender's selection and, ideally, receive the same Quality of Service.

Nevertheless, different receivers may want different levels of service. They may have different capabilities. Also, if it is the receiver that must pay for the flow, as is common in broadcast scenarios, the receiver may be happy with a less than ideal QoS. Finally, in the multicast scenario, not all branches of the flow within the multicast tree can be adequately provisioned to the ideal QoS level. Thus, it would be useful for receivers under such branches to request a slightly less than optimal QoS for their branch of the flow. All these QoS multicasting scenarios fall in the something-is-better-than-nothing category. This scenario applies when the real-time traffic degrades, with loss, but receiving a subset of the traffic is still useful.

When different receivers require that different subsets of the flow's data be protected, the multicast tree will likely become comprised of heterogeneous flows. Figure 4.6 demonstrates heterogeneous flows within a multicast tree. The larger arrows represent that all the flow's traffic is protected, while the smaller arrows represent that only a portion of the flow's traffic is protected. Near the receivers, the arrows reflect the specific requirements of a receiver. Further up the multicast tree, smaller arrows merge with larger arrows to reflect the combined requirements of all the downstream receivers. Finally, the sender receives the combined requirements of all the members of its multicast session.

Integrated Services

Quality of Service in a diverse network such as the Internet requires some set of standard definitions and protocols. Without a set of definitions and characterizations for service quality, it would be difficult to uphold QoS end-to-end over the Internet. That is, if all of the varied

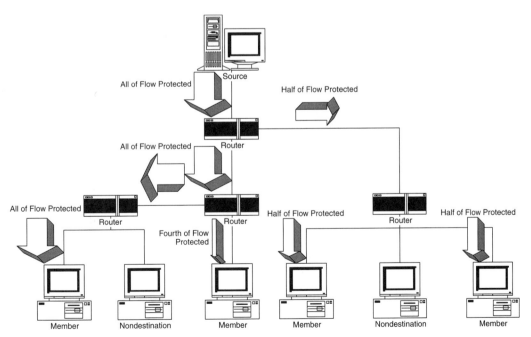

Figure 4.6   Heterogeneous flows within a multicast tree.

devices comprising the Internet simply did their own thing with regard to QoS, there would not be deterministic end-to-end QoS. The communicating endpoints would not know what a heterogeneous QoS network would do with their traffic. Indeed, some degree of homogeneity is necessary. There must exist some consistency in terms of how routing devices interact with the traffic they handle to provide data flows with the Quality of Service they require. The act of prioritizing traffic can be implemented via any conceivable method, but the resulting characteristics of the traffic must be expressed in certain terms.

Once the definitions are in place, devices on the network will have the capacity to accurately describe the needs of their traffic to the network. The network will then be able to interpret these needs and potentially comply. The end result will be that required traffic characteristics can be reliably upheld end-to-end over the network.

The Integrated Services (IntServ) for Internet QoS provides a number of specifications useful for describing service requirements. It specifies categories of applications and requirements for devices that support QoS, and defines a protocol useful for signaling QoS requirements on behalf of applications. We will discuss these IntServ definitions and requirements later in this chapter.

Categories of Applications

There are a number of categories under which application traffic may fall, depending on how tolerant or intolerant the application is to network congestion and other inconsistent network behavior. Broadly speaking, applications can be categorized as being either *elastic* or *real-time*.

Elastic Applications

Elastic applications are the most tolerant to network conditions. They can best be expressed as non-real-time applications. Such applications do not particularly suffer if their traffic is treated unreliably, or at least inconsistently; best-effort service is acceptable as long as some network resources are still available. These applications will operate over a wide range of data rates, delay bounds, and reliability conditions. They will simply adapt to the network's characteristics and slow down or speed up accordingly.

Applications such as e-mail, World Wide Web browsers, file transport, and Internet news are some obvious examples of elastic applications.

Any application that expects the user to wait after clicking a button or typing a command when communicating over the Internet is a likely candidate for an elastic application. Applications that run in the background without any user interaction are also typically elastic.

Applications built on top of TCP can generally be described as elastic. TCP provides the reliability and adaptability over a best-effort network medium. Chapter 2 introduced TCP and provided some insight as to its functionality. From the application's perspective, this protocol makes the Internet appear as a reliable, connection-oriented network. Nevertheless, applications that require exceptional timeliness cannot rely on TCP. Behind the scenes, TCP will slow down or speed up its data rate depending on network conditions. Due to the functionality that delivers all packets in order and without redundancy, TCP will simply queue up subsequent data while it waits for lost packets to be retransmitted. Furthermore, TCP has no control over how the network treats its data. The protocol simply makes the best of whatever network capacity is available in a well-behaved manner that is fair to other competing traffic.

Real-Time Tolerant Applications

It is not always acceptable to make the user of an application wait. If the user is trying to hold an audioconference over the Internet, or is watching a remote video playback, interruptions in service are unacceptable. Such applications communicate time-sensitive information and, thus, are classified as real-time applications.

Real-time tolerant applications are a less sensitive form of real-time applications. They do expect their data will arrive in a timely fashion, but the occasional missing packet or delayed packet will not cause serious problems. These applications are tolerant of some variability in the network, so long as it does not typically exceed a certain well-defined threshold.

Applications can be both real-time and tolerant of network irregularities via additions to their design. A video application, for example, may buffer a few frames ahead. If the timing of frames out of the network is not perfectly consistent, the buffer will isolate the user from such distractions by always showing the buffered frames at consistent intervals. All the user needs to see is the well-executed video feed on the monitor. Figure 4.7 demonstrates the use of buffering to hide the effects of the occasional delayed packet. When the application starts receiving data, it will first buffer a few frames in memory before displaying them to the

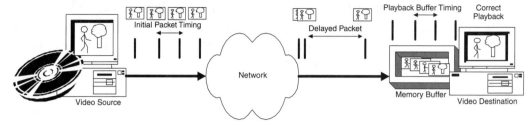

Figure 4.7 Real-time tolerant buffered video application.

user. This buffer will then always have a cache of frames to be displayed in the future. When a packet that contains a new frame is delayed, there will likely be sufficient frames remaining in the buffer to be displayed to the user in a timely fashion. Eventually, the delayed frame will arrive to take its place in the buffer.

Other real-time tolerant applications are inherently tolerant. They are simply forms of elastic applications that require sufficient network resources to behave ideally. Networked computer games are one example of such applications that interact with a user, but not with absolute timing constraints.

Real-time tolerant applications simply require that network resources be available. It is not necessary that their traffic be handled to an exact specification. If the network is not overly congested, and sufficient bandwidth is generally available, such applications will operate acceptably.

Real-Time Intolerant Applications

Real-time intolerant applications are the most demanding of the network. If their traffic is not handled consistently and precisely at all times, such applications will degrade unacceptably. Such applications have very precise timing constraints. Their packets must be delivered deterministically, with minimal latency and jitter.

One can imagine an industrial network that operates stamping machines. The stamping machines listen for a packet from a central computer that notifies them when to stamp metal pieces traveling through the stamp machines on a conveyor belt. The computer must synchronize the timing of the stamp machine so that it will only stamp when there is a piece of metal under the stamp head. Obviously, if this small network operated over the Internet, the routing devices would have to be able to keep the latency of a packet below a well-defined threshold. As the packets from the central computer would likely be generated with consistent timing, it is important that they be received at the stamp machine no later than when the next metal piece moves into place. If the packet delay becomes indiscriminate, the stamp machine will likely miss the metal and some poor technician will soon lose his or her job.

Obviously, the stamp machine network is not at all practical. Nevertheless, it is a useful illustration of a real-time intolerant application. Other applications that would fall under the category of real-time intolerant include plain old telephone calls that are uncompressed and are not buffered. Such audio service would allow for fast-paced conversation, but such conversation would not tolerate noticeable delay between the release of a packet of data onto the network and the resulting audible signal through the destination's speaker. Delay in a two-way conversation is simply unacceptable. If one speaks and then has to wait until the audio data reaches the other party before that party may respond, real-time conversation is simply not possible.

The lines between elastic, real-time tolerant, and real-time intolerant applications are somewhat arbitrary. In the end, different applications have different requirements for the network. Therefore, it is necessary that these requirements be expressed to the network in a fashion that the network can understand and, hopefully, comply with. Table 4.2 provides examples of different kinds of applications and their most closely related service types.

Service Specifications

Given the three broad categories of applications discussed previously, the question arises of how each type of traffic should be treated by network devices. Each category of traffic has particular requirements. There are currently two types of service specifications defined for Integrated Services besides best-effort: *Controlled Load* and *Guaranteed* Qual-

Table 4.2 IntServ Service Types and Their Applications

ELASTIC	REAL-TIME TOLERANT	REAL-TIME INTOLERANT
E-mail	Internet phone applications audioconferencing tool (e.g., LBL VAT)	IP telephony
Web browsing	Video streaming	Interactive video
File transfer	Internet gaming	Control systems

ity of Service. They are roughly targeted at addressing the needs of real time-tolerant and intolerant applications respectively.

Controlled Load

The controlled load service is directed toward real-time tolerant applications. Again, these applications require that, on average, a sufficient amount of network bandwidth is available. If some packets are occasionally delayed or even lost, the situation will not result in a corresponding degradation in the application's performance. These applications were designed to operate over best-effort networks with sufficient available bandwidth.

To support the real-time tolerant applications, controlled load simulates a best-effort quality of service not affected by excessive load. To achieve this, the controlled load service will set aside a specific amount of bandwidth for applications that request the service. This subset of the network device's link capacity will always be available to a requesting application irrespective of other traffic. When all devices devote the same subset of their capacity to the same application, the result is a bandwidth pipe that acts like a best-effort network, devoted to the given application's traffic and no other.

So, controlled load service sets aside a sufficient portion of bandwidth to effectively meet the needs of real-time tolerant applications. What controlled load service does not provide is any fine-grain guarantees. The end-to-end delay experienced by any particular packet over the controlled load service cannot be precisely determined. It will likely fall into a given range determined by the underlying queuing methods cumulatively employed on all devices along the route from the data source to the destination. This means that packets that may have been sent at precise intervals will likely arrive at their destination at different intervals. Each packet will experience an undetermined delay. This skewing of packet intervals via the traffic's progression through the network will likely lead to bursts of packets closely bunched together. Figure 4.8 demonstrates the eventual delay and clumping of packets due to interactions with forwarding devices in the network.

What controlled load service does promise is that, despite the occasional clumping of packets, the average packet rate will remain consistent over large periods of time. In an application that buffers packets before using them, the buffer can absorb the skew due to the occasion-

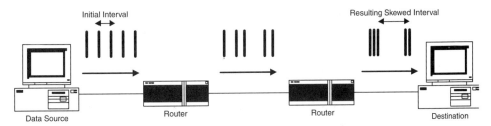

Figure 4.8 Skewed interpacket intervals due to interactions with forwarding devices.

ally delayed packet. The buffer becomes akin to a shock absorber for a car, absorbing the occasional bump in the road. To the driver, the ride remains smooth and, likewise, to the application's user, the video and/or audio playback appears smooth and consistent.

Since a specific amount of available bandwidth is set aside in controlled load service, only traffic that falls within the corresponding data rate will be protected by controlled service. Additional traffic generated by an application above and beyond the amount set aside for controlled load service can expect to receive only best-effort service or worse. Traffic that violates the expected data rate is considered to be out-of-profile for the granted service specification. It is important that applications that require significant reliability for their traffic not send data at a rate higher than that expected by the network components granting the controlled load service. Any additional traffic will be susceptible to loss or excessive delay.

Nevertheless, because the controlled load service does not precisely control packet delay, devices implementing the controlled load service should not penalize bursts of packets from an application. This means that a group of packets that violate the granted controlled load service specification over the short term should not necessarily be treated as out-of-profile. As long as the burst is short-lived, a device receiving the burst should simply buffer the packets and proceed to deliver them in accordance with the granted service specification. Only when the number of buffered packets grows beyond a specific bound will additional packets be considered to be out-of-profile and given just best-effort service.

Guaranteed QoS

Guaranteed Quality of Service is appropriate for applications that are real-time intolerant. Guaranteed QoS provides both bandwidth and a deterministic upper bound on packet delay. This means that a packet in a flow granted a guaranteed QoS specification must arrive at its destination within a defined delay bound. The additional upper bound on the delay requires a more sophisticated way to specify traffic requirements. It also requires that the delay target be computed, hop-by-hop, along the data path, because it is the cumulative maximum delay of all the hops that is important to the application.

Guaranteed QoS is also useful for real-time conversational applications or real-time interactive applications that are intolerant of excessive delay. Such applications will probably only buffer a small amount of data before it must be used. Thus, these applications are sensitive to even the occasional delayed packet, as data will likely be lost with noticeable implications for the user. Obviously, if one is piloting a robot remotely through an obstacle course, there are tight delay bounds between when the operator spots an obstacle and appropriate course corrections can be relayed to the moving robot. If the feedback is not prompt, the constantly moving robot will likely end up hitting the obstacle because the course corrections will arrive too late.

Finally, guaranteed QoS attempts to provision for a specified upper delay bound. This means that the service can guarantee that a packet belonging to a provisioned flow will never arrive later than the specified maximum delay, provided that the flow behaves appropriately. It is important to note that what is specified is an upper bound on the delay, not the average or minimum delay. Packets granted a guaranteed Quality of Service can arrive faster than what is specified by the maximum delay.

An application making a QoS request can control the maximum delay in a mathematically provable way. Basically, an application can decrease delay by increasing the amount of bandwidth requested. As more bandwidth is made available to support a given data rate, more of the data will be able to avoid queuing delays in the network. Looking back at the funnel analogy, increasing the available bandwidth is akin to increasing the size of the neck of the funnel. If the rate at which sand poured into the funnel is less than the rate sand can pass through the neck, there will eventually be no sand in the body of the funnel. At this point, all the sand will simply pour through the funnel and, thus, achieve minimal delay. The relevant components of the guaranteed service will be detailed in later chapters.

Admission Control

Quality of Service can only be achieved if network resources are available. To achieve better QoS, a flow is granted priority use of a subset of the available resources. Nevertheless, the finite physical resources available must be carefully managed in order for QoS to be effectively achieved. This is the role of admission control.

If a flow's requirements are to be provisioned, there must be adequate resources available that are not already committed to servicing other flows. After all, if every flow were simply granted access to all the limited resources available on a network device, the resulting contention between flows would yield nothing better than the classical best-effort Quality of Service. If a network device along a path chooses to provision resources for a particular flow, the resources required must be committed to that flow and no other. If enough bandwidth resources are not available, the network device must explicitly deny any new request for QoS.

There are, in fact, many aspects to admission control. The process of granting access to available resources is the easiest part of admission control. Logically, anyone with the appropriate signaling mechanism could request QoS protection from the network device. However, it may not be acceptable to allow just anyone's flow to actually receive special treatment by the network. Going beyond simple admission control is the concept of policy-based admission control. Policy can be used to determine specifically who gets access to what resources, and when.

A lengthy discussion regarding policy with respect to admission control will be the subject of Chapter 9. For now, it is sufficient to realize that QoS cannot be achieved by anyone if there is no provision for basic admission control that distinguishes between available and committed resources. It is the purpose of such resource admission control to make sure that a particular network device has enough capacity available to deliver better service to all its committed flows.

QoS Specification Parameters

There are a number of general characterization parameters that need to be understood by all IntServ network devices. These standardized parameters have a common and consistent interpretation that allows the discovery and specification of QoS end-to-end over a heterogeneous network.

IntServ Unaware Hops

Because the Internet has such a diverse network infrastructure, it cannot be assumed that every networking element will support the Integrated Services. Even if an entire intranet is QoS-aware, no network is entirely separate in the Internet. An end-to-end session can easily span multiple networks with entirely different QoS capabilities or administrative policies.

The NON-IS_HOP parameter is used to indicate that there are either network elements along the data path that are legacies and therefore not aware of the Integrated Services' specifications, or there are network elements that simply do not support the requested service. The parameter basically takes the form of a flag that is set to indicate the presence of such devices along the path of a data flow. In cases where this flag cannot be set by legacy devices because they were deployed before the Integrated Services specifications were completed, it can be set by IntServ-aware devices that detect the presence of such legacy devices. The parameter can then be relayed to the appropriate endpoints via a QoS signaling protocol.

Number of IntServ Hops

Another useful parameter for the characterization of QoS-aware devices along a data path is the determination of the number of hops that are IntServ-aware. The NUMBER_OF_IS_HOPS parameter is a simple counter that is incremented by every network device along the path of a flow that supports the Integrated Services architecture. Since the number of possible hops in the Internet is limited to 255, this parameter can range from 1 to 255.

Available Path Bandwidth

The path through the network that the data will follow may be comprised of many different routing devices. The device with the least amount of bandwidth available determines the bandwidth available along the entire path. The AVAILABLE_PATH_BANDWIDTH parameter specifies the minimum available bandwidth along the data path. This parameter is supposed to take into account administrative restrictions as well as physical limitations of the available bandwidth. The parameter expresses bandwidth in terms of bytes per second available along the composite data path.

Obviously, a device requesting QoS for a data flow will typically want enough resources so that the data flow can be adequately protected. The AVAILABLE_PATH_BANDWIDTH parameter is useful for determining whether enough resources are available along the path to achieve this result. If enough bandwidth resources are not available, the requesting device may opt to request lower QoS instead to achieve some protection for the flow.

The AVAILABLE_PATH_BANDWIDTH parameter is represented as a 32-bit, or single precision, IEEE floating-point number. This data type is expressed with a 7-bit signed exponent and 24 mantissa bits with 1 sign bit. This composition allows numbers to be expressed up to 1×10^{37}. Since the parameter is in terms of bytes per second, with negative numbers disallowed, it can range from 1 byte per second to 40 terabytes per second. As the numbers grow larger, the precision need not be accurately represented to the very byte per second. Rather, it is sufficient that the parameter be accurate within 0.1 percent of the actual value.

Minimum Path Latency

The IntServ MINIMUM_PATH_LATENCY parameter describes the cumulative smallest latency that would be incurred due to all the devices participating along the path. To calculate this parameter, each device along the path must first determine the smallest possible latency that a packet traveling through it might experience. This delay is basically a factor of the speed of light propagation delay as well as any delay attributed to processing the packet header. That means no packet traversing the device should ever exceed this smallest possible delay time.

Since every device along the path will contribute some delay, the MINIMUM_PATH_LATENCY must represent the cumulative delays of all the devices encountered by a flow. No packet within the flow can expect to experience a delay less than this cumulative delay. Thus, this parameter expresses the absolute lower bound on the overall path latency.

The MINIMUM_PATH_LATENCY parameter is expressed as an unsigned 32-bit integer. This number represents the minimum path delay time in microseconds. Thus, the value may range from 1 microsecond, or $1/1,000,000$ of a second, to $2^{32} - 1$ microseconds, or a little over 2 minutes. Although the parameter may be expressed to the microsecond, accuracy to the nearest hundredth of a microsecond is acceptable. Nodes that cannot accurately estimate their minimal latency will instead set the parameter to its maximum value, which is taken by the endpoints to mean the path latency is indeterminate.

Maximum Packet Size

The PATH_MTU parameter represents the maximum transmission unit that can be supported over the data path. That is, this IntServ parameter represents the maximum allowed packet size that can be transmitted over the data path. Basically, the device along the path that supports the smallest MTU size will dictate the value of this parameter.

The PATH_MTU is not simply a factor of the maximum packet size that can be physically supported by all the network devices along the path. Rather this parameter must take into account the QoS-specific limitations on MTU size as well. As was discussed in Chapter 1, the size of the packet matters. The packets must be small enough that the multiple packets can be efficiently multiplexed without creating excessive delay. Large packets will take longer to transmit, and, thus, potentially produce excessive jitter in smaller packets. Packet size is an extremely important factor in effectively supporting QoS. Thus, the traditional MTU discovery methods that only determine the maximum physical MTU size along the path cannot be employed.

The PATH_MTU parameter is expressed in terms of bytes. It is represented as a 32-bit unsigned integer. This allows the maximum MTU to take on values from 1 byte to $2^{32} - 1$ bytes. It counts the maximum number of bytes allowed in an IP packet along the data path. If larger packets are sent, they will be considered as out-of-profile of the QoS specification and will not be protected under the provisioned service.

QoS Service Specification

Of course, the goal of Integrated Services is to provide a common framework for describing QoS characterization parameters. The most important parameter of all is the QoS service specification itself, or the IntServ TOKEN_BUCKET_TSPEC parameter. This is the parameter used by end devices to request QoS protection from the network.

The TOKEN_BUCKET_TSPEC parameter is actually comprised of multiple values that characterize the data flow in detail. These are the token rate (r), the token bucket (b), the peak rate (p), the minimum policed unit

(m), and the maximum packet size (M). The token rate describes the average data rate of the flow. The token bucket roughly estimates the buffer size that should be allocated to the flow's data to absorb the unavoidable bursting of data. The peak rate specifies the maximum short-term data rate of the flow. The minimum policed unit describes the minimum datagram size, taking into account all but the link layer headers. This value is used to determine the per-packet resources that must be devoted by the IntServ-aware device. The maximum packet size represents the largest packet size that will be allowed to receive QoS-controlled service.

Taken together, the values of the TOKEN_BUCKET_TSPEC parameter can be used by an endpoint to accurately describe the characteristics of its flow. It can also be used to specify a particular QoS request to the network on behalf of an endpoint that would like to receive the specified QoS from the network. The r and p values are each expressed as single precision floating-point numbers. They represent data rates in terms of bytes per second. The b value is a float as well, and is expressed in terms of bytes of IP data. The m and M terms are unsigned 32-bit integers, and are measured in bytes. Chapter 7 will investigate how the token bucket parameters interact with traffic control.

ReSerVation Protocol

Now that traffic can be classified into flows, and service requests can be characterized, only one piece remains missing to round out the specification of the Integrated Services architecture. This missing piece is the protocol that can be used to request a specified QoS from the network. This protocol is the Resource reSerVation Protocol (RSVP). The RSVP protocol will be examined in detail in Chapters 5 and 6. For now, a brief overview is in order.

The RSVP protocol was designed as the primary signaling protocol for QoS in the Internet. It is used to request a specific IntServ service characterization, hop-by-hop, along the data path. It requests the QoS on behalf of a particular flow. The protocol follows the receiver-based, IP multicasting model for reasons of scalability, as addressed in Chapter 3. The protocol is used by the sender to describe the attributes of its data flow. It is then used by the receiver to request a specific level of protection for the data flow. Thus, for RSVP, characterization of the flow is the sender's responsibility, while the receiver specifies its particular service requirements.

Implications of QoS

Quality of Service does not come easily to the Internet. The Internet was not originally designed to support the vision of Integrated Services. Rather, it was a best-effort—highly scalable and fault-tolerant—medium, quite suitable for classic data applications. Now, with the introduction of QoS, the story is changing, and this change has implications not just for the network, but for its users, its applications, and perhaps most of all, for the network's administrators.

Users

QoS will probably make the most favorable impression on the network's users. Although a higher level of QoS will carry a higher price tag, frustrated Internet users most likely will appreciate consistent service. Also, anyone who has ever attempted to carry on an audio conversation over the Internet using best-effort service probably realizes there is much left to be desired. As was pointed out in Chapter 1, even occasional interruptions in service can quickly become unacceptably annoying to a user.

Of course, the trade-off of having higher Quality of Service is that the lower Quality of Service mark may degrade. If more and more of the traffic over the Internet gets classified as being highly important and time-critical, less bandwidth will be available for the classic best-effort traffic. If e-mail takes even longer to deliver, and a Web page takes longer to download, progress will not have been made. Thus, it is important that QoS traffic not stomp out best-effort traffic on the Internet; rather, adequate capacity must be set aside for both.

Chapter 1 demonstrated how some communications technologies can be very wasteful of their capacity. TDM-style networks will set aside a fixed amount of resources on behalf of connections whether or not the bandwidth is actually used. This wasteful aspect of classic real-time networking can be avoided with packet switched networks such as the Internet. That is, when a QoS-provisioned flow is not utilizing all its bandwidth, the remaining bandwidth can be made available to any needy best-effort traffic. In a sense, the beggar best-effort traffic may feed on the remains of the rich man's feast . . . or so the theory goes.

In any case, one can argue that the extensive bandwidth and network infrastructure that must be built to support the bandwidth-hungry real-time traffic of the future will also provide more bandwidth for the classic best-effort traffic. It is certainly better economically and more efficient to have one integrated network instead of many independent and specialized networks.

Applications

Most applications will probably have to be updated to take advantage of QoS mechanisms in the Internet. This is due to the fact that it is the application's responsibility to notify the network, or the QoS interfaces of the protocol stack, of its bandwidth requirements. This means the applications must understand what their requirements are and be able to accurately communicate them to the network.

In some cases, however, applications may not be updated to take advantage of new QoS technologies. These applications will often be legacy applications that were designed before QoS signaling mechanisms were in place. These applications can also be used under a QoS paradigm. If such an application is well known, it is possible that a third party can request or set up QoS on behalf of the legacy application. Essentially, a QoS proxy can be developed for the legacy application.

In the end, a QoS infrastructure will allow real-time applications to take advantage of the Internet, where it would have been nearly impossible before. Voice, video, distance learning, conferencing, collaboration are categories of application content that will be enabled by QoS. It is, after all, vast and diverse content that has been driving the success of the Internet.

Chapter 10 will investigate methods of QoS enabling applications, from interacting with QoS interfaces in the protocol stack to writing proxies that request QoS on behalf of legacy applications.

Administrators and Providers

Network administrators may be the most affected by the move to QoS in the Internet. Already, network administrators are overloaded with the task of managing the classic Internet technologies. More complexity is never a good thing for a busy network administrator. The goal of the job is to keep the network working, above all else. Introducing new fledgling technologies into a stable intranet is probably not the brightest career move for any network administrator.

Nevertheless, for those who move to adopt the new technologies, much can be gained—specifically in the future. Those individuals and organizations that are first to master the new technologies emerging in the Internet will likely be the first in line to reap the rewards of the integrated network paradigm. Besides, nothing worth doing is easy at first.

This book introduces the QoS technologies available and presently being developed for the Internet. In the process, we discuss the pieces that will allow organizations to enable QoS on their networks. Hopefully, fears can be eased and understanding achieved on the realities of QoS in the Internet and the value that QoS could provide.

Summary

This chapter has investigated the basic concepts involved in supporting Quality of Service within the Internet. As the Internet employs a diverse set of networking technologies it is important to design standards for describing QoS requirements. These standards must also describe the required functionality of devices comprising the infrastructure of the Internet in order for them to be QoS-aware. The protocol used to communicate the QoS requirements to the appropriate network devices will be thoroughly investigated in the next two chapters.

CHAPTER 5

Fundamentals of the Resource Reservation Protocol

The Resource reSerVation Protocol (RSVP) provides a general means for an application to communicate its QoS requirements to an Integrated Services Internet infrastructure. The previous chapters have presented the fundamentals of data transport through the Internet. RSVP is not a data transport protocol, but a control protocol that signals QoS requests on behalf of a data flow. RSVP is sophisticated, in that it allows reservations in both the one-to-one unicast and the many-to-many multicast data transport scenarios. This chapter will investigate the fundamentals of RSVP, its usage, and its capabilities.

RSVP Overview

RSVP signals the requirements of a data flow to Integrated Services–capable data-forwarding devices. First, RSVP is used to describe the characteristics of a traffic flow. Second, it is used to reserve resources for the flow from the applicable network devices that service the flow. When resources are reserved for a flow, they are effectively committed to servicing the specified data flow above all other competing network traffic.

RSVP establishes a reservation for a *simplex flow*. A simplex flow is a unidirectional flow traveling from its source to its destination. Thus, RSVP inherently distinguishes between the source and the destination endpoints of a data flow. Throughout this work, the receiver or destination of a data flow is considered the *downstream* endpoint, while the sender or source is considered the *upstream* endpoint. Likewise, nodes along the data path receiving data from the perspective of the data flow are considered *downstream nodes.* Nodes forwarding data from the perspective of the data flow are considered upstream nodes.

Hop-by-Hop Protocol

Integrated Services devices along the data path of a flow must be aware of the flow's QoS requirements if they are to provide any special treatment to the flow's data. There will probably be many such devices along, or comprising, a data path. A resource reservation protocol must be able to communicate with each IntServ device along the data path. To accomplish communication spanning multiple devices, RSVP serves as a hop-by-hop QoS signaling protocol.

Most RSVP messages are transmitted from one node to the next node sequentially through all RSVP-aware nodes along the data path. In order to accomplish such hop-by-hop behavior, a route must effectively be pinned where every neighboring hop knows what its adjacent RSVP hops are for a particular flow. Once the route is pinned down, an RSVP message can be transmitted hop-by-hop upstream or downstream, end-to-end. To transmit a message hop-by-hop it must be specifically addressed for, and sent directly to, the appropriate adjacent hop along the data path. Each hop receiving an RSVP message will first interpret its contents and then address it to the next consecutive hop along the data path. Each hop initially determines the next hop by using its routing table, just like it would do for any packet. This procedure is repeated until the message is eventually received by the intended endpoint.

Through RSVP's hop-by-hop signaling mechanism, all devices along the path of a data flow can be made aware of the QoS requirements of the data flow. Likewise, all devices along the data path have the opportunity to interact with certain RSVP messages. This hop-by-hop interaction enables these devices to update parameters within the RSVP message where appropriate.

RSVP messages are transmitted directly on top of the IP protocol, as opposed to being transmitted over TCP or UDP. RSVP has its own Protocol ID value, specified in the basic IP header (RSVP = 46). Thus, it does not depend on any other protocols such as TCP for reliable delivery, or UDP for application layer interaction. RSVP messages are transmitted as raw IP packets without the need for any transport layer protocol support.

Routing Protocol Independent

RSVP is not a routing protocol, nor is it part of the routing architecture of the network devices involved in packet forwarding. Furthermore, RSVP is not dependent on a particular routing protocol or architecture. The only requirement RSVP has from the underlying routing mechanism is a simple interface, to be used in determining the next downstream node of a potential flow from the device's routing tables. This information enables the RSVP Process to determine the next downstream node along the data path.

Basically, the RSVP message used to pin down a route follows the same path as the data flow that it represents. This simply implies that there is a single shortest-path route through the network that data packets will follow. As was shown in Chapter 2, routing protocols typically find and use the best possible route from a source to a destination. These routes are generally stable over short-to-medium time periods. Nevertheless, routes can and do change from time to time. When routes change, the data packets will simply follow a new path, and so will the corresponding RSVP messages. Thus, RSVP relies on the functionality of the underlying routing architecture to discover or pin down a stable route between the source and destination of a data flow. The protocol's messaging follows this route, allowing it to communicate QoS information about a flow to all relevant devices along the data path.

Sender Advertisements

In the simplex data flow scenario, the source application typically knows the characteristics of the traffic it is capable of sending. It likely knows the data rate, the approximate deviations from this rate, and other traffic parameters. Simply speaking, the sender is, first and foremost, in control of its own traffic. Traffic characterization parameters describe the traffic the source is capable of sending.

RSVP allows the data source to describe the characteristics of the traffic it intends to generate. This information is encoded in parameters within an RSVP message and is transmitted from the source to the destination along the data path. Thus, the destinations, as well as every RSVP-aware device along the path, are aware of the sender's traffic-generating capabilities.

This procedure effectively installs a path state on all RSVP-aware devices along the path of a data flow. Through this path setup mechanism, all the devices along the path become aware of which are their adjacent RSVP nodes for the data flow. Thus, the RSVP-aware devices can pin down the data path. The path state also remembers the traffic characteristics of the data flow as specified by the source application. Appropriately, the RSVP message responsible for communicating the capabilities of the source of a data flow to all downstream devices and the eventual destination(s) is called the *PATH message.*

Receiver-Issued Reservations

Once the path state has been established, and all devices along the path are aware of the capabilities of the source of a data flow, a reservation may be issued. In the RSVP model, the receiver always issues a reservation request for a particular data flow after the corresponding PATH message has been received. This reservation request must then follow, hop-by-hop, the path laid down by the corresponding PATH message. It is important to note that no device will commit its resources to service a data flow until a reservation request has been issued for the flow and accepted by the device along the data path.

The RSVP reservation request contains the receiver's QoS specification for the data flow. That is, the destination of the data flow determines what QoS the flow will actually receive. This determination may be dependent on the destination's capabilities, the application requirements, or other administrative considerations. In any case, different receivers may specify different QoS requirements for the same data flow.

The RSVP message that communicates the reservation request is called the *RESV message.* Like the PATH message, the RESV message is communicated to all devices along the data path. In the case of the RESV, however, the message is sent hop-by-hop upstream from the destination to the data source. This mechanism avoids the possibility that the reverse path may follow an entirely different route through the network. Through the hop-by-hop reservation setup mechanism, all RSVP devices along the original path will become aware of the QoS reservation request. Each device along the path may then individually decide to accept and commit the reservation, modifying appropriate parameters in the RESV message before sending it upstream, or refuse the request altogether due to capacity or administrative constraints.

Soft State Design

The Internet is inherently an unreliable communications network. This fundamental constraint must be a consideration in the design of any protocol expected to operate over the Internet. RSVP is no exception. Still, RSVP is a protocol used to communicate QoS requests through a number of different components along a data path. These requests essentially establish state within participating devices along the path. This state is necessary because the devices must be aware of the QoS requirements specified in the request and must allocate corresponding resources, if they are available, for a data flow. Furthermore, RSVP-installed state can be used to police and shape traffic associated with a data flow, given its QoS specification. When a host no longer requires quality service from the network, the corresponding RSVP state installed on the devices along the path must be removed. In this way, the resources allocated to service the QoS requirements of the flow can be made available to other data flows.

Both the RSVP PATH and RESV messages install state on devices along a data path. The PATH message is used to explicitly bind the data path of a flow and describes the data source's capabilities. The RESV message issued by the destination host then follows the path laid down by the RSVP PATH message hop-by-hop back to the data source. For each hop, the RESV message may install state associated with the specific resource requirements of the destination. This is the state that the forwarding devices along the path will actually use to explicitly allocate resources for a flow, and then police and shape the traffic associated with a flow.

Obviously, when state is installed anywhere on communications devices within an unreliable medium, it is important that lost communication can be handled gracefully. Additionally, when devices along a path are all keeping state in lockstep with one another, issues of route changes must also be considered. Within the Internet, depending on the routing protocols employed, routes can change relatively frequently. When routes change, the path data takes from its source to its destination will also change. As RSVP needs to install state within all RSVP-aware devices along the data path, it is also necessary that the devices along the new path be updated with the correct path and reservation states corresponding to the rerouted flow. Similarly, devices no longer participating along the path due to a route change must be able to delete the inapplicable path and reservation states so that resources may be made available for other QoS requests.

The RSVP soft state model achieves the complex chore of state management. *Soft state* is a method to implicitly manage state across a network. Fundamentally, if an installed state is soft, it is a temporary state. Under this model, state must simply be continuously refreshed or it will be automatically removed. Thus, with respect to RSVP, the PATH and RESV messages must be periodically retransmitted to keep a reservation state active along the data path. This technique is powerful in that it solves the problems associated with lost packets and route changes.

To illustrate the RSVP soft state model in action, first consider the state initiated by the PATH message. The PATH message follows the route determined by the routing tables of the forwarding devices along the data path. In general, this route should prove reasonably stable over short time periods. Route changes are typically incurred due to link or device failures along the data path or the introduction of new routes, both of which are relatively rare situations. The first path state is installed on all RSVP-aware devices between the source and destination. This state will explicitly bind the source information for the data flow. This path state will not remain permanently, however. Essentially, a timeout interval will be specified in the PATH message that limits the period the path state will be remembered by the participating device. This timeout period is reset each time a PATH message for the same data flow is received. Thus, the path state can be persisted by periodically sending PATH messages to refresh the state. As long as the route remains unchanged and the source is still advertising the QoS characteristics of its data flow by sending PATH messages, the state will remain installed on the devices along the data path.

The RSVP reservation state is maintained in a similar manner to the path state. The RESV message installs state upstream hop-by-hop in all RSVP-aware devices comprising the data path. Like the path state, the reservation state will simply timeout if it is not refreshed by periodic RESV messages. Thus, if messages are lost or routes change, the reservation state will be purged automatically.

To compensate for lost refresh messages, the timeout period is typically three times the interval between RSVP message refreshes. Provided that the devices along the path give priority to the RSVP control messages, this redundancy should prove sufficient for keeping state stable along the path.

Confirmations and Errors

Besides the RSVP RESV and PATH control messages, there are three additional control messages primarily used to provide information about the QoS state. These messages are the PATH Error, RESV Error, and Confirmation messages.

The PATH Error and RESV Error messages are used to report any errors that may occur during an attempt to install a path or reservation state along the data path. If any device along the data path cannot install a path or reservation state, it should send a PATH Error or RESV Error message respectively. If a PATH message received by a device along the data path cannot be installed, the rejecting device will send a PATH Error message notifying the source that the path state could not be installed. Similarly, if a RESV reservation request could not be granted due to admission control, policy control, or an error condition, a RESV Error message should be sent back to the destination. Both the PATH Error and RESV Error messages travel hop-by-hop. The PATH Error message will travel upstream, back through each previous hop, toward the source of a flow that originated the erroneous PATH message. Similarly, the RESV Error message will travel downstream, next hop to next hop, toward the ultimate flow destination that originated the offending RESV message. Neither the PATH Error nor the RESV Error messages are refreshed. They are one-shot messages corresponding to a single erroneous PATH or RESV message.

The RSVP RESV Confirmation message is solely for the sake of the application issuing a reservation request. The confirmation message provides a positive indication that the reservation request was, indeed, accepted and provisioned by all the nodes along the data path. This message is initiated by the source of a data flow or merge point once it receives a reservation request. The RSVP Confirmation message is sent directly to the flow's destination and not hop-by-hop through the devices along the data path. As the Confirmation message is not refreshed, it can provide an indication that the QoS reservation was, in fact, properly provisioned, provided it gets delivered without getting lost.

Removing Reservations

RSVP provides two other messages used to explicitly delete state along the data path. These are the PATH Tear and RESV Tear messages.

The soft state mechanism defined previously will automatically remove path or reservation states that have not been properly refreshed. Nevertheless, this mechanism can be quite slow. For example, if an RESV message is refreshed every 30 seconds, and a timeout will not occur until three refreshes have been missed, then the corresponding reservation will not timeout and be removed until after 90 seconds. If the individual issuing the reservation is getting billed for the length of the reservation, the extra 90 seconds may be unacceptable to the pocketbook.

To attempt to more expediently remove undesired states, the appropriate tear messages can be used. These messages quickly notify all the relevant nodes along the data path that the path or reservation state should be deleted. This explicit-state termination mechanism allows resources to quickly be freed for use by other flows.

Extensibility through Objects

An RSVP message basically contains a header that identifies the RSVP version, various flags, the message type, and the length of the message. The header also has a checksum field for verifying that the message is not corrupted, and a sender TTL field useful for determining the number of RSVP-aware hops. The current RSVP version is 1. The one-byte Type of Message field is used to determine if the RSVP message is a PATH or RESV, PATH or RESV Error, PATH or RESV Tear, or RESV Confirmation message. Finally the two-byte Length field is used to determine the size of the entire RSVP message in bytes. The size of an RSVP message is fundamentally limited to 64 Kbytes due to the packet size restrictions imposed by the underlying IP protocol. Further RSVP message size limitations due to the underlying MTU size of the path may also be necessary.

RSVP is fundamentally an extensible protocol. It achieves this extensibility through the use of reusable type/length/value format objects. An RSVP object is simply a variable-sized chunk of data that is given a type for purposes of identification. The RSVP object header consists of a two-byte Length field followed by a one-byte Class Number and one-byte Class Type field. The Length field simply determines the size of the object in bytes including the object header length. The Class Number and Class Type effectively categorize and identify the structures contained in the data portion of the object. The Class Number can be thought of as a general characterization of the object data while the Class Type represents the specific data format.

Figure 5.1 demonstrates the general construction of a complete RSVP message. The IP header identifying the RSVP protocol will typically preclude the RSVP message, since IP is the transport protocol. The RSVP message itself then begins with the RSVP message header as described previously. Following, or contained by, the RSVP message header are the individual objects that comprise the data describing the RSVP message. This generic format is useful for defining all the RSVP messages. The appropriate data objects will simply be included in their corresponding RSVP message.

Styles of Reservations

RSVP allows for different styles of reservations. As the destination of a data flow makes a reservation, it is the receiver's choice how its reservation should be applied. Obviously, a reservation can be made for a lesser amount than that required by the data flow. In such cases, the RSVP-aware devices along the data path will only protect a portion of the actual data flow. When multicast traffic is considered, there is also the potential for more than one sender for the same data flow. The style of reservation gives the destination control over how traffic generated by multiple sources is treated.

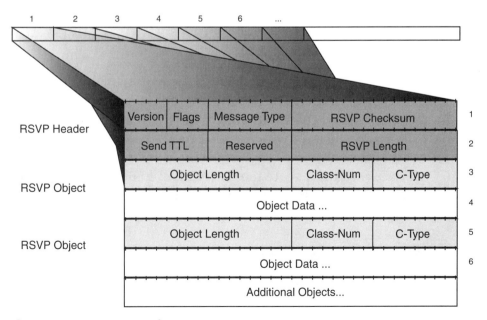

Figure 5.1 RSVP message format.

Distinct Reservations

In some cases, the destination of the multicast data flow would like to be able to reserve a portion of the available bandwidth for each data source. In such cases, the destination will be able to protect traffic from every source. This style of reservation is called the *Fixed Filter* style. Think of this reservation as applying to multiple flows for the same multicast session, each flow being generated by a different source. Each flow can have its own distinct reservation. Thus, each flow can be protected independently from the other flows.

Shared Reservations

In other cases, the destination of a multicast flow may want the sources to share a single reservation. This kind of shared reservation is supported by the Wildcard Filter and Shared Explicit styles of reservation. These styles are useful for applications that want to listen to multiple sources, but no more than one or so at a time. A real-life illustration of these shared reservation styles would be a conference call. During a conference call, there may be several speakers, but each speaker will talk one at a time. If multiple speakers were to talk simultaneously, the conversations would be nearly impossible to follow. Thus, it makes no sense to set aside bandwidth so that every speaker can be heard simultaneously if, at most, one speaker will talk at a time. In such cases, a receiver would likely opt for a shared reservation where enough bandwidth can be set aside for one source to be heard at a time.

The Wildcard Filter lets a destination request that its reservation be shared by all sources for the same session. Effectively, this implies that the sources may come and go, yet the destination would like its reservation to be shared by all of them, present and future. Shared Explicit reservations, on the other hand, allow the destination to pick which sources it wants to share the reservation. In both cases, the bandwidth specified by a single reservation must be shared by the sources selected by the receiver, whether directly or indirectly.

Reservation Styles and the Funnel Analogy

Turning back to the funnel analogy of traffic congestion described in the previous chapter should help clarify the different styles of reservations. Assume that a reservation lays a pipe from the destination to the source of a data stream. This pipe provides an isolated, committed path between the source and destination through which the sifted sand may travel.

To properly illustrate the multicast scenario where multiple sources are contributing to the same session, consider multiple funnels emptying into a single funnel. This funnel then empties into a destination bucket. Each of the higher funnels represents a source dumping data for the same session. The question that reservation style addresses is how pipes are run from the destination to the sources to protect the respective data flows. Figure 5.2 demonstrates the different cases under this analogy for Fixed Filter, Wildcard, and Shared Explicit style reservations.

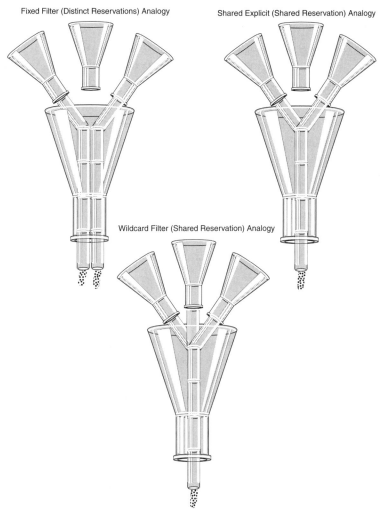

Fixed Filter (Distinct Reservations) Analogy

Shared Explicit (Shared Reservation) Analogy

Wildcard Filter (Shared Reservation) Analogy

Figure 5.2 The funnel analogy applied to different reservation styles.

In the Fixed Filter style of reservation, a hypothetical pipe can be run from the destination to a select number of the sources. Each pipe can be of a different size, and each pipe is independent of the others. This method allows each of the flows to receive a receiver-prescribed level of protection. Thus, sand from all of the selected sources should reach the destination at the prescribed rate. It is important to note that enough space must be available in the neck of the lowest funnel to fit each independent pipe. For a large number of sources, this cumulative pipe size potentially could become quite large. Likewise, the cumulative reserved bandwidth required at a downstream device to support a number of distinct reservations could become quite large.

The shared reservation styles ease the cumulative or aggregate pipe size problem by allowing the sources to share the same pipe. Effectively, a single pipe can be run between the destination and then can be branched out to each of the sources. In the case of a Wildcard style reservation, all the sources would be protected by default. Effectively, the pipe would branch to provide shared protection for each and every source. For a Shared Explicit style reservation, the pipe would branch to protect the flows from a receiver-selected number of the sources. Since the pipe with a fixed size is shared by the sources, there is no cumulative pipe size issue, and bandwidth is available so that other pipes can be laid or, in the case of bandwidth, other reservations can be made. Obviously, the aggregate pipe may not be large enough to protect simultaneous data from all the sources. Thus, the shared reservations are best used in those situations where only a small subset of the sources will send simultaneously.

Messages and Objects

In all, there are seven RSVP messages: the PATH and RESV messages, the PATH Error and RESV Error messages, the PATH Tear and RESV Tear messages, and the Confirmation message. Each of these messages is comprised of the RSVP message header, followed by a set of objects. The objects contain the information necessary for describing the message in question. This section will describe the data objects defined for use with RSVP and their use within their respective RSVP messages.

Data Objects Available in RSVP

Fourteen classes of objects are currently defined in the RSVP specification. These objects comprise the attributes that constitute the RSVP messages. Each class of object in RSVP can contain multiple types that further specify the format of the encapsulated data.

Session Class

The Session Class of objects specifies the destination IP address, protocol address, and destination port of a data flow. The class number for this object is 1. There are two types of session objects currently defined—the IPv4 class type and the IPv6 class type—which support the IPv4 and IPv6 style of addressing, respectively. The session address may be either a unicast or multicast address, depending on the flow being serviced. Figure 5.3 demonstrates the format of the Session Class objects.

The Session object is one of the objects used to identify a flow. In order to identify a flow, its protocol type, destination address, and destination port must all be known. The Session object simply provides this information to accurately describe the destination of a particular flow. It is a required attribute of all RSVP messages, as they all are used to relay QoS information about a particular flow.

RSVP Hop Class

The RSVP Hop Class object is used to identify neighboring RSVP-aware devices along the data path. A device's neighboring RSVP hop is the

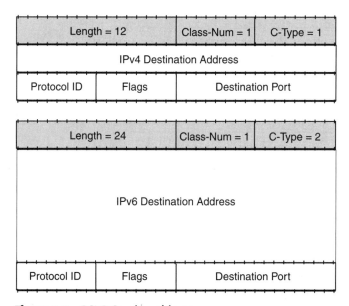

Figure 5.3   RSVP Session objects.

closest RSVP device upstream or downstream along the data path. Even though the neighboring RSVP-aware devices may not be directly connected, any RSVP-unaware forwarding devices between neighboring RSVP hops will not interpret or act on an RSVP message. A device's *next hop* (NHOP) is considered the next neighboring device downstream from the perspective of a data flow. A device's *previous hop* (PHOP) is considered the previous neighboring device upstream from the perspective of a data flow.

The Hop Class object is basically comprised of an IP address and a logical interface handle. The two class types defined for the RSVP Hop Class provide address formats compliant with the IPv4 and IPv6 addressing, respectively. The logical interface handle attribute is represented in both object types. This parameter is useful for uniquely identifying a specific interface on a device. This number represents the physical interface connecting the neighboring node with respect to the data flow. Figure 5.4 graphically demonstrates the format of the RSVP Hop objects.

Integrity Class

The Integrity Class object is used to provide security to RSVP messages. This object provides a means of performing an integrity check on an

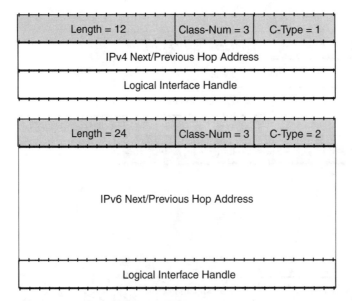

Figure 5.4 RSVP Hop objects.

RSVP message. Integrity implies that a known and trusted device sent the RSVP message and, therefore, the message is legitimate. The specific application of RSVP integrity will be demonstrated in Chapters 6 and 9, which cover the security aspects surrounding resource access in the Internet. The Integrity Class object is optional in all RSVP messages. It is selectively used in those cases where message security and validation are important considerations.

Time Values Class

The Time Values Class object is used to provide timing information about RSVP messaging. Since RSVP is a soft state protocol, messages must be periodically refreshed. It is useful to control this interval between message refreshes. In some cases, such as devices where many flows are handled, too many refreshes can lead to degradation in performance. Figure 5.5 demonstrates the format of the Time Values object.

Error Specification Class

As error conditions can always arise, the Error Specification Class is used to identify and report errors that may occur. Typically, the RSVP RESV Error and PATH Error messages use this object to specify a particular error condition. Additionally, the RESV Confirmation message may also specify an error condition. Error conditions can occur anywhere along the data path and are always with respect to an RSVP RESV or PATH message.

The Error Specification object is comprised of an address field as well as flags, error code, and error value fields. Two flags are defined that determine whether a reservation is still in place after the error condition, or if the application is at fault. Both flagged conditions are with respect to an RESV message. The Error Code field is used as a generic categorization of the error value. Given that any device along the data path can generate an error message, the Error Specification object contains the IP address of the generating device. Again, the Error Specifica-

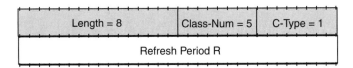

Figure 5.5 RSVP Time Values object.

tion Class has two types—one for specifying IPv4 format addresses and one for IPv6 addresses. The format of the Error Specification object is shown in Figure 5.6.

Scope Class

The Scope Class object encapsulates a list of sender IP addresses. This object is used to record a set of senders in order to avoid message looping in certain multicast scenarios. Two types exist for this class that can be used to identify a list of IPv4 and IPv6 addresses, respectively. The use of this object will be demonstrated in Chapter 6 when the Wildcard Filter style of reservations is discussed in detail. Figure 5.7 shows the different formats of the Scope object.

Style Class

The Style Class is used to specify the particular style of RSVP reservation. Since the style is with respect to a reservation, all RSVP RESV messages must carry a style object. Currently there are three styles of reservations defined: the Fixed Filter, Wildcard, and Shared Explicit styles. The first style applies to reservations that are distinct for each flow. The two remaining styles apply in scenarios where a reservation is

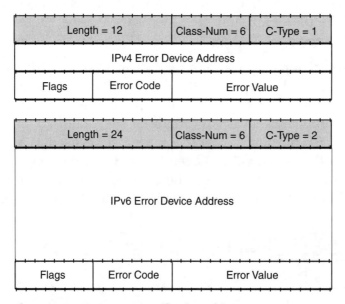

Figure 5.6 RSVP Error Specification Objects.

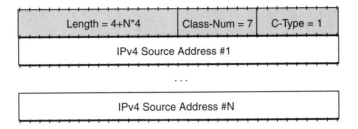

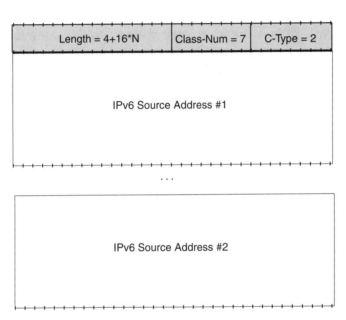

Figure 5.7 RSVP Scope objects.

shared across multiple flows for the same session. A variety of multicast cases arise where multiple senders may share a reserved flow. It is important to note that different styles of reservations can never be mixed for the same session. Figure 5.8 demonstrates the format of the Style object.

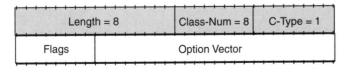

Figure 5.8 RSVP Style object.

Flow Specification Class

The Flow Specification Class defines the IntServ-compliant characteristics of a data flow. This class is used in reservation messages to define the receiver's requirements for the data flow. The different formats of this object will be discussed at the end of this chapter, when Guaranteed Service and Controlled Load are reviewed in the context of RSVP.

Filter Specification Class

The RSVP Filter Specification Class object is used by RESV messages to identify a particular source of a data flow. It is most useful in the multicast case where multiple sources are contributing to the same multicast session. This object is typically used in conjunction with the Flow Specification object to describe the desired QoS a particular data flow should receive. The Filter Specification Class is used in RESV, RESV Error, and RESV Confirmation messages to specify source information where required.

The Filter Specification Class object is comprised of the source's IP address and additional demultiplexing information. Three types of this object are defined. The first type is composed of an IPv4 format address and a field for specifying the source application port. The other two types are comprised of an IPv6 format address field with a source application port in one case, and an IPv6 flow label in the other. Figure 5.9 illustrates the RSVP Filter Specification Class objects.

Sender Template Class

The Sender Template Class of objects identifies a sender address and some additional demultiplexing information. This object is required to uniquely identify a flow's source in RSVP PATH messages. It effectively identifies the sender device and originating application for the PATH message. There are three types of this object that directly correlate in function and format to the Filter Specification Class of objects previously defined. The only difference is that the Sender Template Class is used in the PATH and PATH Error messages.

Sender TSpec Class

The Sender TSpec Class object is used by the source of a data flow to specify the traffic characteristics of its data flow. It is a required object in PATH messages, since it is used to describe the data flow generated by a source.

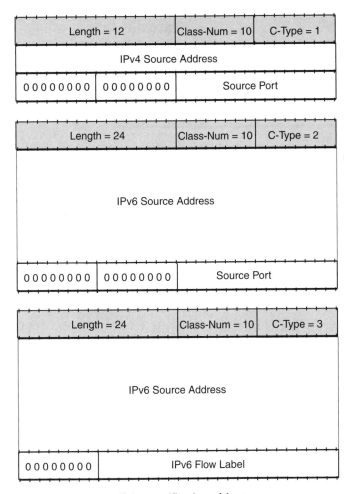

Figure 5.9 RSVP Filter Specification objects.

Basically, the Sender TSpec object describes the data flow using the IntServ parameters for token buckets. The attributes for this object include the token rate, token size, peak rate, minimum policed unit, and the maximum packet size. The meaning of these attributes was discussed in Chapter 4. Figure 5.10 demonstrates the wire format of the Sender TSpec object.

AdSpec Class

The AdSpec Class object is used by forwarding devices along the path of a data flow to describe the kind of services, the service-specific performance attributes, or the amount of QoS resources available for a reservation. The object is carried in PATH messages and is updated by the

Length = 36		Class-Num = 12	C-Type = 2
Version Number	Reserved	IS Length	
Service Number	Reserved	Service Data Length	
ParamID=127	Parameter Flags	Parameter Data Length	
Token Rate (IEEE Float)			
Token Bucket Size (IEEE Float)			
Peak Data Rate (IEEE Float)			
Minimum Policed Unit			
Maximum Packet Size			

Figure 5.10 Sender TSpec object.

forwarding devices along the data path that intercept the PATH message. The devices that receive a PATH that supports the AdSpec object should update the AdSpec only if there is no AdSpec in the incoming PATH message, or if their available resources or abilities to support a service are less than what is specified in the incoming PATH's AdSpec. The AdSpec Class object allows the destination application to gauge how large a reservation can be accepted by the network. Of course, this object is informational only, and available resources can always change after the PATH message is sent. This object is optional in PATH messages. We will revisit the AdSpec object in greater detail in Chapter 6.

Policy Data Class

The Policy Data Class object encapsulates information useful for making policy decisions with respect to an RSVP message. Information in this object may be used to authenticate a user, provide credit card billing information, or provide other useful policy-related data. This object is optional in the PATH, RESV, PATH Error, and RESV Error messages. Chapter 9 will provide additional information on this object and specify its interaction within a policy framework for RSVP.

Reservation Confirmation Class

The Reservation Confirmation Class carries the IP address of a destination. If a destination wants a RESV Confirmation message to be sent when its RESV message is accepted by the source, this object is carried in the RESV message. It simply identifies the destination that asked to receive a confirmation message. The sender of a corresponding PATH message will issue a RESV Confirmation message for all destinations that provide this object in the RESV message. If a destination does not wish to receive confirmation that its reservation was successfully installed, it should simply omit this object from its RESV messages. Figure 5.11 demonstrates the format of this class.

Reservation Setup Messages

The two RSVP messages involved with path setup and resource reservations are the PATH and RESV messages respectively. This section will investigate the formats for these messages and their interpretation by network devices.

Path Message

The RSVP PATH message is used to discover the path of a data flow and bind this route for use by RSVP. It is generated by the data flow's source and is eventually received by the data flow's destination, or destinations in the multicast case. The PATH message identifies the data flow, and its source, and describes its traffic characteristics. This information needs to be received by each and every RSVP-aware device along the data path. The PATH message allows the RSVP nodes along the data path to discover their RSVP-aware neighbors, advertise their capabilities, and install state relevant to the data flow.

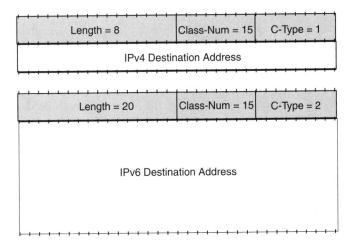

Figure 5.11 RESV Confirmation objects.

The PATH message is addressed from the source to a destination at the IP header level. The destination address may be unicast or multicast. PATH messages are addressed this way so they will be routed appropriately by RSVP-aware and RSVP-unaware devices alike. A PATH message also specifies protocol 46 in the IP header. RSVP-aware devices recognize protocol 46 as the RSVP protocol. Thus, RSVP-aware devices will intercept all IP packets that specify this protocol ID. Intercepted messages will then be delivered to the RSVP process on the device.

If an RSVP message received by a networking device is a PATH message, the RSVP process interprets the message and will establish a path state for the message if one doesn't already exist. The PATH message contains a Session object describing the destination address and port information. It also carries an RSVP HOP object that identifies the interface of the previous RSVP-aware device along the data path (PHOP) that generated the PATH message. This is effectively the neighboring upstream RSVP-aware device. A Sender Template and Sender TSpec object identifies the source and the traffic characteristics of the data flow. The Session, PHOP, and Sender information uniquely identify the path state for a flow. The Time Values object is included in the PATH as well, and describes the refresh interval of the PHOP. Based on this refresh timer, a device can determine when to timeout the associated RSVP path state. An AdSpec object, if included, is used to describe the kind of services and resources available on the participating upstream devices. Finally, a Policy Data object may be included in the PATH specifying any policy information relative to the source or PHOP of the data flow. Figure 5.12 graphically demonstrates the format of the PATH message as its attributes relate to the network environment.

Once an RSVP path state is installed on a device, the device should forward a corresponding PATH message out all relevant interfaces as determined by routing. Such outgoing PATH messages must have updated values for the RSVP HOP and, optionally, AdSpec objects. As each interface on the device will probably have a unique IP address, this information should be reflected in the corresponding outgoing PATH message as the PHOP. Different interfaces may also have different resource constraints. This information can be reflected for each outgoing PATH message in the AdSpec object if it is more restrictive than the AdSpec in the incoming PATH message or if no AdSpec was specified in the incoming PATH. The installed path state must be refreshed periodically in accordance with the value specified within the Time Values

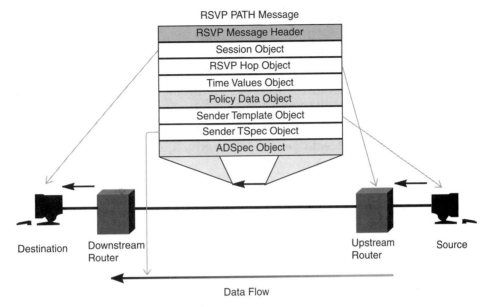

Figure 5.12 RSVP PATH message format.

object. Simply sending a refresh PATH message to all applicable downstream RSVP devices accomplishes this task of keeping the path state alive in the neighboring downstream device.

RESV Message

Once a path state is installed along the data path, a destination may opt to make a reservation request. This is accomplished when the destination generates an RSVP RESV message specifying the requested QoS characteristics for the data flow. The RESV message is transmitted hop-by-hop from the destination back to the data source. The message simply follows the reverse of the path established by the PATH messages.

The RESV messages are addressed from the sending downstream hop to the previous upstream hop. The IP header source address field simply contains the address of the node that generated the RESV message and the destination address contains the unicast address of the PHOP to which the RESV is destined. The PHOP information is obtained from the corresponding path state installed on the sending device for the same session.

When a PHOP receives a RESV message it will be interpreted by the device's RSVP process. This process will check to see if there is at least one valid path state installed for the same session. If a valid path state exists, the reservation will be processed and, if admission control succeeds, a reservation state will be installed. This implies that resources will be applied to service the corresponding flow. The RESV message contains the Session object that identifies the destination address of the data flow. An RSVP HOP object is included that describes the downstream device interface that produced the RESV message (NHOP). A Time Values object describes the refresh interval of the NHOP. Optionally, a Reservation Confirmation object may be included if the destination wishes to have the reservation explicitly confirmed. Additionally, a Policy Data object may be included to describe policy information relevant to the destination or NHOP.

The rest of the RESV message's format depends on the style of the reservation specified by the Style object. If it is a Wildcard reservation, there will be a Flow Specification object describing the QoS characteristics for the shared reservation. A Scope object may also be included in the Wildcard case if there was more than one PHOP for the RESV message. If the reservation style is Shared Explicit, then a single Flow Specification object will be specified for the shared reservation along with a list of Filter Specification objects. The Filter Specification objects explicitly identify the list of sources to which the shared reservation applies. Finally, a Fixed Filter reservation will specify a number of Filter Specification and Flow Specification object pairs that describe the requested QoS characteristics for each flow. Figure 5.13 illustrates an RSVP message and how its contents refer to various network devices or hosts along the path of a reservation.

Once a reservation state is successfully installed on a forwarding device, the device must prepare outgoing RESV messages for this state for all applicable outgoing interfaces. Since multiple RESVs may be received for the same session, it is possible to merge reservation states. Merging in RSVP can be quite complex and will be covered in detail in Chapter 6. For now, it is important to note that a different set of Flow Specification objects and a different set of Filter Specification objects may be generated for each of the interfaces out which a RESV message needs to be sent. The RSVP HOP object should be set to the forwarding interface out which the RESV is sent. The HOP object is interpreted by the upstream RSVP-aware device to determine what NHOP generated the message. As with the PATH message, the Time Values object should reflect the refresh interval of the downstream RSVP-aware device.

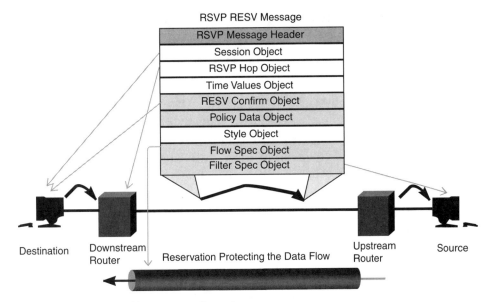

RSVP RESV Message

| RSVP Message Header |
| Session Object |
| RSVP Hop Object |
| Time Values Object |
| RESV Confirm Object |
| Policy Data Object |
| Style Object |
| Flow Spec Object |
| Filter Spec Object |

Destination · Downstream Router · Reservation Protecting the Data Flow · Upstream Router · Source

Figure 5.13 RSVP RESV message format.

Tear Down Messages

Although RSVP is a soft state protocol where state will simply timeout if it is not explicitly refreshed, merely waiting for state to timeout may take too long. When reservations are being billed, or when QoS requirements are highly transient, it would be helpful to have an explicit mechanism for removing RSVP state along the data path. To accomplish this, RSVP defines two messages for quickly removing path and reservation states respectively.

PATH Tear

The PATH Tear message is sent by the source of a data flow to remove any state associated with a corresponding PATH message. PATH Tear messages travel downstream and follow the data path just like PATH messages. The messages may be sent when the source application is exiting and, thus, no more data is generated. They are also generated if a path state times out on any intermediate node along the data path.

The IP header of a PATH Tear message is addressed from the sender of the path to the session address. All RSVP-aware devices along the data path intercept this message as it is identified as protocol 46. The message contains the Session, RSVP HOP, and the Sender Template and Sender

TSpec object pair. The Session, HOP, and Sender Template objects are used to uniquely identify the PATH state that is to be removed.

Once a device receives a PATH Tear message, it will forward a corresponding PATH Tear message out all its outgoing interfaces associated with the data flow. In this case the PHOP field should be updated to reflect each applicable outgoing interface just as in the case of the PATH message. Via this procedure all applicable devices along the data path should be able to remove their path states quickly. Nonetheless, the PATH Tear message may be lost at some point along the data path due to the unreliable nature of the Internet. In such cases, the soft state model will eventually clean up the legacy path state throughout the network.

RESV Tear

The RESV Tear message removes reservation state from all devices along the data path. Like the RESV message, the RESV Tear message travels hop-by-hop along the reverse path from the destination to the source. The RESV Tear may be initiated by a destination that no longer requires a reservation to remain in place. In cases of reservation state timeout, intermediate nodes will also generate RESV Tear messages.

The RESV Tear message is sent from the node generating the message and is addressed to the upstream PHOP. The message contains the Session, RSVP HOP, and Style objects. In the case of an RESV Tear message for a Fixed Filter and Shared Explicit style reservation, one or more Filter Specification objects will identify the specific flows for which reservation state is to be removed. This information is used to uniquely identify the reservation state to be removed.

When a device receives an RESV Tear message, it needs to forward it to all upstream PHOPs that correspond to the deleted reservation. The RESV Tear is unicast to all applicable PHOPs such that they know the reservation state is to be deleted. In a case where multiple flows are specified for the same reservation, only a subset of the reserved flows may need to be removed. In the case of a Shared Explicit reservation, a subset of the sources may be identified in an RESV Tear message. This basically specifies the flows that are no longer supposed to receive protection under the shared reservation, and the reserved paths to the corresponding sources should be pruned. Specific scenarios where reservation states are removed will be detailed in Chapter 6.

Error Messages

Situations will often arise where path states cannot be installed or reservation requests cannot be accepted. Situations like these create the need for explicit error notifications within the RSVP protocol. To facilitate error-reporting capabilities, RSVP defines the PATH Error and RESV Error messages that identify error conditions related to the PATH and RESV messages respectively.

PATH Errors

PATH Error messages are used to describe problems associated with processing or installing PATH messages. They may also be used to report administratively defined constraints imposed on the creation of path state within the network infrastructure. Any RSVP-aware device along the data path may generate a PATH Error message. This message is transmitted hop-by-hop along the reverse path as determined by the path state. Eventually, the error message will reach the source of the corresponding PATH message that may then choose to take corrective actions or to report the condition to the user. It is important to note that intermediate upstream devices that are not the source of a data flow should not act on the PATH Error messages. Rather, such devices should simply forward the message to the appropriate PHOP for the data flow in error.

Since the PATH Error is to be sent hop-by-hop from the device initiating the error back to the data source, each device must address the message to the next PHOP. To identify the device that originated the error message as well as the error condition, the PATH Error contains the Error Specification object. To uniquely identify the offending PATH state, the PATH Error message will contain the Session, Sender Template, and Sender TSpec objects as well. Due to the fact that an error condition can arise because of administratively defined policy restrictions, the PATH Error may also carry a Policy Data object.

RESV Errors

The RESV Error message is used to communicate an error situation with respect to a reservation state. If an RESV cannot be installed due to capacity admission control, administrative constraints, or message errors, the device that rejects the RESV will initiate an RESV Error. Any RSVP-aware device in receipt of an erroneous RESV request can initiate an RESV Error. This error message is transmitted hop-by-hop downstream toward the destination that generated the corresponding RESV message. On receipt of the RESV Error message, the destination may decide to take corrective action, such as reducing the amount of its reservation and retrying, in case there was a capacity admission control failure.

RESV Errors are addressed to the unicast address of the next downstream hop, and are thereby transmitted hop-by-hop from the originator of the error to the destination. This message contains the Session, RSVP HOP, and Error Spec object as well as the Style, Filter Specification, and Flow Description objects as found in the RESV message. These objects uniquely identify the reservation state at fault. The Error Spec object identifies the device originating the error message as well as an informative error code identifying the circumstances under which the error occurred. Policy data can also be included in the RESV Error to specify error conditions arising due to policy authorization failures within the network. Optionally, a scope object may be included in the case of Wildcard reservations.

It is important to note that the RESV Error message allows only one Filter Spec to be included. This means that a Fixed Filter reservation that may have contained multiple Flow Specs and Flow Descriptors could degenerate into a number of RESV Error messages, each specifying the individual erroneous flow.

When an RESV fails due to capacity admission control limitations, an RESV Error will be generated. If the failed RESV was an update of a previous reservation request, the previous reservation state will be left in place despite the error condition due to the updated request. RESV Errors arriving at downstream nodes will not result in the removal of reservation states. Such states will either have to be explicitly torn down, updated, or allowed to timeout before they will be deleted.

The Confirmation Notification

RESV Confirmation messages are used to notify a destination that its reservation request was successful. The RESV Confirmation is generated by the source or merge point in response to an incoming reservation that provided a valid RESV Confirmation object. This object within an RESV indicates the specific node that wants to receive confirmation after the successful installment of its reservation. The node that requests confirmation may either be a receiver of a flow or any node along the path of a flow. Receipt of an RESV Confirmation at a destination is wholly probabilistic. There is no guarantee that this one-shot message will be received. Confirmations are simply to be used as informational messages to help assure the destination that its reservation request was successful.

The Confirmation message is sent directly from a source or merge point to the destination and the underlying IP header is addressed likewise. The RESV Confirmation message specifies the Session, Style, and Flow and Filter description for uniquely identifying the reservation state that succeeded. An Error Spec object is used simply to identify the node generating the confirmation (no error code should be specified). An RESV Confirmation object is also included as copied from the RESV message.

Types of Service

Chapter 4 introduced the Controlled Load and Guaranteed Service. RSVP allows for both service types to be specified by destinations via the Flow Specification object. This section will investigate the Flow Specification attributes and interpretation for both service types. It is important to note that these service types are fundamentally incompatible and therefore cannot be merged. It is the responsibility of the destination applications to consistently choose the same service type for the same session. Attempting to request or merge incompatible service types for the same flow will result in an RESV Error.

Controlled Load

The Controlled Load service type provides QoS consistent with that achieved through a lightly loaded network with similar capacity. This type of service is best applied to applications that are real-time tolerant. On average, the Controlled Load service will provide the bandwidth reserved by a receiver but makes no firm guarantees on delay bounds. The Controlled Load description meets the token bucket traffic handling properties for a flow required by the network's forwarding devices.

The format of the Controlled Load Flow Specification object is demonstrated in Figure 5.14. This object contains header information identifying the service type as Controlled Load. This service type requires the token bucket parameters described in Chapter 4. The token bucket includes the token rate, token bucket depth, peak rate, minimum policed unit, and maximum policed unit. The token bucket parameters for the token rate, token bucket size, and the peak rate are all specified as IEEE single precision (32-bit) floating-point numbers. The token bucket parameters only describe a flow from a bandwidth or capacity perspective. Each device along the data path interprets these parameters consistently and without alteration. No parameters are included that describe the delay characteristics of the data flow. Chapter 7 discusses the parameters in more detail.

If a shared reservation is created for the Controlled Load service type, different Flow Specifications may have to be merged. Essentially, this process involves taking the largest of the Flow Specifications that are to be merged and forwarding it upstream. For Controlled Load this involves calculating the appropriate token rate, peak rate, and token bucket size of all the combined reservations. In all cases, it is not possible for the controlled reservation flow specification to exceed the Sender TSpec for any particular flow. If the flow specification is larger than its corresponding Sender TSpec, the value for the Sender TSpec's token bucket will simply be employed on behalf of the reservation. Details of RSVP merging, with specific examples, will be presented in Chapter 6.

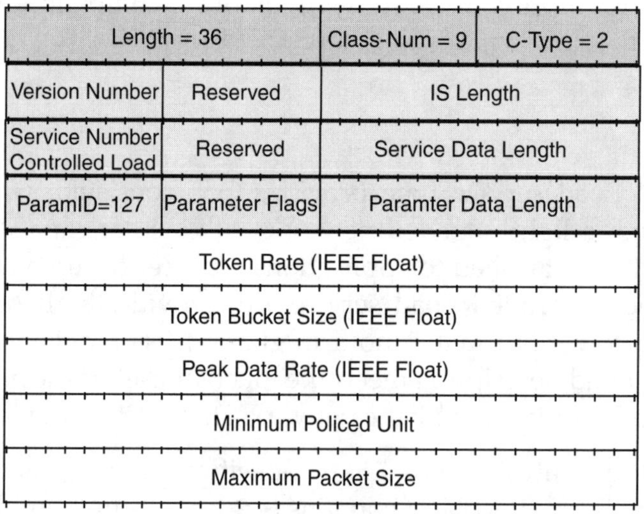

Length = 36		Class-Num = 9	C-Type = 2
Version Number	Reserved	IS Length	
Service Number Controlled Load	Reserved	Service Data Length	
ParamID=127	Parameter Flags	Paramter Data Length	
Token Rate (IEEE Float)			
Token Bucket Size (IEEE Float)			
Peak Data Rate (IEEE Float)			
Minimum Policed Unit			
Maximum Packet Size			

Figure 5.14 Controlled Load Flow Specification object.

Guaranteed Service

Guaranteed Service goes beyond Controlled Load in that it addresses the complex issues associated with delay bounds. This service guarantees a maximum upper bound on delay. Applications that are real-time intolerant are the best candidates for the guaranteed service type.

The Guaranteed Service Flow Specification object contains the same token bucket information found in the Controlled Load case. It also contains an additional resource specification (RSpec) term that identifies a rate and a slack term. These terms are based on the principle that increasing the reserved bandwidth will decrease the delay associated with queuing, as discussed in Chapter 4. Each hop has the ability to modify these terms as is necessary to provide the requested QoS. Figure 5.15 demonstrates the wire format of the Guaranteed Service Flow Specification object with the added RSpec term.

As with Controlled Load reservations, Guaranteed Service reservations may have to be merged. This process is somewhat more complex since the Guaranteed Service presents a vector of flow-description parame-

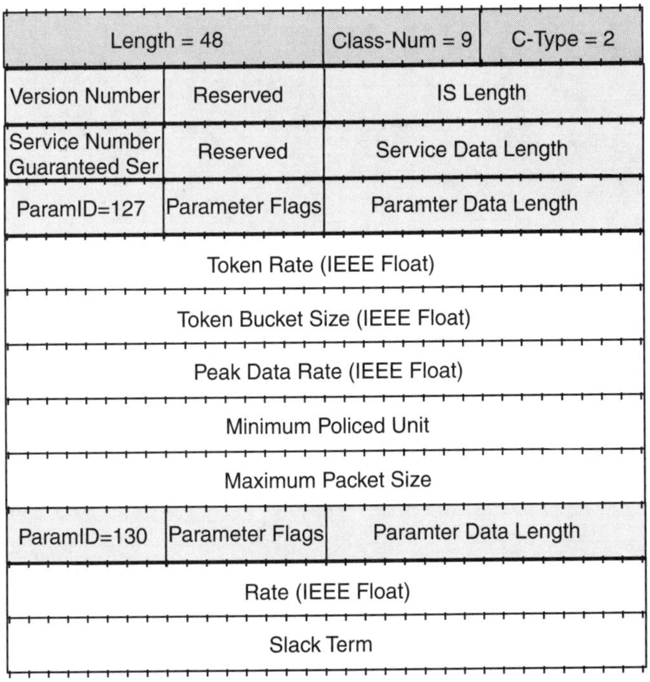

Length = 48		Class-Num = 9	C-Type = 2
Version Number	Reserved	IS Length	
Service Number Guaranteed Ser	Reserved	Service Data Length	
ParamID=127	Parameter Flags	Paramter Data Length	
Token Rate (IEEE Float)			
Token Bucket Size (IEEE Float)			
Peak Data Rate (IEEE Float)			
Minimum Policed Unit			
Maximum Packet Size			
ParamID=130	Parameter Flags	Paramter Data Length	
Rate (IEEE Float)			
Slack Term			

Figure 5.15 Guaranteed Service Flow Specification object.

ters that do not always compare as being larger or smaller. Merged Guaranteed Flow Specification objects may result in a new Flow Specification object that is at least as large as those being merged. Chapter 6 will provide a more detailed description of this merging process.

Summary

This chapter described the basic functionality of the RSVP protocol. It also examined the wire format of, and operation of, the RSVP messages. This process illustrated the protocol's object attributes and their use with the RSVP messages. Now that the basics have been described, Chapter 6 will delve into the operational aspects of this QoS signaling protocol. There we will see RSVP merging in action in multicast environments, as well as other specific details about the protocol.

CHAPTER 6

Advanced Concepts in RSVP

RSVP has been introduced as the QoS signaling protocol for the Internet. It carries the information necessary to describe an application's service requirements to the network infrastructure. In order for QoS to be effectively provisioned by the network it is necessary that devices in the network be able to protect the appropriate traffic. This process involves the interaction between the RSVP protocol and various traffic and admission control components. Additionally, forwarding devices typically support multiple interfaces over which traffic is received and sent. In the multicast scenario, multiple RSVP messages for the same session may have to be merged according to the appropriate RSVP message-processing rules before a combined RSVP message can be forwarded. Finally, RSVP must be able to protect itself against abuse. Such abuse may range from illegitimate RSVP messages to denial of service attacks. In this chapter we will discuss the details of RSVP and its interactions with the various components in network devices.

RSVP Components

There are several components necessary to properly support RSVP on a device. The exact components vary somewhat depending on whether the implementation is located on an end host or a forwarding device such as a switch or a router. Besides a process required to handle the RSVP messaging, a method is needed to classify and control traffic, and to provide both policy and capacity admission control, as well as to interact with the underlying routing architecture.

In RSVP, the end hosts must be able to signal their QoS requests to the network infrastructure. The network, in turn, must be able to either successfully provision the QoS request or signal an error condition. This process involves every RSVP-aware device along the data path. Each device must successfully allocate resources on all of its relevant forwarding interfaces or notify the requesting host of any failure. This section will detail the specifics of this process from end host to end host, including the network in between. Consider Figure 6.1 as a simplified illustration of a number of hosts connected via an RSVP-aware network.

Host

Typically, the source and destination of an RSVP message will be a host system running an RSVP-enabled application. Such a host may be the data source, data destination, or both. The host must also support an RSVP signaling stack with which an application may interact. The host should support a traffic control component to keep produced traffic within its specified bounds. Finally, a host might employ a policy module to keep resource usage under administrative control. Figure 6.2 demonstrates the various interacting components necessary to support RSVP on a host. We will describe each of the RSVP components found on a host.

Application

An *application* is the process running on a host that is the ultimate source or destination of a data flow. It is the application that actually generates a data flow and knows the characteristics of its traffic. Additionally, the application that receives a data flow knows the desired properties of the flow. Examples of applications range from interactive, videoconferencing applications that have specific requirements for network bandwidth and delay, to streaming or presentation applications that simply have bandwidth requirements.

If an application is sending traffic to be protected, the application should have the ability to cause a PATH message specifying the characteristics of the traffic to be sent. If an application is receiving a flow and desires the flow to receive protection from the network infrastructure, the application should be able to create an RESV message specifying the

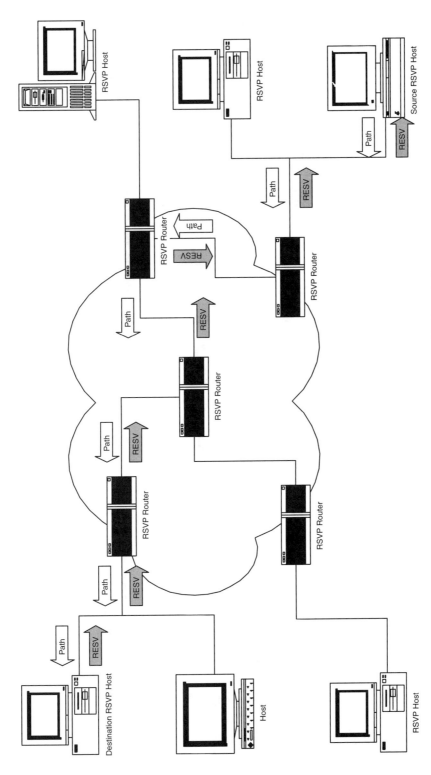

Figure 6.1 Illustration of host and network devices comprising an RSVP-enabled network.

Host System

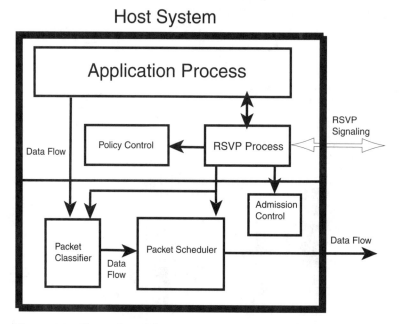

Figure 6.2 Illustration of the RSVP components on a host.

QoS it wishes to receive. If the application is to act as both the source and the destination of a data flow, both PATH and RESV messages will have to be issued on its behalf. In this case, the PATH will describe the characteristics of the traffic the application will generate, while the RESV will request the QoS desired for any incoming traffic from applications on other hosts.

RSVP Process

The purpose of the RSVP process running on a host is to handle the specifics of RSVP signaling. This process must be able to interact with applications requiring QoS support from the network. It must have access to the network interface on the host and be able to deliver raw RSVP messages to the network. Likewise, all RSVP messages received on the host's network interface must be delivered to this process.

The RSVP process keeps all states relevant to the establishment and maintenance of path and reservation state. The application will typically inform the RSVP process of its requirements and characteristics through a basic Application Programming Interface (API). Based on information provided by the application through such an interface, the RSVP process will know whether to establish a path or reserve state or to remove an existing state. The RSVP process will then continue to refresh the path or reserve state on behalf of the application. The interface between the application and the RSVP process on the host will be described in detail in Chapter 10.

Traffic Control

On the host, traffic control is comprised of three components: admission control, packet classification, and packet scheduling. These components are responsible for keeping the allocated resources within acceptable limits, classifying packets that are to be protected, and scheduling packets for transmission consistent with their corresponding QoS specification. The traffic control component is responsible for providing link layer–specific information to the RSVP process. Essentially, this is the component that provides the Integrated Services–specific functionality and information.

In some cases, hosts may not support full traffic control functionality. Rather, the host may depend on the network infrastructure to classify and prioritize its traffic. In such cases, hosts only signal their traffic characteristics and requirements without specifically controlling their traffic. This scenario is perfectly valid for hosts that are primarily data receivers and not senders of QoS data.

Admission Control

Admission control is responsible for keeping track of resource consumption on a particular interface and making sure sufficient resources are available to support a resource request. When resources are requested, admission control will first verify that sufficient bandwidth is available on the host's interface. If sufficient resources are available, admission control will allocate the required resources in support of the corresponding flow. These allocated resources are effectively deducted from the pool of available resources. If sufficient resources are not available to support a resource request, the request must be rejected. When a resource request is torn down or removed due to a soft state timeout, the corresponding allocated resources will be made available for use by future resource requests.

Packet Classifier

The packet classifier on a host is responsible for identifying packets corresponding to a provisioned flow. This identification is necessary because outgoing packets for a provisioned flow will likely receive special treatment before they are admitted into the network. Packets are uniquely identified as belonging to a particular flow by their source and destination address, protocol ID, and source and destination ports. Together, these five fields are called the *five-tuple.* This information is used to map the packet to a particular QoS class designated for the corresponding flow.

Packet Scheduler

The packet scheduler is responsible for ensuring that packets generated by the source application are in-profile with the specified QoS. The packet scheduler is a link layer component aware of the particularities of the underlying communications medium. Scheduling is important to ensure that the packets leaving the host fit their prescribed traffic profile. If the flow exceeds the allocated data rate, the network will potentially drop the excess packets. Packet scheduling on the source host keeps the traffic it generates in check before it is put on the network.

Exactly how the packet scheduler treats in- versus out-of-profile packets can depend on the underlying link layer technology and its abilities. The scheduler can delay bursts of packets, effectively shaping the traffic to be in-profile. If the data rate is in excess of that provisioned by the reservation, excess packets may be re-marked to be treated as best-effort by the network. Finally, excessively out-of-profile packets may simply be dropped and never transmitted to the network.

Policy Control

If a host has a secure operating system that isolates user and administrative functionality, it is possible to perform policy control from the host. The policy control component may be responsible for enforcing administratively imposed constraints on which RSVP messages may be issued, how much a type of resource can be allocated, or who may be allowed to issue resource requests. Additionally, policy control on the host can create the appropriate policy data object to be carried in a PATH or RESV message initiated by the host. Network devices can use this information to authenticate the RSVP message as belonging to the host, a user, or an application. In any case, because of trust issues, policy control is only an optional component for hosts.

Router

Like the host, an RSVP-aware forwarding device will support an RSVP process. A forwarding device will also support several network interfaces and a routing mechanism. The RSVP process on a forwarding device such as a router will require access to the routing process. It will also need to interact with the traffic control component that is employed with respect to each interface on the device. Policy control can also be added to determine who gets the available resources and under what conditions. Figure 6.3 demonstrates a forwarding device with the components necessary to support RSVP.

Interconnections

Routers and other forwarding devices typically consist of several interfaces. Each interface supports a link for data transmission. A collection of devices linked together through their interfaces forms a network. A data flow then travels through a device via its interfaces. As a convention, an interface can be considered as incoming or outgoing with respect to a data flow. That is, if the interface receives a packet from a data flow, it is an incoming interface for that data flow. Similarly, if the interface forwards or transmits an outgoing packet for a data flow, it is an outgoing interface for the data flow.

Because RSVP signals resource allocation requests for a unidirectional (or simplex) data flow, RSVP expects interconnects between devices to

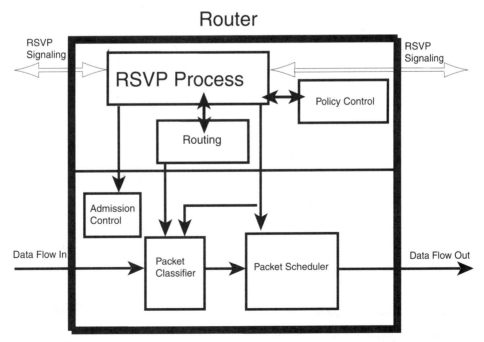

Figure 6.3 Illustration of the necessary RSVP components on a router.

be simplex as well. This means the outgoing interface for a data flow has full control of the traffic on a link in the outgoing direction. Because the outgoing interface has full control of the resources on the simplex link, it is responsible for managing its resources appropriately to avoid oversubscription. Downstream, the corresponding incoming interface is simply a passive receiver of traffic arriving over the simplex link. All provisioning of resources is performed on the upstream device's outgoing link.

RSVP considers bidirectional communication to be established through the use of two devoted simplex links, one for each direction. Thus, a bidirectional interface can be a passive receiver of traffic from the incoming simplex link and at the same time be the active sender of traffic out the outgoing link. This concept of devoted simplex links for both directions is important to the proper provisioning of resources in RSVP. Such links are called *full-duplex* links where communication can be established independently in both directions simultaneously. Obviously, if a single link were shared by both interfaces, there would need to be an additional mechanism by which two or more interfaces connected by the same link could collaboratively share the resource. Such shared links, where there is only one link available for communication in both directions, are called *half-duplex* links. Effectively, only one device can communicate on the link at a time. Methods by which such half-duplex resources can be appropriately provisioned for QoS will be examined in Chapter 8. For now, forwarding devices will be considered as supporting full-duplex connectivity for all interfaces. Figure 6.4 demonstrates a full-duplex interconnection strategy supporting simultaneous communication in two directions.

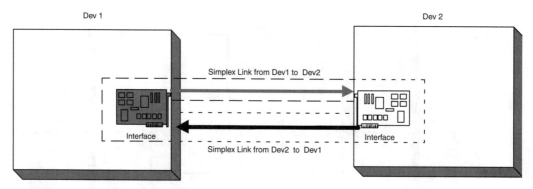

Figure 6.4 Illustration of full-duplex interconnects.

RSVP Message Processing

The RSVP process on a router is required to deal with all the RSVP messaging. It must be able to receive and interpret PATH and RESV messages, as well as their corresponding error and tear messages. On a forwarding device, the RSVP process must also take into account routing over multiple interfaces. The RSVP process must then build state for the relevant RSVP messages. Specifically, this process maintains reservation and path state that include the relevant incoming and outgoing interfaces for each state.

A valid PATH message will cause a Path State Block (PSB) to be created by the RSVP process. The PSB retains all the relevant information in the corresponding PATH message as well as all the applicable outgoing interfaces for forwarding the PATH message to its destination. Future PATH messages will be compared to the existing PSBs in order to determine whether they are new, updated, or refresh messages.

A valid RESV message will cause a Reservation State Block (RSB) to be created by the RSVP process. The RSB retains all the relevant information contained in the associated RESV message. In all cases, this includes the session information, NHOP, style, flow specification, and the outgoing interface on which the reservation is to be applied. For an FF-style reservation, each filter specification identifying a single flow will have its own RSB. In the SE case, a list of relevant filter specifications identifying a group of sources will be stored in a single RSB. In the WF case, the source list implicitly includes all sources. Incoming RESV messages will be compared against the existing RSBs to determine what is new, updated, or is simply being refreshed. New and updated RESV messages are then cross-checked to verify that applicable PSBs exist for the reservation. Simply put, PATHs must be installed before an RESV can be issued.

The RSVP process is responsible for maintaining the RSBs and PSBs. This means it is responsible for forwarding the messages to their relevant NHOPs or PHOPs. It is responsible for generating periodic refresh messages for the installed RSB and PSB states. It is also responsible for watching for erroneous RESV or PATH messages and generating the appropriate error messages. If tear messages are received, the corresponding RSBs and PSBs should be deleted and the tear message forwarded to the relevant PHOP or NHOP. Finally, the RSVP process is responsible for verifying that the local state blocks are periodically refreshed or timed-out and deleted.

The RSVP process will interact with traffic control to determine how flow specifications are compared, updated, and merged. Additionally, the RSVP process will perform admission control on an outgoing interface-by-interface basis. Finally, the RSVP process is responsible for installing the relevant flow information in the traffic control components so that the corresponding traffic will be provisioned as requested.

Routing Process

The RSVP process on a forwarding device will interact with the underlying routing process to determine to which outgoing interfaces the incoming PATH messages should be forwarded. In the case where the session is a multicast address, multiple outgoing interfaces may be candidates for forwarding a PATH message. The RSVP process will use the routing information to assign the appropriate local PHOP interface information for each outgoing PATH message. The RSVP process will then forward the PATH message out all the applicable outgoing interfaces for the given session.

Policy Control

Policy control is an important capability for a forwarding device. This is the component that is responsible for deciding who gets to make reservations and who doesn't. It is responsible for enforcing administratively imposed constraints determining the usage for RSVP. It is also responsible for interpreting any information encapsulated within the RSVP Policy Data object. Policy control over RSVP will be examined in detail in Chapter 9, including its interaction with the RSVP process.

Traffic Control

Traffic control is a crucial component of any RSVP-aware forwarding device. It is the responsibility of such devices to functionally provide QoS. In order to be able to provide QoS, forwarding devices must be able to properly provision their resources with respect to a select number of flows. The traffic control component provides the link layer specific classifying, scheduling, and policing capabilities. It also provides link layer–specific Integrated Services information for the RSVP process.

Admission Control

On a forwarding device, admission control happens on the outgoing interface from the perspective of a data flow. This interface is the same interface that receives reservation requests for a flow. When an RESV message is received on the outgoing interface, the RSVP process will perform admission control with respect to that interface. This process must take into account all currently provisioned RSVP reservations to determine the remaining resources available. If sufficient resources exist, the reservation will be committed and the required resources allocated. If the available resources are insufficient, an RESV Error will be generated and sent to the offending downstream hop.

Classifier

Packet classification also occurs on the outgoing interface from the perspective of a data flow. Once a reservation for a flow has been accepted by admission control, a filter identifying the flow's traffic will be installed in the classifier. The classifier simply examines the header information of each outgoing packet and determines whether it is due QoS protection. The header information to which the filter is typically compared includes the source and destination IP address, protocol ID, and the source and destination ports specified in the packet.

Packet Scheduler

Finally, the packet scheduler operates with respect to the outgoing interface. Once a packet has been classified as belonging to a protected flow, the packet scheduler will make sure that its QoS requirements are satisfied. This will typically mean that an in-profile data packet arriving for a protected flow will be transmitted in a timely fashion over the outgoing link. The packet scheduler may also take steps to ensure that a flow's traffic is kept in-profile. This means that bursty incoming traffic will be shaped to avoid aggravating the condition of the flow. Allowing too many data packets for a single flow to collect back-to-back will eventually cause downstream nodes to mark some of the clumped packets as out-of-profile. The result will be loss of packets inside the network, even if the packets were initially conforming when sent by the source.

Advertising Data Path Capability

Chapter 5 discussed in some detail the characteristics of the PATH message as well as the Sender TSpec object. Although the Sender TSpec sufficiently describes the traffic characteristics of the data flow as sent by the source, it does not contain information about the kind of service that can be provided by devices comprising the data path. Chapter 4 described a number of Integrated Services parameters that require the interaction of devices along the data path. These include the NON-IS_HOP, NUMBER_IS_HOPS, and AVAILABLE_PATH_BANDWIDTH, as well as the MINIMUM_PATH_LATENCY and PATH_MTU parameters. Additionally, the Guaranteed Service type requires a more detailed analysis of the path's forwarding delay characteristics. The AdSpec object optionally carried in the PATH message provides this IntServ information, which is updated hop-by-hop along the data path. It is the mechanism by which RSVP provides its *one pass with advertising* (OPWA) functionality.

The AdSpec Object

As described, the AdSpec object is contained in the RSVP PATH message and is manipulated hop-by-hop along the data path. It provides a number of service-specific parameters as well as several default parameters describing the characteristics of the data path. This information is used by the receiving application to determine the available service types, the minimum capacity of the data path, and other characteristics of the data path. This information, in turn, is used to construct an appropriate reservation for the traffic.

The wire format of the AdSpec object is divided into functional blocks. One block is used to represent the general characterization parameters of the flow; the second is used to specify the availability of the Controlled Load Service; and the third is used to advertise the Guaranteed Service and describe its parameters. If a forwarding device along the data path cannot update a particular functional block or blocks, a specific flag in the block's header should be marked. The presence of this marked flag implies that the parameters specified in the block may not be accurate due to the fact that at least one device along the data path did not update them. If any of the service–specific blocks are absent, the receiving application is advised that any QoS specification related to the service may not be fully supported by the nodes on the path.

General Characterization Parameters Block

The General Characterization Parameters block of the AdSpec object carries four values. The NUMBER_IS_HOPS parameter counts the number of Integrated Service–compliant hops along the data path. It is incremented by each IntServ hop the PATH message encounters along the data path, which should be equivalent to the number of RSVP-aware hops. The AVAILABLE_PATH_BANDWIDTH parameter estimates the largest data rate a destination can hope to reserve from the network. This value reflects the maximum bandwidth available for the whole data path. The path's bandwidth is reflected in the minimum bandwidth available on any particular device along the data path. Each forwarding device increases the MINIMUM_PATH_LATENCY parameter by the minimum amount of time it will take the device to forward a packet. This parameter reflects the shortest possible delay a packet can expect from the data path. Finally, the PATH_MTU parameter reflects the maximum packet size that can be forwarded, given QoS constraints. Packets larger than this size will likely not receive the required level of QoS protection.

Controlled Load Service Block

The Controlled Load Service block typically has no values besides a header. Additional service-specific overrides of some of the values described in the General Characterization Parameters block may be included in this block when appropriate. Such overrides provide a service-specific version of the prescribed value if it is different from the general case. Typically, the Controlled Load block is included only to advertise to the destination that Controlled Load is an acceptable service type for the flow.

Guaranteed Service Block

The Guaranteed Service block of the AdSpec object is used to provide delay bound information about the data path. Devices along the data path that support Guaranteed Services will modify the bound information to describe their local worst-case delay characteristics. Any device that does not support Guaranteed Service and therefore cannot update the delay bounds values must set the Service Not Supported bit in the Guaranteed Service block's header.

The Guaranteed Service block contains information about the total rate-independent delay term (D) and the rate-dependent delay term (C). These terms are modified hop-by-hop along the data path. Each device will add its local delay characteristics to the received C and D terms to produce a total end-to-end delay bound for the entire data path, Ctot and Dtot. Another set of C and D terms is used to describe the worst-case delay characteristics since the last traffic-shaping device. These are the Csum and Dsum terms.

The C term is used to describe the delay a packet may experience due to the data rate of the flow. This term is typically expressed as a function of the transmission rate. The value of C is described in units of bytes.

The D term is used to represent the worst-case delay a packet will experience due to its transmission through a device, given its queuing characteristics. This term is expressed in terms of microseconds. As an example of a worst-case D delay, consider a TDM link that will only send a packet from a flow every 10 time divisions. If a packet arrived just after its allocated time slot, it may have to wait 10 time slots to be transmitted. To account for such a potentially worst-case scenario, the error term D should be set to 10 time slot times, thereby providing an upper bound for such potential delay.

In Chapter 7, we'll describe the traffic control components in greater detail, and we'll also investigate the Controlled Load and Guaranteed Service models.

Merging Reservations

When considering multicast flows, the problem of merging reservations arises. Reservations must be merged for scalability reasons. Multicast trees are dynamically generated and grow arbitrarily from downstream nodes. New branches can be formed in the tree without the involvement of upstream devices. The result is a topology where a multicast flow will selectively divide and travel multiple routes to multiple destinations simultaneously. Effectively, the multicast flow is analogous to a tree. Rooted at the source of the flow, it will eventually branch out to a select number of destinations.

In the multicast scenario, a PATH message will, as always, be addressed from the source to the multicast destination. This means that the PATH messages will be generated at the source and forwarded through all downstream hops interested in or registered as receivers for the multicast group, just like the data flow itself. Effectively, path state will be installed on all RSVP-aware devices involved in routing the multicast flow.

Once a member destination receives a PATH message for a multicast flow, it may choose to issue a reservation via an RESV message. The amount of resources requested is entirely up to the destination. This is compliant with the receiver-based model for IP multicasting. Obviously, multiple destinations may issue RESV messages for the same multicast flow. These RESV messages will travel, hop-by-hop, upstream toward the source. These various reservations will eventually meet at some point along the data path. Again, referring to the tree analogy, RESV messages travel down the branches toward the root of the tree, or the multicast source. Eventually these messages will meet at the trunk of the tree. This proverbial meeting of reservations results in a merger of the intersecting reservations. The result is a single reservation that adequately represents the requirements of all the merged individual reservations.

The devices where reservations meet are called *merge points*. Specifically, within a merge point reservations may meet either at the incoming or outgoing interface of the device with respect to the data flow. If two reservations are received on the same outgoing interface from the same link, the RSVP process will merge them before admission control is applied. If two separate outgoing interfaces receive reservations for the same data flow, these reservations will be merged into a single reservation before they are forwarded out the incoming interface. Figure 6.5 represents these scenarios for merging reservations within a forwarding device.

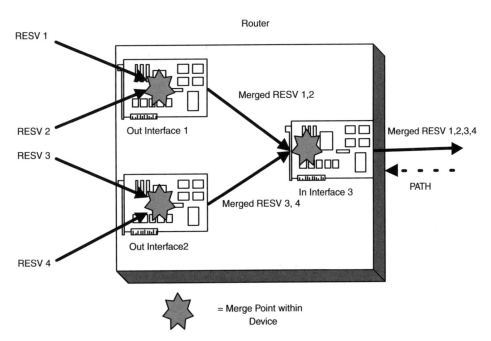

Figure 6.5 Illustration of possible merge points within a network device.

Heterogeneous Reservations, Homogeneous Filters

Although different destinations may issue different reservations for the same session, these reservations can differ only in terms of the quantity of resources to be reserved. Reservations specifying different styles of service cannot be merged by RSVP. The first reservation received for a session sets the precedent for any subsequent reservations.

An application issuing a reservation for a different style than a reservation previously accepted for the same session will be given an error notification. This error will be triggered when the new reservation intersects a previous reservation with a differing style. This is the point where the two reservations otherwise would have been merged. Since the reservations are inherently incompatible, however, the merge point will issue a RESV Error message for the subsequent incompatible reservation.

Additionally, reservations specifying different types of services cannot be merged, since they too are considered incompatible. This means a reservation that has specified the Controlled Load Service type cannot be merged with a reservation for Guaranteed Service or vice versa. Service-type merging is not necessarily impossible, but it would add complexity to the message-processing rules for RSVP with questionable applicability.

Neither of the preceding restrictions on filter or service type merging should be of any significant concern. This is due to the fact that very similar applications will be participating in the same multicast session. These applications will likely have similar QoS requirements with respect to filter and service types. Thus, the consistency between their filter and service types should be obvious even before a reservation is issued. If it is not obvious which filter type should be chosen, this information can be negotiated via some out-of-band method. RSVP is not responsible for helping applications participating in a multicast session decide which filter or service type they should use.

Fixed Filter

Fixed Filter (FF) reservations are issued when a destination wishes to independently protect all flows from a select number of sources. Merging Fixed Filter–style reservations is a relatively straightforward task. FF reservations are only merged for the same session with respect to a common traffic source. Each and every source for a session will have its flow protected for all reserving destinations. Not every destination need get an independent flow from the same source. Obviously, that would defeat the purpose of multicasting. Rather, each reserving destination will eventually share a reservation for the same flow produced by the common source.

Figure 6.6 demonstrates the salient points regarding FF merging. Here two sources (S1 and S2) are connected to a router (R1), and two destinations (D1 and D2) are connected to another router (R2). The appropriate path states have already been established. Assume D1 begins by issuing an FF RESV message to R2 for sources S1 at 10 Kbits per second and S2 at 10 Kbits per second. The bits-per-second rate used in this example is only for illustrative purposes. In reality, the resources required would be described using the token bucket set of parameters. This reservation request will be forwarded to R1 and then to S1 and S2, reserving the required bandwidth for each independent flow along the way. A total of 20 Kbits per second will be reserved along the link between D1 and R2 as well as along the link between R2 and R1 to account for both flows. The link between S1 and R1 will reserve 10 Kbits per second, as will the link between S2 and R1.

Once these flows have been successfully reserved, D2 issues an FF reservation for S2 only at 20 Kbits per second. The result is that this reservation will be received by R2 and merged with the reservation state for S2's flow. The result of the merge will be the larger reservation for S2 at 20 Kbits per second. The resulting RESV message will be propagated upstream toward S2. The total bandwidth reserved between R1 and R2 will now increase to 30 Kbits per second, and the bandwidth reserved on the link between S2 and R2 will reserve the shared 20 Kbits per second. D1 will now benefit from the resulting increased reservation between R2 and S2 shared with D2.

When upstream nodes for an FF reservation state generate RESV Error messages, these messages must be routed to the appropriate offending destinations. This routing of RESV Error messages must take into account merging. The FF RESV Error messages are issued on a flow-by-flow basis. The routing procedure is simple enough when only one destination exists for the given flow; the RESV Error is simply delivered, hop-by-hop, back to the origin of the offending reservation request. But when two or more destinations share the same flow, only a subset of the destinations may be responsible for the failure upstream. In some cases, those endpoints not directly responsible for the RESV Error may receive

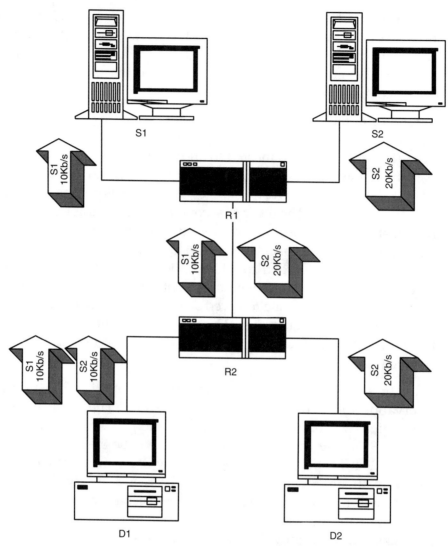

Figure 6.6 Illustration of FF-style reservation merging.

notification of it, too. Generally, an RESV Error will be caused by an admission control failure on an upstream node, and the erroneous Flow Specification in the RESV Error can be selectively matched to the Flow Specification objects of the original excessive reservation requests.

A destination has the ability to issue an FF RESV Tear for any subset of its reserved flows. When an RESV Tear message for a Fixed Filter reservation is received at a merge point, one of three possibilities exists. First, the RESV Tear may delete all reservation states for the flow on a device and will continue to be forwarded upstream. Second, the RESV Tear may cause a revised RESV message to be generated by the merge point and sent upstream. As a third possibility, the receipt of the RESV Tear may not cause any Tear or modified message to be sent upstream.

At a merge point, the RESV Tear message will cause a recalculation of the merged Flow Specification, given the remaining reservation states for the remaining flows. If the RESV Tear removed the last reservation state for a flow at the merge point, the RESV Tear will be forwarded to the corresponding PHOP for the flow. If other reservation states exist, and the removed Flow Specification was greater than any other for a flow, the resulting merged Flow Specification will be smaller than previously specified. This updated Flow Specification will then have to be sent to the appropriate PHOP. Finally, if the removed reservation state for a flow had a smaller Flow Specification than any other existing reservation state, there will be no change to the Flow Specification and no additional information will need to be forwarded to the PHOP for the flow.

Consider again Figure 6.6 as an example for the three cases described for updating an FF session's merge point. Here, two sources and two destinations are illustrated for an FF session. Destination D1 has an established FF reservation with S1's flow. Destinations D1 and D2 share an FF reservation with S2, with D2 having made the larger reservation of the two. If D1 were to send an RESV Tear for its established reservation to S1, the reservation state for S1's flow would be removed and, since no other reservations exist for S1, the RESV Tear would continue to propagate to S1. If D2 were to send an RESV Tear for S2, the merged Flow Specification would have to be recalculated for S2, resulting in a smaller local reservation state and an updated RESV to be issued to S2. If instead, D1 were to send an RESV Tear for S2, the local reservation state for D1/S2 on R2 would be deleted. The Flow Specification would be recalculated to yield no change, since D1's reservation was smaller than D2's. No updated RESV would have to be sent to S2 in this scenario.

Shared Explicit Filter

The Shared Explicit (SE) style of reservation is issued when a destination wishes a select number of hosts to share the same reservation. In the Shared Explicit case, all reservations meeting at a merge point for the same session will be merged. Thus, all flows will probably share a single merged reservation at some point. Only reservations that do not share a common merge point will remain distinct.

Figure 6.7 illustrates a merged SE scenario. Here again, two routers (R1 and R2) connect to two sources (S1 and S2) and two destinations (D1 and D2). Assume again that the appropriate path states have been established. In this example, suppose D1 begins by issuing an SE RESV for S1 and S2 for 10 Kbits per second. Since the reservation is shared, only 10 Kbits per second are reserved on the link between D1 and R2 as well as on the link between R1 and R2. Meanwhile, the links between S1 and R1 and S2 and R1 each are also reserved for 10 Kbits per second. The result is that both S1 and S2's flows will share the single merged reservation for 10 Kbits per second between D1 and R1. Next, suppose the destination D2 now issues an SE RESV for 20 Kbits per second but only explicitly specifies S2's flow. The result will be that D1 and D2's reservations will be merged at R2, producing a reservation for 20 Kbits per second to be forwarded upstream to R1. The link between R1 and S2 will then be reserved for 20 Kbits per second, while the link between S1 and R1 will remain unchanged.

When RESV Error messages are received at a merge point for an SE session they must be routed to the appropriate reserving destinations. The error message will specify the erroneous flow specification and possibly the subset of applicable filter specifications. This information can be used to limit the number of destinations that actually receive the error message.

If a destination's reservation has been removed due to a timeout or SE RESV Tear message, merge points will have to reevaluate their corresponding reservation states. Essentially, the process is the same as previously described for the Fixed Filter case. If the reservation to be removed was the only reservation for the explicit list of shared flows, the local reservation state will be deleted and the RESV Tear message will be forwarded upstream. If the resulting list of filter specifications or the computed Flow Specification changes as a result of the removed reservation, an updated RESV will be forwarded upstream. Finally, if the removed reservation results in no change of state, no updated RESV will need to be sent upstream.

To illustrate how an SE RESV Tear or timeout will affect the RSVP signaling, consider again Figure 6.7. If D1 decides to reduce the scope of its reservation by removing S1 from its filter specification list, all states associated with S1's flow will be deleted on R2. Then R2's merged reservation to R1 will be updated to reflect the removal of S1 from the filter

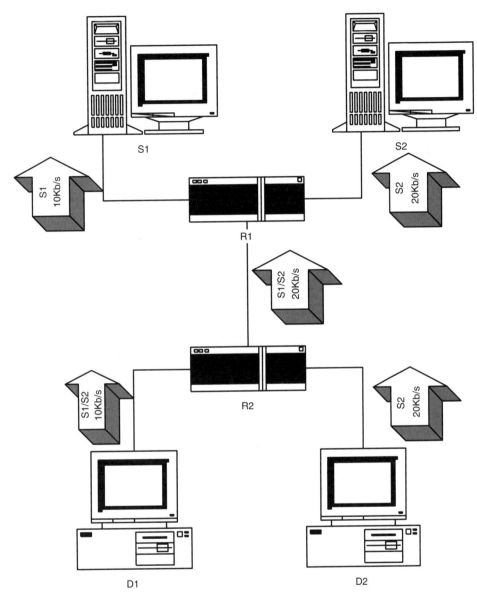

Figure 6.7   Illustration of SE-style reservation merging.

specification list. This will in turn cause R1 to remove its state associated with S1's flow, and S1's link to R1 will no longer have a reservation for the flow. Meanwhile, the merged reservation of 20 Kbits per second for S2 will remain unchanged. If, on the other hand, D2 were to tear its reservation for S2, the flow specification would be recomputed at R2 to be just 10 Kbits per second. This updated flow specification will then be reserved between R1 and R2 as well as between R1 and S2. In this case, the filter specification list for the merged reservation will remain unchanged. Finally, if D1 were instead to reduce the scope of its reservation by removing S2 from its filter specification list, R2 would not have to make any changes to its forwarded merged reservation. The computed flow specification and the filter specification list would remain unchanged for R2's PHOP, R1.

Wildcard Filter

Wildcard Filter (WF) reservations are issued when a destination wishes all possible sources for a session to share the same reservation. WF reservations effectively provide protection to all sources for a session. Whenever WF reservations meet, they are merged. This merged reservation represents the maximum flow specification of all the WF RESV messages received by the merge point.

Figure 6.8 illustrates how WF reservations may be merged. This time there are three destinations (D1, D2, D3) directly connected to the same router (R2). Two sources (S1 and S2) are connected to another router (R1). Assume that the appropriate path states have been established. Suppose that D1 begins by issuing a WF reservation for 10 Kbits per second. The result will be that the link between D1 and R2 will be reserved for 10 Kbits per second, as will the links between R1 and R2 and between S1, S2, and R1. If D3 then issues a WF reservation for 30 Kbits per second, all the links except those between D1 and R2 will be updated to the merged flow specification of 30 Kbits per second. Finally, if D2 sends a WF reservation for 20 Kbits per second, its link to R2 will be reserved for 20 Kbits per second, but the resulting merged reservation from R2 will still remain at 30 Kbits per second.

Increasing a WF reservation may cause an admission control failure at an upstream node. If this occurs, a WF RESV Error will be issued for the problematic RESV. If a new, larger reservation was previously merged with established smaller reservations on the path, the RESV Error message should be routed to the offending destination. In this case when the RESV fails at a node it would be obvious that the larger reservation is the culprit of a capacity admission control failure. Thus, the erroneous Flow Specification provides the only insight as to which original reservation was responsible for the RESV Error.

When WF reservations are torn down or timeout, the merge point for these reservations must recalculate the merged reservation. In the WF

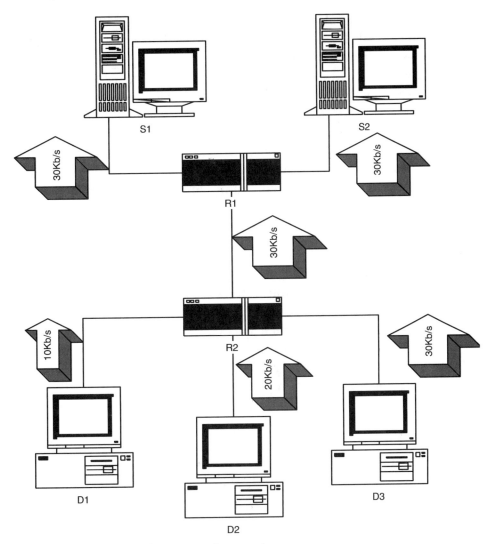

Figure 6.8 Illustration of WF reservation merging.

case, this process must only take into account the potential change in the merged flow specification. If there is no change in the merged flow specification, the merge point will only have to remove the reservation state attributed to the corresponding NHOP. However, if the merged flow specification changed as a result, an updated reservation will have to be sent to all upstream PHOPs for the session. If the removed WF reservation is the only reservation in place for the session at the merge point, the RESV Tear message can simply be forwarded upstream to all the relevant PHOPs.

Figure 6.8 illustrates what happens when the WF reservation state is removed. If D2 were to send an RESV Tear message, the result would affect only the link between it and the merge point, R2. The merged flow specification would remain at 30 Kbits per second. If D3 were then to remove its reservation for 30 Kbits per second, the result would be that a new merged flow specification would be calculated to be 10 Kbits per second, and all the remaining reserved links would reflect this change. Finally, if D1's reservation were torn after the other two reservations were torn down, the RESV Tear would be propagated to all upstream nodes, effectively removing all reservation states.

Avoiding Multicast Loops

Because Wildcard Filter (WF) reservations do not explicitly select sources, the possibility exists for infinite RESV message loops. These loops are related to the auto-refresh, soft state mechanism used by RSVP. Basically, if a WF reservation forwarded by a node out on a particular interface finds its way back to the same node, a cycle will be created. This cycle will continue to refresh itself even after the host that initially generated the reservation stops. Figure 6.9 demonstrates just such a looping of source-independent shared reservations. Here, two routers, R1 and R2, have four interfaces and are connected via two of these links. Each router directly supports one source and one destination for the same session. Source S1 is connected to R1 via interface i8, and destination D1 is connected to R1 via interface i7. Source S2 is connected to R2 via interface i1, and destination D2 is connected to R2 via interface i2. Without any scope, an RESV message from D1 with WF style will be forwarded to S1 via i8 and S2 via i5 on R1 to i3 and i1 on R2. At R2, this RESV may be forwarded back to R1 via i4 to i6. This WF RESV arriving on R1's i6 will then be merged into i8's reservation state for S1 and i5's reservation state for S2. The result is an auto-refreshing loop that cannot be removed by D1 timing-out its state or by an explicit RESV Tear from D1. Obviously, such loops are entirely unacceptable, and a mechanism must be provided to avoid them.

The RSVP Scope object exists to solve the potential problem of WF reservation loops. The Scope object is used in WF RESV and RESV Error messages. It contains a list of source addresses for the multicast session. As every interface on a node will have a path state for all upstream sources, the appropriate sender lists can be generated for every hop.

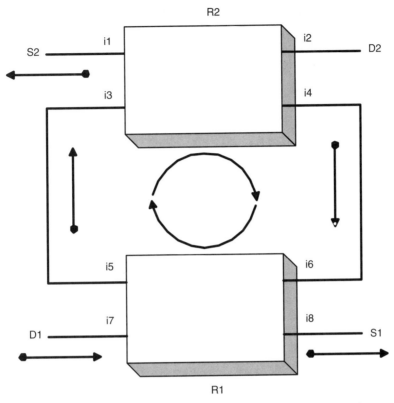

Figure 6.9 Illustration of potential auto-refreshing WF reservation loop.

The algorithm used states that a merged WF RESV is forwarded only if a Scope object can be calculated to contain at least one source address. The Scope object is computed via a three-step process:

1. The union of all the corresponding incoming RESV messages' Scope objects creates the merged WF RESV Scope object. If an incoming RESV arriving on an outgoing interface does not contain a Scope object, one is created consisting of all the sources that route through this outgoing interface for the same session. The sources that route through this outgoing interface are known by the installed path state set up by the PATH messages that are forwarded out the outgoing interface.

2. Any sources local to the device will be removed from the Scope object computed as just described.

3. An intersection of the sources in the computed Scope object and sources that are reachable by the incoming interface over which the

RESV will be forwarded is computed. If the intersection is a null set, there are no sources in common with the incoming interface, and the RESV will not be forwarded over the incoming interface. The forwarded Scope object contains the list of sources in the intersection.

Figure 6.10 demonstrates how the Scope object removes the possibility for auto-refreshing WF RESV loops. Here the previous topology is demonstrated again, only this time with the inclusion of a Scope object. D1 will send a WF RESV with a scope object identifying the sources S1 and S2. A Scope object will be calculated for i5, given the preceding rules, to consist of only S2. Likewise, a Scope object will be calculated for i8 consisting of only S1. When the WF RESV message arrives on R2's interface i3, it will contain a Scope object identifying S2 only. Given the aforementioned rules, a WF RESV to be sent out i4 will not have any entries for its Scope object. Thus, no WF RESV message will be sent out R2's interface i4, and no looping will be incurred.

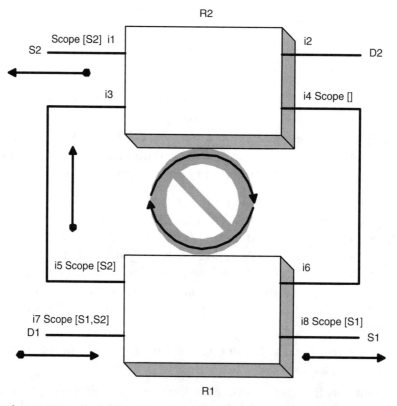

Figure 6.10 Illustration of WF reservation loop avoided through the use of the Scope object.

One unfortunate side effect of the Scope object is that it limits the source-based scalability that could otherwise be achieved by the Wildcard Filter type. Obviously, if a destination is receiving a large number of PATH messages from a large number of sources, every source will have to be represented in a single Scope object for a corresponding RESV message from the destination. Effectively, the Scope object is carrying out a form of explicit sender selection at the downstream hops. Due to the fact that the Scope object is limited in size according to the maximum size possible for an RSVP message, the maximum number of explicitly selectable sources is limited. The result may be that some flows may not receive the desired QoS protection.

Steps for Merging Flow Specifications

When reservations for the same session meet, their flow specifications will be merged. Merging flow specifications is not as simple as illustrated previously, because flow specifications are multiparameter vectors. One vector is not strictly greater or less than another vector. Some values of the vectors will be larger and other values may be smaller. To resolve this issue, a merged flow specification can be thought of as a vector that is mathematically at least as large as each of the original flow specifications. This calculation of the merged flow specification is called the *Least Upper Bound* (LUB). The opposite of this calculation is called the *Greatest Lower Bound* (GLB). The GLB flow specification is at least as small as any of the original flow specifications.

Effectively, computing the merged flow specification is a three-step process performed between the RSVP process and the traffic control component.

1. First, an effective flow specification is calculated for an outgoing interface based on the reservations from all the NHOPs for the same session arriving on this outgoing interface. Calculating the LUB from these incoming reservations produces the necessary result. This result is the pairing of an effective resource specification (Re) and an effective traffic specification (Resv_Te).

2. Next, all the applicable PATH's TSpecs are summed via the traffic control component to calculate the effective upper bound for the combined flow's traffic specification (Path_Te).

3. The combined (Re, Resv_Te) and Path_Te vectors are given to the traffic control component, which will compute the effective flow specification as the minimum of the Resv_Te and Path_Te values.

The last step is a sanity check that ensures the reservation does not exceed the total resources required to support all the applicable flows. Reserving more than this amount would be an obvious, if not malicious, waste of network resources.

Controlled Load

Merging flow specifications for the Controlled Load (CL) service is relatively straightforward. To compute a merged CL flow specification from two or more CL flow specifications simply involves finding the LUB of two token buckets. This is a device-independent calculation that involves the following five steps:

1. Take the largest token bucket rate.
2. Take the largest token bucket size.
3. Take the largest peak rate.
4. Take the smallest minimum-policed unit.
5. Take the smallest maximum packet size.

Merging flow specifications as described previously must also take into account the resources required to support all the flows. Computing the sum of all the applicable Sender TSpecs does this. The sum is calculated via the following five steps:

1. Sum the token bucket rates for all TSpecs.
2. Sum the token bucket size for all TSpecs.
3. Sum the peak rate for all TSpecs.
4. Take the minimum of all the TSpecs minimum policed unit.
5. Take the maximum of all the TSpecs maximum packet size.

Guaranteed Service

Merging flow specifications for the Guaranteed Service (GS) is a bit trickier and is highly device-dependent. This is because the GS Flow Specification is specified as two vector values. It does use the same token bucket vector of values as CL, and the same operations apply. But GS also adds an RSpec consisting of two additional values: a rate and a slack term. These are merged in a manner similar to the TSpec—the largest rate and smallest slack term are chosen. Nevertheless, the merged Rspecs are first calculated based on a mathematical inequality and may differ from the originally received Rspecs.

Avoiding Denial of Service

Denial of service basically constitutes any action, malicious or innocent, that improperly prevents others from establishing resource reservations. Killer reservations are one way to cause a previous reservation state to be lost along the data path. These are reservations that are simply too large to pass admission control for all upstream hops.

Before examining the killer reservation problems and their solutions, it is important to realize that the receipt of an RESV Error will not necessarily cause state to be torn down. Reservation state is only removed in response to the receipt of a corresponding RESV Tear message or the elapse of a timeout period without receipt of a reservation refresh message. Thus, a downstream node receiving an RESV Error from an upstream node will simply pass the message along without deleting the corresponding local reservation state.

KR-I

The first variety of killer reservations is those caused by an attempt to increase the resources consumed by an established reservation. It is acceptable for a host making a reservation to attempt to issue a larger reservation after a previous reservation was established. Essentially, a host may attempt to probe the limits of its reservation allowance by issuing progressively larger reservations. Eventually, a reservation attempt may fail. KR-I is the problem that would arise if the result of a failing reservation update meant that the previously accepted reservation was lost.

Such a problem may also occur when multiple reservations have been merged. Subsequent reservation attempts may increase the size of the merged reservation. The resulting larger reservation may fail at an upstream node. If this failure were to result in the loss of the previously accepted merged reservation, all downstream merged flows would lose the protection of the reservation.

To solve the problem of merging reservations, two rules are specified in RSVP. The first rule states that if an accepted reservation is updated with a larger reservation that fails capacity admission control, the previous reservation state will be conserved. As with any reservation state, the previous reservation state must be refreshed by downstream nodes or it will be lost. Obviously, the client issuing the excessive reservation update will have to likewise fall back to the previously accepted reservation state once the failure has been detected.

The second rule states that once an updated reservation fails admission control at a device, that device should not tear the previous reservation states on upstream nodes. Leaving the previous successful reservation in place on upstream nodes will allow a host to recover its previous reservation along the entire data path.

KR-II

The second kind of killer reservation is the result of continuously attempting to establish a reservation too large to be accepted by an upstream node. By keeping the excessive reservation in place on all downstream nodes, smaller reservations that merge with the larger reservation would also not be accepted by upstream nodes. This is because the resulting merged reservation would likewise be excessively large and would thus fail upstream. This form of killer reservation is caused by the excessive reservation being both first and persistent, drowning out all other smaller reservations merged into it.

Blockade State

To solve the second kind of killer reservation problem, downstream nodes have to be intelligent about how they treat merged reservations that fail upstream. They must be able to selectively block a persistent reservation that causes failures upstream for other merged reservations. Blockade state is an additional state reserved for merge points that helps prevent the KR-II problem.

Blockade state is created when a merge point receives a reservation error from an upstream node. Essentially, this reservation error will cause the offending reservation to be temporarily blocked or ignored by the merging process on the device. The result is a merged reservation taking into account all aspects of the reservation state except for those associated with the offending reservation. This merged reservation may then proceed upstream and hopefully will be successfully installed along the entire path. It is important to note, however, that the blockade state is only temporary. After the blockade state times-out, the persistent larger reservation will again be processed and the larger merged reservation sent upstream. If the merged reservation fails again, the smaller successful reservation should remain in place upstream from the point of failure, an RESV Error will be sent, and a new blockade state will be established for the failing reservation. Thus, the blockade state solves the second variety of killer reservation problem.

RSVP and Legacy Environments

As the Internet is made up of such a diverse and inconsistent variety of networking technologies, the idea that every device on the Internet will be able to support RSVP overnight is simply not realistic. So the question then becomes one of how RSVP can work with legacy networks that do not yet fully provide QoS functionality.

The RSVP PATH message passes through RSVP-unaware nodes. This is because the PATH message is addressed exactly like data packets from the flow to which it corresponds. As with any IP packet, the PATH message will be routed end-to-end from its source to its destination. The only difference is that RSVP-aware devices will know to intercept the IP packets based on the RSVP protocol ID. These devices will modify the PATH messages with their hop information before forwarding the message downstream en route to the corresponding destination(s).

Aside from the PATH and RESV Confirm messages, all the other RSVP messages are routed hop-by-hop up or down the data path. For example, RESV messages are passed upstream to the PHOP corresponding to the information known by the local path state. As the PHOP is an RSVP-aware device, the RESV message is simply routed RSVP-hop-by-RSVP-hop, routing through RSVP-unaware devices or clouds of devices. The result is that RSVP messages can be effectively routed end-to-end regardless of how many RSVP-ignorant devices may comprise the data path.

Sometimes RSVP RESV messages may be inconsistently routed though non-RSVP clouds. Such inconsistent routing may lead to RESV messages appearing at the correct upstream device but on the wrong interface of the device. This possibility of RSVP messages arriving on the wrong interface can be detected by the use of the Logical Interface Handle (LIH) parameter found in the RSVP HOP object. The LIH identifies a unique interface on a device, providing finer granularity of information than the device's address. The PATH message contains both the LIH and IP address of the upstream device in its HOP object. When an outgoing PATH message is sent downstream to the NHOP, it sets up a path state at that NHOP. The path state on the downstream device determines to which PHOP address an outgoing RESV message is destined and this PHOP's LIH. The installed PATH message's HOP object information is returned to the PHOP when the NHOP builds its outbound RESV message. When an RESV message is received on its destined PHOP, the LIH of the RESV's HOP object is compared with the LIH of the receiving interface. If the RESV's LIH is different, then the RESV message must have been rerouted to the wrong interface. Though this mechanism, a PHOP can determine when RSVP messages have been rerouted in non-RSVP clouds, subsequently mapping the inbound RESV to its correct local interface.

Of course, just being able to route RSVP messages through non-RSVP clouds of devices does not provide QoS. If the devices do not support RSVP, it is likely they don't understand the Integrated Services–defined service types. The result is that some devices won't protect the reserved flows. Nevertheless, in general, having a flow protected along 90 percent of the data path is far better than leaving the flow completely unprotected. Additionally, intelligent placement of RSVP-aware forwarding devices in relation to legacy devices can still achieve sufficient QoS behavior from a heterogeneous network. For example, provisioning for important flows via RSVP through bottlenecks and aggregation points in the network can be quite valuable. RSVP is simply a tool, and networks need to be engineered to take advantage of the protocol's capabilities where they are the most useful.

RSVP Security

Unfortunately, not every RSVP message can be assumed to be what it seems. Without security mechanisms, RSVP messages are subject to the whims of those who may have malicious intent. RSVP messages may be intercepted and modified or simply generated with falsified data. As reservations may be accounted and those who issue reservations billed, falsified reservations have the potential to cause expensive problems. Additionally, service may be denied to valid users by the unauthorized reservation of resources.

In reality, RSVP is probably perfectly usable even if it is not particularly secure. Typically, networks can trust the devices that comprise their infrastructure. In controlled environments, the hosts may also be trusted. Additionally, granting reservations should not lead to any serious problems with security as, for example, providing credit card information may. RSVP is a service and can be considered equivalent to packet forwarding, which is also inherently insecure. There is very little individuals may gain by falsifying RSVP messages, aside from denial of service attacks. Nevertheless, for the overly paranoid, RSVP does define additional security mechanisms.

Message Integrity

RSVP messages may optionally carry an Integrity object. This object provides a method by which the legitimacy of an RSVP message may be verified. Performing a form of cryptographic checksum over an RSVP message generates the data necessary for the Integrity object's digest before the RSVP message is sent on to its destination. On the receiver, the generated Integrity object can then be cross-checked with the contents of the received message to determine if any data was modified. If a received RSVP message fails its integrity check, the RSVP message should simply be silently discarded.

It is important to notice that RSVP messages with the Integrity object are not encrypted. The data within the RSVP message is always readable. The integrity check simply confirms that an illegitimate device did not manipulate the original data. Performing a keyed hash across the contents of the RSVP message is sufficient to generate the Integrity object. Specifically, a hash result is obtained after combining the data with a secret key. If both the sender and receiver of the RSVP message know the same key information, the message's integrity can be verified by rerunning the same hash algorithm on the message's receiver.

The Integrity object for RSVP also provides a method for determining the sequence of the RSVP messages. This sequence number information is included in the Integrity object. The hash used to generate the Integrity digest is then applied to the entire RSVP message, including the sequence number. A receiver will accept only messages with sequence numbers larger than those already provided in previous messages.

Overall, the RSVP integrity process is simpler and faster than more extreme security measures such as data encryption. Still, it provides a mechanism by which network devices can validate that the RSVP messages they receive have been generated by trusted parties. When network resources become a precious commodity, such security provisions will be an important tool for protecting the network.

The Chain-of-Trust Model

The integrity mechanism requires that RSVP-aware devices be able to share secret keys by which they can authenticate one another's RSVP messages. This implies a chain-of-trust model whereby connected devices share the same secret keys. Connected nodes must also keep state on previous sequence numbers related to their neighbors' RSVP signaling. This allows the peer nodes to determine if subsequent RSVP messages carry a number greater than that described in the last message sent from one peer to another.

Other trust models exist whereby keys can be obtained from a trusted third party. This third party is effectively able to distribute the necessary information for authenticating RSVP messages. It also provides a simpler way to manage security mechanisms for RSVP, as the network administrator need not configure each and every device on the network with the appropriate secret key.

Summary

This chapter delved into the obscure details of the RSVP protocol and its interaction with network devices, examining applicable components required to support RSVP on hosts and routers. These are the RSVP process, traffic control, and policy control components. Other details of RSVP covered in this chapter include RSVP's ability to advertise the capabilities of the data path, merging reservations for multicast sessions, and ways to deal with denial of services attacks. The next chapter will discuss in detail the various aspects of traffic control.

CHAPTER 7

Traffic Control

As we discussed in Chapter 6, traffic control is an important part of ensuring that the requested QoS is delivered by the network infrastructure. The Internet's infrastructure consists of various link layer technologies and topologies that have limited resources for servicing QoS flows. Due to the fact that network resources are only finite, there must be mechanisms for ensuring that traffic can be controlled so that QoS may be properly provisioned. This chapter will investigate the details of traffic control, including both the requirements and functions of the various traffic control components.

Traffic Control Overview

In the typical usage model for the Internet, all packets are treated in the same way and effectively given best-effort service. However, when an application successfully requests QoS for a particular flow, packets from that flow must be identified and given appropriate service to ensure end-to-end QoS. Let us first consider what it takes to provide such QoS:

- A standard way to specify the desired QoS characteristics of a flow is needed.

- A method and a protocol for signaling the QoS requirements of a flow to the network are needed. (RSVP provides such a facility.)

- An *admission control* procedure is needed at each network node to verify that necessary resources are available to meet the QoS requirements and, if so, reserve the resources such as buffers and link bandwidth to be used by the admitted flow.

- Once a flow's QoS request is admitted and its packets start flowing through the network, its packets must be identified and distinguished from the packets belonging to other flows at each network node in the path. A *packet classification* mechanism is needed in hosts and routers for this purpose.

- To ensure that the flow receives the QoS requested, packets in the flow must be given access to reserved resources at each node in a timely manner. A *packet scheduler* is needed for this purpose. When an application requests a QoS guarantee from the network, it essentially enters into a bilateral agreement with the network. Under this agreement, the network must ensure that the requested resources are granted to the admitted flow and the application must behave to ensure that its flow does not exceed the specified traffic characteristics. Network nodes must take steps to protect themselves and well-behaved flows from rogue flows that exceed their traffic specifications. A packet scheduler typically provides such functionality. It includes a firewall mechanism to ensure that packets in each flow are separated or protected from traffic in other flows. In addition, *traffic policing* is often used in conjunction with a traffic scheduler to ensure that a flow does not violate or exceed its traffic specifications.

The admission control module, packet classifier, and packet scheduler together constitute the traffic control component of an RSVP-aware forwarding device.

Figure 7.1 illustrates the RSVP and traffic control components inside a router. Note that this is a simplified view and actual implementations may vary. Given an RSVP-based QoS reservation, these components interact as follows:

1. An RSVP RESV message arrives at the RESV agent in the router. After the RESV message is processed to verify its correctness and to extract its contents, the RESV agent invokes the admission control module. The agent passes the FlowSpec to the admission control component that includes the Integrated Services (IntServ) parameters and the service type requested.

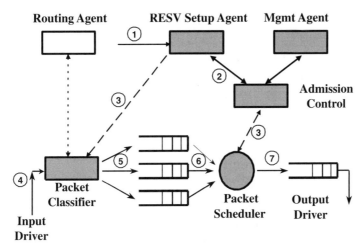

Figure 7.1 Illustration of traffic control components.

2. The admission control module uses its admission control algorithm and information on available resources to determine whether or not to accept the RESV request. If the request is accepted, the admission control module returns its decision to the RESV agent.

3. After successful admission, the RESV agent passes the packet filtering information to the packet classifier that describes how to identify the packets in the admitted flow. As described earlier, this information provides a five-tuple consisting of source and destination IP address, transport protocol identifier, and source and destination port numbers. The packet classifier maintains an internal database of such filtering information for several flows.

   Similarly, the admission control module also contacts the packet scheduler and passes it information such as the FlowSpec parameters (e.g., token bucket parameters) so that the scheduler can schedule the packets in the flow appropriately.

4. As the traffic arrives at a router, the input driver receives each packet and passes the packet to the classifier.

5. The packet classifier searches its filtering database to identify the flow to which the packet belongs and then enqueues the packet in an appropriate queue. Depending on the scheduling mechanisms used, the scheduler may use a separate queue for each flow, or flows may be aggregated into a single class or queue for scheduling purposes.

   In some implementations, the arriving packet may first be passed to the packet scheduler and the scheduler may invoke the classifier as part of its processing. For the purpose of this discussion, however, we will treat the two components separately.

6. Given one or more input queues, the packet scheduler uses its scheduling algorithm to pick a packet from one of the queues and schedules it for transmission over the outgoing link. This is a crucial step as, to a large extent, it determines the kind of QoS the flow receives at this node. The scheduler takes into account both delay and bandwidth requirements of the flows to prioritize the order of selection and transmission of packets from multiple flows.

7. When the time for packet transmission arrives according to the schedule, the scheduler passes the packet to the output driver for transmission. More than one packet may be queued to be transmitted at the output link, depending on the speed and nature of the transmission link.

The following section first discusses the QoS specifications used to describe a flow's QoS requirements and then the traffic control components in detail.

QoS Specifications

RSVP relies on the Integrated Services framework for the specification of a flow's QoS requirements. Under the IntServ model, a QoS specification consists of two parts, the Tspec, or traffic specification, as described in the source's Sender Tspec or the receiver's FlowSpec, and the Rspec, or receiver specification. The Tspec describes the traffic characteristics of a flow generated by a sender, whereas the Rspec specifies the performance requirements expected by a receiver and the level of resources to be reserved for the flow.

In the Internet both best-effort and real-time traffic is expected to be bursty. Real-time traffic is bursty because it is typically compressed and consists of a group of packets generated and transmitted at a variable rate. Therefore, the traffic characteristics of a flow are best described using a token bucket model. The token bucket described here models a traffic flow as a train of bursts with gaps between the bursts, where each burst consists of one or more packets bunched together. In the following, we will first describe the token bucket model and then discuss both the Tspec and Rspec parameters and their significance.

Token Bucket Model

The purpose of the token bucket model is to describe the flow of traffic as it enters and travels through the network. The idea is to take an arbitrary flow of traffic and shape it to fit a traffic model based on certain, measurable parameters so that it is easy to describe at what rate and size it arrives at a network element. Given such a traffic specification, it is then simple to talk about the amount of network resources a flow will consume and how it can be serviced.

One of the easiest methods for shaping a traffic flow is to present it as a regular stream of packets with a uniform time interval between successive packets of the same size. The leaky bucket model proposed by Turner [Leaky-Bucket] converts an input flow into such a stream. Figure 7.2 illustrates the model. Each flow has its own bucket of size b bytes. As a flow of packets arrives, each packet is placed in the bucket. At any time, the bucket can only accommodate a maximum of b bytes. A packet of size d bytes ($d < b$) can be placed in the bucket provided the bucket has d bytes of space left; otherwise, the packet is discarded. At the bottom of the bucket is a traffic regulator that sends out traffic at a constant rate of p bytes/sec. Thus, a packet (of size d bytes) at the top of the bucket is held for the amount of time d/p before it is transmitted.

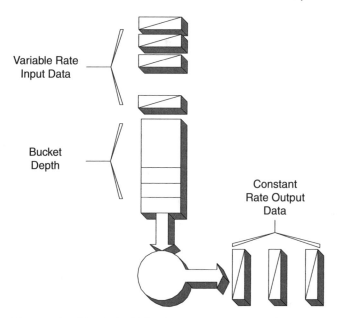

Figure 7.2 Simple leaky bucket.

As a result, what you get out of a leaky bucket is a data flow transmitted at a constant rate. Obviously, this model is especially suitable for fixed-rate data flows. However, if the data flow rate is highly variable and bursty, it must choose a rate p equal to its peak rate to avoid getting its packets discarded at the entry to the bucket. This is so because if p is chosen to be less than the peak rate, when a burst of traffic arrives at the peak rate, it will fill up the bucket and lead to packet discard. In practice, many datagram flows tend to be quite bursty with a peak–to–average data rate ratio of as much as 5 to 10. For example, consider a compressed video stream for a video produced at 30 frames per second. A burst of packets will arrive at every 30 milliseconds, corresponding to each frame. Considered over a longer time scale, the stream may have a transmission rate of 100 Kbytes/sec. Nevertheless, an occasional scene change may produce a burst of packets at a rate of 500 Kbytes/sec over a short interval, corresponding to the first few frames in the new scene. The timely delivery of these frames is necessary so the receiving application can provide a smooth and continuous picture. Such a flow is called a variable bit rate (VBR) flow.

The leaky bucket scheme will require the VBR flow to be shaped at the occasional peak rate to avoid data loss. However, if network resources are reserved at the peak rate, this will lead to waste of network resources, as the VBR flow only rarely sends data at its peak rate.

The token bucket scheme is a variation of Turner's leaky bucket. Figure 7.3 shows the token bucket operation. An important difference is that the token bucket scheme uses the bucket for managing the flow regulator rather than controlling the flow's arrival of data. In a token bucket system, the rate r is the rate at which tokens are placed in the bucket. Assume that each token corresponds to one byte of data. The bucket has a capacity of b bytes and tokens are placed in the bucket at r bytes/sec. If the bucket fills, newly arriving tokens are discarded.

When a packet arrives, it is placed in the buffer on the left. Suppose a packet of size d bytes is at the front of the buffer on the left. To transmit the packet, the regulator must remove d tokens from the bucket. If the bucket does not contain a sufficient number of tokens (d), the packet must wait for d tokens to accumulate in the bucket before it can be transmitted.

If the bucket is full and a burst of packets arrives into the buffer on the left, a burst of packets (equal to b bytes in size when added together)

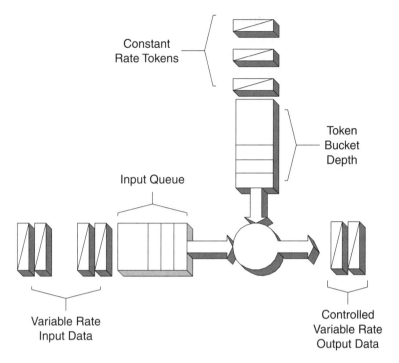

Figure 7.3 Token bucket.

will leave the regulator immediately with no gaps in between. Contrast this with the leaky bucket scheme, which would convert such a burst into a stream of packets leaving at a steady rate.

The token bucket scheme guarantees two things. First, it will never send out more than $(b + r \times t)$ bytes of data over any time interval t for a flow with token bucket parameters b and r. Second, the long-term, average transmission rate of such a flow will be r bytes/sec. Thus, the token bucket scheme is more flexible than the leaky bucket. It allows bursty traffic to be sent without having to request a data rate equal to the peak data rate, but bounds the burst size to b bytes. The only problem with the token bucket system is how the burst of packets is introduced into the network. Suppose that a flow is idle for some time and the bucket fills completely. When the flow is active again, it can send b bytes of data at the link transmission rate without stopping. This can potentially deprive other flows from access to network resources for the duration of the burst. Moreover, such a behavior may require a large amount of buffering at network devices along the path.

To avoid such a problem, many researchers have proposed using a token bucket model that combines the basic token bucket scheme with a leaky bucket. Figure 7.4 illustrates such a token bucket model. The scheme consists of two parts. On the left is the token bucket system previously described. The output from the regulator in the token bucket is not transmitted, but, instead, is placed into a leaky bucket of size b and the leaky bucket regulator transmits data out of that bucket at a peak rate of p bytes/sec. The peak rate p must be much larger than r, so that a burst of data can still be transmitted, while not completely starving other traffic. Overall, the combined scheme permits bursty traffic to be sent, limited to a burst of b bytes, with a long-term average rate of r and a peak rate of no more than p. A traffic flow transmitted using such a scheme is thus characterized by three parameters, namely, $<b, r, p>$.

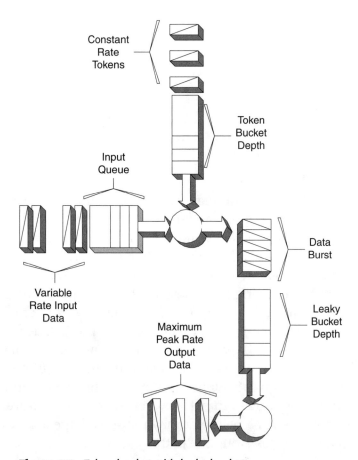

Figure 7.4 Token bucket with leaky bucket.

Sender Tspec

Under the Integrated Services model, the sender Tspec describes a traffic flow using the parameters $<b, r, p, m, M>$, The first three parameters (b, r, p) are the token bucket parameters as previously described. In addition, M specifies the maximum datagram size in the flow and m specifies the minimum policed unit. The parameter m is used by network nodes to estimate the correct amount of bandwidth to be allocated to the flow. Note that the application can specify only the minimum size of packet it generates in terms of the data or payload within a packet. Additional headers get tacked on the data to create the packet that gets transmitted over a particular link layer technology. So the network nodes use the value of m to compute the maximum bandwidth overhead needed to carry a flow's packets over a specific link layer technology. This computation is based on the ratio of m to the link layer header size [RFC2210]. The maximum size M is needed by nodes to determine whether or not they can service such a packet, and the sender can choose M based on the maximum transmission unit (MTU) supported over the path.

Receiver Rspec

A receiver uses the Rspec to specify the amount of resources it wishes to reserve to obtain a desired level of performance. When a receiver sends a RESV message, it includes an RSVP FlowSpec object consisting of a traffic specification (receiver Tspec) and an Rspec. The Tspec parameters $(r, b,$ and $p)$ are set to reflect the traffic parameters of the receiver's desired reservation. The Rspec specifies the type of service desired and service-specific parameters.

In the case of Controlled Load (CL) service, the receiver specifies only the Tspec parameters corresponding to the desired bandwidth allocation, and no Rspec parameters are specified other than the service desired (CL).

In the case of Guaranteed Service, the receiver will specify the Tspec and two service-specific parameters in the Rspec. These parameters are the required service rate R, which must be no less than the token bucket parameter r in Tspec, and a slack term. The receiver selects the R and S terms to obtain the desired bandwidth and delay guarantees. We will explain the use of these two terms later following the description of packet scheduling later in this chapter.

Policing and Shaping a Flow

The ability to describe the characteristics of a traffic flow is necessary to properly provision resources in a network's infrastructure. Once an appropriate traffic specification is determined, it is important to ensure that a flow stays within its traffic specification and does not send excess traffic. If flows were allowed to send excess traffic, the network resources will not be able to be accurately provisioned. It is also necessary that a flow maintain its traffic characteristics as it travels through the network. These are the functions of traffic policing and shaping in the IntServ model.

Policing is a term used to describe the enforcement function. It is typically implemented at hosts or at the edges of the network where a traffic flow is first introduced into the network. In RSVP, a flow's traffic is described using the aforementioned token bucket model. It is the job of a regulating agent to enforce a flow's Tspec using a token bucket system as shown in Figure 7.4. For each flow, this regulator allocates an input buffer to hold the packets arriving at the regulator. The regulator also maintains a flow state in terms of a flow's token bucket state and the peak rate to be enforced at the output of the regulator. Using this model, application traffic will be forced by the regulator to stay within its described bounds or risk delay or even loss. Meanwhile, the network can be assured that flows maintain their specified traffic characteristics, allowing accurate resource provisioning.

Now that we have seen what policing does and why, it is important to point out that per-flow policing can be expensive. Thus, it is advantageous for hosts to police their reserved traffic and remove this burden from the network's infrastructure. Such a distributed model is only effective, however, if the hosts can be trusted to actually police their traffic. When the hosts cannot be trusted, it is left to the network infrastructure to perform policing in order to guarantee that misbehaving flows do not negatively impact the QoS received by other conforming flows.

Figure 7.5 shows the QoS components inside a host. Here, applications can be seen as interacting with the Operating System's protocol stack. The applications are responsible for describing their traffic characteristics and the protocol stack is responsible for ensuring the flows are compliant before they are released into the network. The packet scheduler that resides at the output interface is responsible for the policing func-

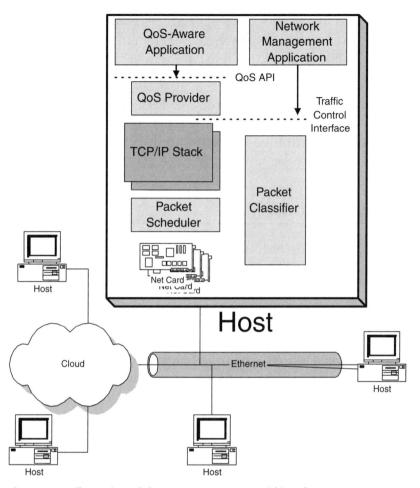

Figure 7.5 Illustration of the QoS components within a host.

tion. In addition, the scheduler may also schedule packets from multiple flows so that the packets from each flow obtain a proportional share of the bandwidth and, if applicable, experience the necessary delay bound. The latter function is similar to the scheduling performed at routers, as will be discussed later in this chapter.

Shaping is a concept similar to policing, only shaping typically applies to flows inside the network. Assuming that a flow has already been policed to its traffic specification, its journey through the network may still lead to the eventual clumping of its packets. The result is a well-behaved flow that may experience loss simply due to the compilation of packet delays experienced within the network itself. To avoid the potential for such loss, shaping can be used to reshape a malformed flow back into its described traffic characteristics. Again, a shaper will utilize the token bucket mechanism as shown in Figure 7.4. However, in the case of a shaper, ample buffer space will be provided such that large bursts of data from the flow can be held while they are shaped.

Now that we have seen how shaping and policing can be used to ensure that a flow maintains its traffic characteristics, it is time to delve into the details. Next, we will investigate the functions of the packet classifier component.

Packet Classification

In today's Internet, a traditional router performs two main tasks in forwarding a packet. First, it must look up the packet's destination address to determine an outgoing interface to be used for forwarding the packet toward its destination. This task is a form of packet classification in which the router looks at one of the fields in the packet header. Second, it must *switch* (transfer) the packet from an incoming link to one of the outgoing links based on the address lookup. With recent advances in hardware-based switching, the speed of packet forwarding mainly depends on the efficiency of the address lookup algorithm.

Until recently, the address lookup task was relatively easy. A router maintains a forwarding database that consists of destination IP addresses and the next hop router to which packets should be forwarded. In the case of unicast traffic, when an IP datagram arrives, the router only looks at the destination IP address (either in part or full) to decide how to forward the packet. In some cases, for multicast traffic, the router will also examine the source IP address in the header of an incoming IP datagram to decide how to forward it.

Routers at the periphery of the Internet need to maintain only a small forwarding database consisting of a few hundred entries and, in such cases, packet lookup or classification algorithms may use a simple mechanism such as a hash table lookup algorithm. However, as the Internet has grown, the number of possible destinations and destination networks has grown, leading to a huge growth in the number of forwarding table entries. For a router at the core of the Internet, the number of entries may reach tens of thousands or higher. In that case, the efficiency of the table lookup algorithm plays a major role in determining the speed and efficiency of packet forwarding. This is especially true as link speeds continue to grow to gigabits per second (Gbps) and beyond. In the last few years, several algorithms have been developed for fast address lookup [Scalable, Small] that solve this problem, allowing such routers to handle gigabit speed links with ease.

However, fast address lookup solves only part of the problem for routers that support QoS mechanisms. Remember that an RSVP-enabled flow is identified by looking at more than one field (IP destination address) in the IP header. In particular, the packet classifier must look at as many as five fields in the IP header and higher transport protocol header (<src IP addr, src port, IP protocol ID, dest IP addr, dest port>) of an incoming datagram to determine to which flow it belongs. Typically, this requires a classification algorithm that must find an exact or best match by examining five fields in the packet header(s). If the match is obtained by examining fields in sequence, the process will be much slower compared to a single address lookup. Moreover, such a lookup must be done efficiently to handle the link speeds in the multi-Mbps or higher. This requirement is definitely an impediment to deployment of RSVP at backbone routers that forward traffic at Gbps or more.

Fortunately, the current research suggests that efficient lookup algorithms exist that can find the best matching filter for a packet at gigabit speeds even when the lookup table contains as many as 100K entries [L4Lookup]. Many switching and router vendors are incorporating such algorithms in their hardware lookup implementations, easing the fear of bottlenecks to QoS deployment. Another way of reducing the lookup overhead is to rely on a single "flow label" field in the IP datagram header to identify a flow. Internet Protocol version 6 (IPv6) makes such a provision by including a "flow label" field in its IP header. The flow label would then be used as a single, contiguous filter in the forwarding table, allowing use of much simpler and efficient lookup algorithms. As IPv6 gains in popularity, the simplicity of this approach should benefit QoS deployment.

Packet Scheduler

As illustrated by the simple example in Figure 7.1, a packet scheduler operates at a multiplexing point where traffic from one or more input links arrives and then gets classified into one or more queues or classes. Each of these classes contains one or more flows, depending on the scheduling algorithm. Each class may represent a traffic class based on the desired performance properties or may represent an administrative class based on how a link is shared among multiple organizations. The scheduler's job is to control the interactions among different classes and to deliver the desired performance for each of the classes. As we examine different alternatives for packet scheduling, we will keep the following desirable properties in mind, as they are important for delivering the necessary QoS:

- *Protection among flows:* The scheduler must ensure that misbehaving flows do not affect the performance of well-behaved flows that stay within their traffic specifications. Otherwise, if a rogue flow sends traffic at a high rate, it can capture a large portion of the link bandwidth and prevent other flows from getting their due share. The scheduler must prevent this by building firewalls among flows, and this is usually achieved by maintaining a separate queue for each flow.

- *End-to-end guarantees:* Depending on the desired IntServ service class, flows need guarantees on bandwidth, delay, or both, and the scheduler must incorporate mechanisms to assign resources to meet these needs.

- *Flexibility in allocating resources:* In particular, the scheduler must be flexible in allocation of resources so that it can separately control per-packet delay from the bandwidth allocated to a flow. For example, some scheduling algorithms might bundle delay and bandwidth parameters together in determining the amount of resources to be allocated. In such cases, bundling might lead to inefficiency in resource utilization if a flow with a low delay requirement is artificially assigned higher bandwidth than necessary to meet its delay requirements.

- *Integrated support for both real-time and best-effort traffic:* Because a large fraction of Internet traffic consists of best-effort traffic, it is important that the scheduler support both best-effort and real-time traffic together, without starving the best-effort traffic.

- *Simplicity and efficiency of implementation:* Acceptance of traffic control mechanisms by network equipment vendors is important for widespread deployment of RSVP and IntServ. The scheduling algorithm used must be simple to implement and should lead to efficient resource utilization. In particular, the time and space requirements of the scheduling algorithm are important in determining its efficiency. Given a set of queues with certain maximum lengths, the time to order them according to the sequence of transmission and time to pick the next packet to be transmitted among the packets eligible for transmission determine the time complexity of an algorithm.

In the following, we will describe some of the scheduling algorithms used in practice and discuss their usefulness in providing end-to-end QoS guarantees.

FCFC Scheduling

Most of the traditional Internet routers use first-come, first-serve (FCFS) service on output links. In FCFS, the packets are serviced in the order in which they are received and are assigned to an output queue for transmission in sequence. If a rogue flow sends packets at a high rate, it can fill up most of the buffers in the output queue and, thus, can take up an arbitrary fraction of output link bandwidth, denying service to other, well-behaved flows. In practice, this is not a major problem in the Internet as long as most of the traffic uses TCP as the transport protocol because TCP exercises congestion avoidance and control at the source host. Under TCP's congestion control, each flow periodically examines the available bandwidth at bottlenecks along the path and reduces sending rate when it detects congestion [Comer-TCPIP]. Therefore, flows using TCP typically receive a fair share of available bandwidth. However, if a rogue flow uses a faulty TCP implementation or another transport protocol that does not exercise restraint, it can keep increasing its share of the bandwidth at the expense of others and FCFC scheduling cannot prevent this.

Simple Priority Scheduling

Fundamentally, FCFS scheduling does not distinguish among requirements of different flows. As the Internet has grown in popularity, the kind of traffic carried is no longer limited to data transfer using TCP. Instead, multimedia applications such as real-time audio- and video-conferencing and presentations also send traffic using the Internet and need timely delivery of their traffic. One of the simplest approaches to distinguish among flows is to employ a priority scheme in which outgoing packets are ordered by priority and the highest-priority packets among buffered packets are always transmitted first.

This scheduling algorithm is simple, efficient, and only takes $O(1)$ time in making the scheduling decision as long as the nonempty queues are always ordered according to decreasing priority.

Priority can be assigned to flows based on their QoS requirements. For example, audio packets that request the smallest delays are given highest priority. Audio packets can then be followed in priority by video packets that demand higher bandwidth but can tolerate higher delays, and so on. However, there are some drawbacks to the simple priority scheme. First, even if the admission control algorithm ensures that resources are not overcommitted in the long run, individual flows at lower priority cannot be guaranteed a resource share over a smaller time scale. For example, when bursts of higher-priority packets arrive at about the same time, lower-priority packets remain backlogged until all the higher-priority packets are transmitted. This will lead to resource starvation for lower-priority flows and also results in very high delays for other flows. Second, it is difficult to provide per-packet guarantees on delays for individual flows. This is true even for flows given highest priority. For example, audio flows consist of small packets (e.g., 64 bytes) and each packet may need a stringent guarantee on per-packet delay. However, under the priority scheme, there is no distinction among packets in the same priority class. Therefore, each arriving packet must wait for all the previous packets with the same priority to be transmitted first, resulting in unpredictable delays.

Simply put, basic priority schemes are not suitable when per-flow QoS guarantees must be met.

Round-Robin Scheduling

An alternative form of scheduling uses a round-robin scheme (called *RR scheduling*), in which the scheduler visits each nonempty queue in turn, and services one packet for each visit. This enforces some fair sharing among different classes of traffic and prevents any flow from obtaining an arbitrary share of output link bandwidth. Again, the scheme is simple to implement. It is also efficient, as it takes the scheduler only a constant amount of time to make the scheduling decision because the scheduler only needs to look at the next nonempty queue to select the next packet for transmission.

However, the scheme suffers from two drawbacks. First, it does not offer any flexibility in allocating bandwidth proportional to the requirements of individual flows. Second, it does not take into account packet lengths. In an IP network, datagrams are of variable size, and thus RR scheduling can result in unequal sharing of bandwidth. For example, consider Figure 7.6, in which a scheduler selects from a set of input queues on the left for transmission over the output link on the right. Assume that all the packets in the first queue are each 100 bytes long, whereas all the packets in the nth queue are 1000 bytes long. In the case of RR scheduling, flows in the nth queue will end up getting a much larger (about 10 times) share of bandwidth than flows in the first queue. Moreover, there is no control over the amount of bandwidth allocated to each queue.

A variation of RR scheduling is *weighted RR* (WRR), in which each queue is assigned a weight proportional to the share of the bandwidth assigned to it. For example, consider Figure 7.6 again. Assume that each queue i is assigned a weight W_i. In WRR scheduling, the scheduler services W_i packets from queue i every time it visits the queue. Thus, if the weights are assigned to take into account the different packet lengths and bandwidth allocation, WRR can achieve appropriate link bandwidth sharing. This does assume that the average packet length for each flow is known in advance, which may not be the case for many flows. However, WRR does not meet another requirement. It does not take into account delay requirements of individual flows. Packets in a flow that tolerate very short delays (e.g., audio) must wait for their turn until packets from other nonempty queues are serviced in a RR fashion. Later, we will describe a variation of RR scheduling, called deficit round-robin scheduling (DRR), that addresses some of these deficiencies.

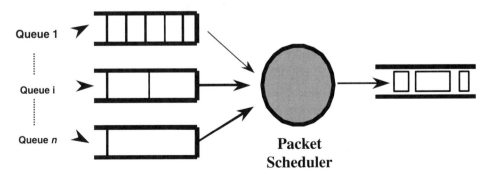

Figure 7.6 Scheduler examines packets in multiple input queues on left and selects a packet for transmission by placing it in an output queue on the right.

Weighted Fair Queueing

So far, we looked at scheduling algorithms that are increasingly effective in providing *flow isolation* among multiple flows and also provide fair or proportional sharing of bandwidth among different flows. An ideal algorithm for fair sharing was proposed by Demers et al. [Fair-Queuing] called *bit-by-bit round robin* (BRR), in which each flow sends one bit at a time in round-robin fashion. Figure 7.7 illustrates the concept where the scheduler simulates Time Division Multiplexing (TDM) model over N flows. One flow is assigned to each TDM channel and a bit from a different flow is serviced in each time slot. So when a packet arrives for F1, a single bit from the packet will be transmitted and one bit from the other flows will be transmitted before transmitting another bit from the same packet. As a result, at any point in time, each flow gets an equal share of the bandwidth.

Since it is impossible to implement such a scheme in practice, Demers et al. suggested an approximation of BRR called *fair queuing* (FQ) that simulates BRR. Under FQ, when a packet arrives for a flow, the scheduler calculates the time when the packet's last bit would have been transmitted by the router using the BRR scheme. Based on this departure time, the packet is then inserted into a queue of packets sorted by their departure times. A variation of FQ is *weighted fair queuing* (WFQ, again suggested by Demers, et al.), in which flows are assigned different weights to reflect their bandwidth or delay requirement. Under WFQ, the servicing discipline is the same as FQ, except that, in each round, the number of bits transmitted by a flow is proportional to its weight rather than a single bit as assumed under BRR.

WFQ has most of the desirable properties listed at the beginning of this section. First, WFQ builds firewalls among flows because each flow is serviced according to its fair share.

Second, WFQ provides great flexibility in resource allocation to meet a variety of goals such as link sharing or providing guaranteed delay

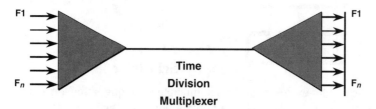

Figure 7.7 Simulation of a TDM model for N flows.

bounds. Under link sharing, the service objective is to allow sharing of link bandwidth based on predefined criteria such as type of protocol (TCP, IPX, or SNA), type of application, or the source of traffic (source subnet or the organization that pays for the share of a link). An important property is to allow such sharing while building firewalls, but at the same time allow any mix of traffic to use the link if the spare capacity exists. WFQ facilitates link sharing because a separate class can be used to aggregate flows that meet the same criterion and a weight assigned to each class based on its allocated capacity. Under WFQ, excess traffic is serviced only when a class with allocated capacity does not have any backlogged traffic. WFQ can also integrate real-time traffic handling with the servicing of best-effort traffic. This is because the best-effort traffic can be allocated a fixed share of the link bandwidth to avoid starvation. Furthermore, any capacity left unused by the real-time flows can be used to forward the best-effort traffic in WFQ.

Third, assuming that a flow traverses a series of WFQ schedulers at routers along its path, WFQ can be used to provide an end-to-end guarantee on both bandwidth and a worst-case delay bound. Note that WFQ guarantees bandwidth because each hop guarantees its share of bandwidth based on the weight assigned. The weight can be computed based on the reservation request that specifies the token bucket parameters. Because a share of bandwidth is guaranteed at each hop, Parekh and Gallager [GPS] have proved an important bound on worst-case end-to-end delay suffered by each packet in a flow traversing a series of WFQ schedulers. Their result is based on the service rate R assigned to a flow at each WFQ scheduler. The higher the service rate, the faster the packets in the flow are serviced at each hop, leading to smaller end-to-end delay. Thus, a receiver can choose its service parameters carefully to request a service rate R that will yield the desired delay bound based on the use of WFQ scheduling in the path. For example, given the token bucket parameters (b, r, p) in the Tspec, the receiver must choose the service rate R (in Rspec) to be larger than r. As R becomes larger, the end-to-end delay will go down because the delay-incurred waiting for service at each node will decrease.

The Guaranteed Service class makes use of this result. Note that end-to-end delay has two components, namely, a fixed component determined by transmission and propagation delay and a variable component (queuing delay). The queuing delay is determined by the Tspec (the token bucket parameters) and the Rspec that specifies the service rate R that an application requests. A detailed analysis of how the WFQ scheduling delivers an end-to-end delay bound based on GS parameters is presented elsewhere [RFC2212]. We will describe it in much simpler terms here.

Consider a source that specifies the token bucket size of b as part of its Tspec $<p, r, b, m, M>$ and assume that the reservation requests a service rate of R. Given a source constrained by a token bucket (b, r) and serviced at a service rate R (R no less than r), Parekh and Gallager have proved that the delay experienced by such a flow at an ideal BRR scheduler is bounded by b/R.

Let us understand this result in the light of a WFQ scheduler that approximates an ideal BRR scheduler. For the sake of simplicity, let us ignore Tspec and Rspec parameters other than b and R ($R > r$). In this case, given a source sending a flow with Tspec (b) and Rspec (R) specified, we can assume that such a flow will send a burst of no more than b bytes at a time. In addition, we will assume that the flow will be serviced by a series of WFQ schedulers on the path at the same service rate R. Let us further simplify our discussion by assuming that the burst consists of a single packet of size b bytes and restricting our understanding of end-to-end delay to only one packet transmitted over the flow. Parekh and Gallager have proven that the end-to-end delay experienced by such a packet is the sum of three parts:

1. b/R seconds of time taken to service b bytes at the rate of R bytes/sec. Even though the packet traverses a series of WFQ schedulers, the series acts as if the packet was serviced by a single WFQ scheduler, ignoring the transmission delay at each hop.

2. An additional delay is experienced at a WFQ scheduler if the packet arrives just after it would have received service under BRR approximation. Note that, the flow is guaranteed to be visited and serviced at the rate R, so a packet of size b bytes will get a chance for service in no longer than b/R units of time. This delay must be summed over all but one of the nodes on the path to account for the worst-case situation where it arrives at each WFQ scheduler just after it would have received service.

3. Assuming the link speed is L (bytes/sec) at each hop, the packet will experience a transmission delay of b/L at each hop summed over all the hops in the path.

Admittedly, this is a very simple analysis based on an ideal situation. In practice, the GS specification accounts for variations in link speeds, packet sizes, and peak rate. In addition, it also accounts for variations in WFQ implementations by allowing the service elements on the path to specify error terms (C and D) that account for their variation from the strict WFQ interpretation.

WFQ and Guaranteed Service

Guaranteed Service is specified assuming that the behavior of each network node that supports the service can be modeled using the so-called fluid server operating at a service rate R. The advantage of this model is that one can describe the service a flow will receive at a reserved rate R independent of the current load at a node or the number of other flows being serviced. The fluid server model was introduced by Parekh and Gallager and has the properties described earlier. For simplicity, we will assume that a node employing the aforementioned ideal BRR scheduler mimics such a fluid server.

As part of the RSVP AdSpec, each node i exports C_i and D_i parameters that describe the level of service that it can provide to flows that go through it. The receiver receives these parameters and interprets them in the context of the desired service rate R. In particular, C_i and D_i capture the deviation of the node i from a fluid server that is operating at rate R. The receiver can use this information to compute the end-to-end delay it can expect at rate R. Recall that we discussed how end-to-end delay can be computed based on Parekh and Gallager's result, assuming an ideal fluid server. The error terms C_i and D_i specify that a flow served at rate R will be delayed by additional $(C_i/R + D_i)$ units at node i due to its deviation from the ideal behavior. Given a sum of error terms along the path, a receiver can now compute the maximum end-to-end delay to expect when using Guaranteed Service.

For GS, a receiver's Rspec specifies a slack term S in addition to service rate R [RFC2212]. The slack term signifies the difference between the desired delay and the delay obtained by using the service rate R. This slack term can be utilized by the network element to reduce its resource reservation for the flow. A receiver can use a combination of R and S terms to decide the level of resource reservation to request. For example, the receiver can trade additional delay for a reduced reservation, thereby increasing the probability of its reservation to succeed or reducing the bill if it is being charged for service. It can also use the information to adjust its own expectations. Consider a video player receiving a video presentation that makes a reservation at rate R. Suppose the end-to-end delay expected using the rate R (with $S = 0$) is just 100 milliseconds. Further suppose that the player can buffer 250 milliseconds of video before playing it back without jeopardizing the playback quality. The player can afford to specify a slack term of 150 milliseconds and considerably reduce the required level of resource reservation without affecting the perceived quality.

Drawbacks of WFQ

One significant drawback of FQ (and WFQ) is that it requires maintenance of a sorted queue and an insertion into a sorted queue. This is expensive when a large number of flows are involved, increasing the cost of router implementations. In addition, WFQ requires maintenance of per-flow Scheduler State and that increases the memory space required in WFQ router implementations.

Deficit Round-Robin Scheduling

A cheaper approximation of fair queuing scheduling called *deficit round-robin* (DRR) scheduling [Efficient-Fair] addresses some of the shortcomings of WFQ scheduling. Unlike WFQ, which can provide guarantees on both delay and bandwidth, DRR focuses only on fair sharing of bandwidth similar to weighted round-robin (WRR) scheduling. Recall that WRR requires that the average length of packets in flows be known in advance in order to fairly allocate bandwidth to individual flows. DRR removes that requirement.

A DRR scheduler associates a flow-specific parameter called a *deficit* with each flow that is initialized to 0. In addition, the DRR scheduler uses a quantum size to decide how many bytes of data to service from each flow during each visit. The scheduler works as follows:

1. Each time the scheduler visits the queue, it tries to service quantum bytes from the queue.

2. If the packet at the head of the queue is no larger than the quantum in size, the scheduler services the packet. If the packet is larger in size than the quantum, the scheduler adds the quantum to the flow's deficit counter and postpones servicing it to the next round.

3. During each visit, if the sum of the flow's deficit counter and the quantum size is larger than the size of the packet at the head of the queue, the packet is serviced and the deficit counter is reduced by the packet size.

Consider an example where the quantum size is 500 bytes and there are three flows, F1, F2, and F3, with packets of sizes 800, 300, and 900 bytes in their queues, respectively. In the first round, the deficit counter of F1 will be increased to 500 with no packet serviced. Also in the first round, the packet from F2 is serviced and its deficit counter becomes 200 (500 − 300). Finally, the packet from F3 is not serviced and its deficit counter is also increased to 500. In the second round, the packet from F1 will be serviced with its deficit counter set to 200 (500 + 500 − 800). Meanwhile, F2's queue is empty and its deficit counter will be reset to 0. Finally, the packet from F3 will be serviced with its deficit counter set to 100. Note that credits are not allowed to be accumulated by flows when no packets are in the queue to avoid unfairness in the future. Contrary to the preceding example, the quantum size must be chosen such that it is larger than the maximum packet size allowed to ensure that at least one packet is serviced in each round.

In the weighted version of DRR, each flow is assigned its own quantum based on the desired share of bandwidth. For example, if the default quantum is 500 bytes and a flow is assigned a quantum of 750 bytes, that flow gets 50 percent more bandwidth than the other flow if only two flows are active.

The biggest advantages of DRR are its simplicity and ease of implementation, which make it very attractive for both software and hardware implementations. The only disadvantage of DRR is that, unlike WFQ, it does not by itself provide strong latency bounds because a small audio packet may be delayed by a quantum's worth for every other active flow at each node along its path.

The weighted version of DRR is suitable for implementation of Controlled Load service, as it can offer a CL flow bandwidth guarantee, irrespective of the amount of traffic on other flows. To meet the CL service requirements, however, the quantum size assigned to each CL flow must be based on its token bucket parameters (Tspec) and the admission control function must limit admission of other flows to ensure that a CL flow is given timely service. Note that a CL flow with token bucket parameters $<p, r, b>$ is constrained to send no more than $(b + r * t)$ bytes over any time interval t. If the DRR scheduler can ensure that $(b + r * T)$ bytes from each flow would be serviced in each DRR round lasting time interval T, each CL flow will receive the appropriate service.

Summary

This chapter described the traffic control function at routers and hosts that is necessary for providing end-to-end QoS guarantees. Specifically, it described the traffic classification and packet scheduling components of traffic control. We also discussed the different packet scheduling algorithms and their suitability for providing various QoS guarantees. The WFQ algorithm was shown to have all the desirable properties for providing such guarantees, but it is expensive to implement. The DRR variation on fair queuing is simple and efficient to implement and can provide the service necessary to implement link sharing and bandwidth guarantees. This chapter also discussed a special form of scheduling called policing that enforces the traffic specifications of a flow.

PART THREE

QoS Applications and Deployment

CHAPTER 8

Odds and Ends—Differentiated Services and the Last Mile Problem

As a signaling protocol, RSVP allows applications to request specific QoS from the network. The Integrated Services (IntServ) framework [RFC 2211 and 2212], described in Chapter 4, defines classes of network service such as Controlled Load and Guaranteed Service. Network applications must specify the class of service they desire and specify the appropriate service parameters in their QoS requests carried by RSVP. RSVP, together with the IntServ service class specifications, is largely independent of the underlying networking technologies. The Internet consists of networks built out of many subnetwork technologies such as IEEE 802-style LANs (Ethernet, Token Ring, FDDI, etc.) and ATM. Each of these technologies exhibits different dynamic behavior in the presence of traffic and, in some cases, provides explicit mechanisms for QoS. For example, IEEE 802 has recently defined prioritized traffic classes for IEEE 802-style MAC layer technologies [802.1D, 802.1Q], whereas ATM technology supports the establishment of both point-to-point and point-to-multipoint virtual circuits (VCs) with a specified QoS. In addition, recent efforts to provide QoS support for aggregated traffic inside the core of the Internet have led to the development of Differentiated Services (DiffServ). In contrast to RSVP's per-flow orientation, DiffServ networks classify packets as belonging to one of a small number of aggregated flows based on the setting of bits in the TOS field of each packet's IP header.

To achieve the necessary end-to-end IntServ service classes across the Internet, it is necessary to define a consistent mapping of the IntServ service classes onto specific subnetwork technologies. The IETF Working Group, Integrated Services over Specific Link Layers (ISSLL), has addressed this issue and this chapter will describe the mapping mechanisms developed for various link layer technologies. In the case of DiffServ, it is important that the aggregation mechanisms interoperate effectively with hosts and networks that provide per-flow QoS in response to RSVP signaling. This chapter will also explore how these two technologies can work together to provide a more scalable network architecture that still achieves QoS.

Shared Media and Subnetwork Bandwidth Management

Earlier, in Chapter 6, we described RSVP as capable of reserving resources over a simplex data link. RSVP was designed for QoS signaling in a WAN environment, where routers are interconnected over full-duplex point-to-point links. Once again, consider two routers interconnected over a full-duplex point-to-point link. Each router has an outgoing interface to the link over which it, and it alone, can transmit data. In this model, the router has complete control over the amount of data it sends over the outgoing link. When such a router supports RSVP-based admission control for QoS management, it assumes its traffic control component is responsible for the outgoing interface in that this component is solely in control over how many reservations to accept, polices accepted flows, and provides for flow separation.

Thus, RSVP is designed to reserve bandwidth over full-duplex links that allow simultaneous bidirectional communication through two essentially independent simplex links. Nevertheless, this assumption is not valid when an interconnection link (or network) is shared among two or more devices. For example, half-duplex links provide bidirectional communication, but only in one direction at a time through a link shared by both endpoints. Similarly, when several hosts are interconnected using an Ethernet cable or a dumb Ethernet hub, the transmission link capacity is a shared resource and each host cannot independently allocate bandwidth without potentially overcommitting the link's resources. This section will describe enhancements to the RSVP protocol and methods for mapping IntServ service classes over shared subnetworks.

IEEE 802 Networks

The Institute of Electrical and Electronics Engineers (IEEE) Project 802 has developed a number of standards for many different local area network (LAN) technologies. The specific underlying LAN technologies include Fiber Distributed Data Interface (FDDI), Token Ring, and Ethernet, among others. These technologies are collectively referred to as IEEE 802-style LAN technologies. They all offer the same, best-effort datagram service to higher-level protocols such as Internet Protocol (IP) over a shared medium. In addition, IEEE 802 has defined standards for interconnecting or bridging multiple LAN segments using devices known as "MAC bridges" or "switches." IEEE 802 has also defined a notion of user_priority or traffic class to be associated with the transmission and reception of all frames in IEEE 802-style networks. In the following pages we briefly describe the IEEE 802 service model and characteristics of 802-style LAN technologies.

IEEE 802 Service Model

IEEE 802 networks typically consist of a group of end stations, or hosts, interconnected using a media access control (MAC) technology such as Ethernet or Token Ring. Under the IEEE 802 service model, end stations transmit frames using a method designed to mediate access to a shared link or subnetwork. Each frame carries a payload type that identifies the type of data carried, contains a link layer identification of the source and destination of the frame, and encapsulates higher-level protocols and data as payload. End stations are identified using link layer MAC addresses that are completely independent of the addressing conventions used by higher-layer protocols such as IP. In an IEEE 802-style network, each MAC layer technology uses its own frame format. In addition, even though IEEE 802 specifies 48-bit MAC address formats, each MAC media technology uses its own methods for encoding the addresses. For example, the IEEE 802.3 standard defines the frame format and media access procedure for Ethernet, whereas the IEEE 802.5 standard defines it for Token Ring technology.

Some of these networks, such as FDDI or Token Ring, also support a notion of user_priority or traffic class. The user_priority is a simple scalar value associated with the prioritized transmission and reception of all frames. It is supplied by a sender using the MAC service and is presented to the receiver along with the data in the frame. The frame formats used by each of the IEEE 802 LAN technologies differ from each other, and some formats define methods for carrying the user_priority value, whereas others do not. In other words, the 802 world presents a number of different frame formats with varying capabilities.

The IEEE 802.1D standard specifies the operation of MAC bridges that connect LAN segments of similar or different MAC technologies. For example, a MAC bridge could be capable of connecting a Token Ring segment to an Ethernet segment. To facilitate communication of MAC addresses to higher-level formats, the specification also defines a single reference format—the so-called IEEE 802 canonical format for MAC addresses. The standard also defines an extended frame format and a consistent way to carry the user_priority value over a bridged network consisting of Ethernet, Token Ring, FDDI, and demand priority networks.

When the user_priority value is carried in packets, the downstream nodes along the path can use the value as a label to discriminate among packets in different streams and offer differentiated service to groups of streams at each priority level. The IEEE 802.1D specification does not dictate how the user_priority value is to be used, but does specify a default mode of operation where switches that implement priority queuing can use static priority queuing. Later in this chapter, we will describe a method of using the user_priority value (also referred to as the traffic class) in conjunction with RSVP-based admission control to achieve integrated services over IEEE 802-style networks.

In order to understand the problems in mapping IntServ service classes over shared or switched LAN technologies, we will briefly describe the shared and switched Ethernet technologies.

Shared Ethernet

Ethernet is the most commonly used LAN technology today. Ethernet is a type of shared medium network technology standardized by the IEEE under the designation IEEE 802.3. In its most basic form, Ethernet is based on the concept of broadcast-style communication.

The basic operation of Ethernet is that a number of hosts are connected to a shared medium such as the so-called yellow wire or a coaxial cable. As the medium is shared, all hosts connected to the network receive every frame sent on the wire. Hosts use this property of broadcast communication to listen for frames addressed to them and to determine if the medium is currently being used by another host for communication. If two or more hosts attempt to broadcast simultaneously, they will detect the collision by observing the frame they send. If the frame is garbled, a collision has occurred. The sending hosts will back off for a random period of time and then again attempt to transmit. The more failed attempts, the longer the random back-off period they will wait before trying again. A real-life analogy to Ethernet is a number of people having a meeting. Typically, only one person will hold the attention of the room at a time, even when the comments are directed to a particular individual. If two people attempt to talk at the same time, it is only polite for both to pause temporarily and then try again.

Unfortunately, communication over a shared medium such as shared Ethernet has its limitations in terms of supporting different service classes. First of all, because the medium is shared, it is not sufficient to perform admission control at a single host. Instead, a method for accounting resources at all the attached hosts is necessary to avoid over-subscribing the link. Second, shared Ethernet does not discriminate among different user_priority values and, therefore, hosts must act responsibly to allow the higher-priority reserved traffic to get precedence over other traffic. Finally, the shared link cannot scale in support of a large number of hosts. Each transmission is broadcast to every host sharing the link, making the medium unusable by more than one host at a time. In addition, the amount of effective bandwidth available to each host is reduced as more hosts are added to the shared medium. These issues limit the usefulness of shared Ethernet as a LAN technology for large QoS networks.

Switched Ethernet

To address some of the limitations of shared Ethernet and to exploit the use of point-to-point links among hosts on a LAN, shared Ethernet has evolved to support MAC-level bridges or switches leading to switched Ethernet technology. One of the important aspects of shared Ethernet that limits its scalability is the notion of a "broadcast region." All the hosts attached to a shared yellow wire or a dumb hub form a broadcast region where each frame transmitted is received by all the attached hosts. This renders the shared medium incapable of more than one transmission at a time. In a switched topology, on the other hand, each switch supports a number of ports to which one or more hosts are attached via full- or half-duplex links. Each link that attaches the host or hosts to the switch can act as a shared segment that only has to support the hosts directly connected to it. The switch, then, effectively limits the broadcast region to the much smaller scope of the shared segment. For each of its ports, the switch acts as a MAC-layer bridge and forwards frames from one port to another based on the frame's destination address, filtering the traffic from ports that do not need to receive it. The IEEE 802.1D standard specifies the rules on forwarding and filtering traffic among broadcast regions attached to a switch. A switch basically allows the network to be organized into a hub-and-spokes structure, where the switch acts as a hub to which hosts are connected like spokes on a wheel. Switches can then be further interconnected using point-to-point links, acting as axles between the wheels, to form a complete switched network topology.

Figure 8.1 provides an example of switched segment topology for a LAN, and shows how an Ethernet topology can scale up to accommodate a large number of hosts. The switch in the middle supports three ports, and each of the ports has a shared Ethernet segment (yellow wire) with several hosts attached to it. Each of these shared segments forms a localized broadcast region where the attached hosts receive all frame transmissions and share the available bandwidth. This localized broadcast region is equivalent to the traditional shared Ethernet. Nevertheless, the switch does not continue to forward broadcast traffic on the shared segment to other segments unless the broadcast traffic is actually destined for hosts on the other segments. By localizing the broadcasts in this way, hosts on other segments are free to use their segment's bandwidth for concurrent communication.

Because the switch forwards frames among segments, it usually uses a buffer at each port to queue up the outgoing frames that must wait for a previously arrived frame to complete transmission. A switch will also make use of queues to temporarily store frames when a port comes under contention. That is, if two connected segments are trying to send information to a third segment through the switch at the same time, this kind of queuing is required to hold the excess traffic until it can be transmitted. If the switch implements the latest revision of IEEE 802.1D that specifies the use of priority values, the switch will include multiple queues to separate traffic specifying different priority values into different priority queues.

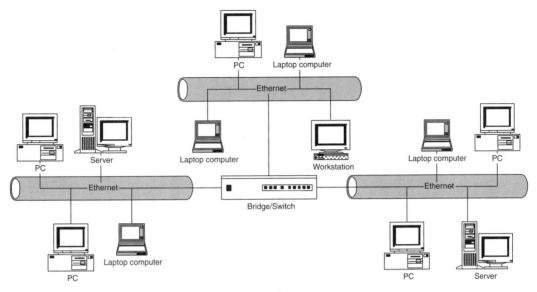

Figure 8.1 Illustration of a switched Ethernet topology.

The SBM

In a shared networking technology such as Ethernet, all the devices (hosts, bridges, or switches) attached to a shared segment get an equal chance to use the medium. This effectively achieves only a best-effort delivery service. Note that even in a switched topology, as shown in Figure 8.1, hosts may be attached to a shared segment. Moreover, even when two devices (such as switches) are directly connected via a half-duplex point-to-point link, the devices still share the link, meaning that only one device can send at a time. For the rest of the discussion, we will refer to such segments as "shared segments" and a network consisting of such segments as a "shared network." Standard RSVP-based admission control does not work in the case of shared segments because multiple devices share the capacity of the link. RSVP requires that admission control meter and properly provision the traffic sent by each party to avoid overcommitting resources and to ensure QoS. In the case of a shared segment, no one device controls the segment or can account for its use.

The Subnetwork Bandwidth Manager (SBM) solves this problem by providing a way of managing the shared resources of a shared segment. The SBM is an extension to RSVP signaling and a method for RSVP-based admission control over IEEE 802-style networks [SBM]. It enables devices attached to a shared segment to volunteer as a "resource broker" for the shared network resources. The resource broker (SBM) is responsible for admission control, and all the devices attached to the shared segment use an extension to the RSVP protocol (called the SBM protocol) to request network resources from the SBM. We will describe the basic operation of SBM by example.

Consider the simple shared segment shown in Figure 8.2. Here, a router and a host are connected to a shared segment brokered by an SBM. The SBM-based admission control procedure works as follows:

1. DSBM Election: Devices attached to the segment run a fault-tolerant election protocol to elect a Designated SBM (DSBM) that is responsible for managing resources on the segment. All other devices act as DSBM clients. When a device (DSBM client) starts up, it first determines whether a DSBM exists on the attached segment and, if so, it diverts its outgoing RSVP messages to the DSBM. If the shared segment is a full-duplex, point-to-point link, an election is not necessary as the device at each end of the link can act as DSBM for its outgoing interface, just as expected by RSVP.

2. The DSBM uses a special MAC and IP address (a reserved multicast address) to listen to incoming requests from the DSBM clients. This address is referred to as the "DSBM address."

3. To request QoS, DSBM clients use the services of the DSBM in conjunction with RSVP. When a DSBM client sends or forwards a PATH message, it first sends it to the DSBM using the DSBM address instead of sending the RSVP message directly to the session address (as is done in standard RSVP processing). When the DSBM receives the PATH message, it creates and maintains the path state according to standard

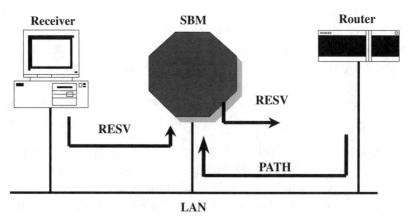

Figure 8.2 Illustration of a simple shared segment managed by an SBM.

RSVP processing rules. Before forwarding the PATH message, the DSBM updates the RSVP_HOP object (PHOP info) to include its own DSBM interface address. Thus, the DSBM effectively inserts itself into the chain of RSVP nodes in the path from an RSVP sender to its receiver. Again, Figure 8.2 illustrates how a DSBM inserts itself in the path of the standard RSVP signaling.

4. When a receiver sends out an RSVP RESV message, that message traverses back to the sender hop-by-hop, retracing the path previously used by the corresponding PATH message. When the RESV message reaches the shared segment, it automatically ends up at the DSBM. The DSBM includes an admission control agent that keeps track of the resources consumed on the segment from all installed reservations and determines whether or not to accept subsequent reservations based on the remaining resources.

Enhancement to Standard RSVP

The addition of a DSBM to RSVP admission control results in some extensions to RSVP message processing rules and objects. In the following, we summarize the SBM extensions to RSVP:

- Path Message Forwarding: On a shared segment, it is required that the DSBM clients discover their DSBM and then forward their PATH messages to the DSBM. To accomplish this, a dynamic binding mechanism is needed such that DSBM clients, including Layer 2 devices such as link layer bridges, can discover their DSBM and send it PATH messages. To facilitate such communication, the DSBM is addressed using a logical address rather than a physical address. An IP multicast address (224.0.0.16) is reserved as the "DSBM Logical Address" and its corresponding MAC address is also reserved, so that even a link layer bridge can easily identify the PATH message addressed to the DSBM. To avoid propagating the messages directed to a DSBM across subnets, the address is chosen from a range of local multicast addresses so that a router (or similar network layer device) that connects one LAN to another will not forward messages directed to a DSBM beyond the shared LAN. All DSBM clients always forward the PATH messages by addressing them to the DSBM Logical Address.

  In addition, it is logical that the DSBM will reside on a link layer device such as a bridge and may not be able to understand and use network layer IP addresses. Also, when a PATH message propagates from one DSBM to its next hop destination, the next link layer hop will include a DSBM client, which, again, may not be able to use IP addresses. To obviate the need for the client link layer device to understand IP addresses, the DSBM uses another logical address (AllSBMsAddress) to forward the PATH messages to its clients. This address is, again, a reserved IP multicast address and has its corresponding link layer multicast address so that devices that can only handle MAC-level addresses can easily identify PATH messages forwarded to them.

- In standard RSVP processing, the RSVP_HOP object is used to keep track of the next hop (downstream node in the path of data packets in an RSVP-enabled flow) and the previous hop (upstream nodes with respect to data flow). These objects allow PATH and RESV messages to pin down and then traverse back up the data path between a sender and a receiver. For example, when a node forwards a PATH message, it includes its own address in the RSVP_HOP object so that the next hop node will know the previous hop address to use when forwarding a subsequent RESV message back toward the sender. The addresses included in the RSVP_HOP objects are IP network layer addresses.

- When a PATH message traverses a LAN consisting of shared segments, the PATH message will traverse additional nodes that host DSBMs for intervening shared segments. As previously stated, these nodes are typically link layer devices such as MAC bridges that may not understand IP addresses. Such devices may also not know how to route RSVP messages to the next or previous hop router or host (a network layer device) using its IP address.

To avoid requiring link layer devices to understand IP addresses and to avoid requiring them to route messages based on IP addresses, the SBM introduces new RSVP objects called the LAN_NHOP and RSVP_HOP_L2. Just like the RSVP_HOP object, RSVP_HOP_L2 object identifies the MAC address of next hop or previous hop nodes participating in the SBM signaling process. For example, when a network layer device forwards the PATH message over a shared segment, it includes its IP address in the RSVP_HOP object and the corresponding MAC address in the RSVP_HOP_L2 object. Having both the IP and their corresponding MAC addresses available simplifies processing for link layer devices that operate strictly with MAC addresses, such as LAN switches and bridges. When a link layer device receives such a PATH message, it will remember the addresses given in both HOP objects and use the MAC address later for forwarding a RESV message back to the previous hop.

Similarly, when a network layer device (node A) forwards a PATH message to the next network layer hop such as another router or host (node B) attached to a shared network, the message is likely to visit DSBMs on the path hosted by strictly link layer devices. To simplify link layer operation, node A includes the IP address and corresponding MAC address of the next hop network layer node B in the LAN_NHOP object. This allows the intervening link layer devices to use the MAC address in the LAN_NHOP object to correctly forward the PATH message toward its next network layer hop, node B.

Another object introduced by SBM is the TCLASS object that is discussed later in this section.

- PATH Message Processing: Again, Figure 8.2 shows how a DSBM effectively inserts itself in the RSVP signaling path of a LAN. The process will begin with the arrival of an RSVP PATH message on the managed segment. The node responsible for forwarding the PATH message from the network layer to the link layer is also responsible for identifying the next network layer hop. The next network layer hop is the next IP-aware node for which the PATH is destined. This information is then added to the PATH message as an additional LAN_NHOP object that specifies both the network and link layer addresses for the next IP hop. The PATH message must be forwarded to the DSBM for the managed segment via the DSBMLogicalAddress previously described. On receiving the PATH message, the DSBM will perform the appropriate RSVP message processing rules, including inserting itself as the PHOP, and then will proceed to forward the PATH message on to its destination via the AllSBMsAddress. The corresponding SBM host or router listening for messages with the multicast AllSBMsAddress will then receive a PATH message identifying it in the LAN_NHOP object. The destination will then install a corresponding path state, as expected with RSVP message processing.

- *RESV Message Processing:* In DSBM PATH processing, as in standard RSVP processing, when an RSVP node receives a PATH message, it creates a path state and remembers the previous hop that sent it the PATH message. However, in the case of the DSBM, both the network layer address (given in the RSVP_HOP object) and the link layer address (in the RSVP_HOP_L2 object) are remembered as part of the path state. When an RESV message arrives for the DSBM, it will find a corresponding path state for the reservation. If the path state exists, the DSBM will check with its admission control component to determine if sufficient resources are available for the reservation. If resources are not available, an RESV error will be generated. If sufficient resources are available, the DSBM will allocate the required resources for the reservation. The DSBM will then use the local path state's MAC address of the previous hop to forward the RESV message upstream. As expected, the DSBM will overwrite the RESV's RSVP_HOP and RSVP_HOP_L2 objects with its own addresses before forwarding the RESV message on toward the PHOP. This process will continue until the RESV reaches the source or the first network layer device on the data path to the source.

Mapping Integrated Services onto IEEE 802-style Subnets

The model proposed by the Integrated Services working group requires RSVP routers to isolate traffic flows from each other during their transit across a network in order to enable QoS. Additionally, RSVP routers provide per-flow service in terms of traffic control at each outgoing interface. The motivation for traffic flow separation is to provide protection to the Integrated Service flows from misbehaving flows and other best-effort traffic that may share the same data path. In this model, routers along the data path make packet handling decisions based on the RSVP session, flow, and filter information and use this information to classify, queue, and forward the corresponding data packets. Nevertheless, this approach is inappropriate for use in the IEEE 802 environment, where per-flow classification and handling is expensive with increasing switch speed, and where devices may only incorporate use of simpler classification mechanisms such as 802.1D user priority.

To map integrated services such as Controlled Load or Guaranteed Service over IEEE 802-style LANs, the SBM and ISSLL [802-srvc] use an "aggregated flows" approach based on the use of link layer priority values or traffic classes. Under this approach, each flow is assigned to one of the available link layer traffic classes and is provisioned as part of this class as the flow traverses the 802-style LAN. Traffic flows requiring similar service are grouped together into a single traffic class, where the switches' admission control and class selection rules ensure that the service requirements for traffic in each of the classes are met. This approach can work effectively even with switches implementing only a simple priority queuing mechanism to differentiate among traffic classes.

Under this model, routers or hosts (network layer devices) on the boundary of an 802-style LAN that transmit traffic flows onto a shared link layer segment should perform per-flow policing to ensure that individual flows do not exceed their provisioned traffic specifications. In addition, these boundary devices are responsible for labeling the MAC-level frames belonging to provisioned flows with a user_priority value to identify their aggregated service class. The fundamental questions that must be addressed are: (1) Who determines the mapping between IP-level traffic flows and link-level classes and (2) how is this mapping conveyed to the boundary devices responsible for marking frames?

One approach is to have the standard meaning of the different traffic classes be universally defined. For example, a set of traffic classes might be identified as user priority 1, corresponding to best effort; user priority 2, corresponding to traffic with guarantee of a maximum delay bound of 100 ms; and so forth. These standard mappings would be used by boundary devices to decide how to map an IP flow with a given traffic specification into a particular service class and mark its data frames accordingly. Though simple to implement, such an approach is too restrictive in terms of mapping a wide range of flow requirements into a few static service classes.

A better approach would be to use a more dynamic mapping that takes into account a variety of factors such as the LAN's topology, traffic control capabilities of switches, current traffic load, and the amount of traffic already admitted in each class.

The approach adopted by ISSLL relies on boundary devices asking the link layer network to specify which traffic class should be used for a given IntServ traffic flow. Given a flow specification, the devices in the LAN can provide a value back to the requestor that specifies the traffic class to be used. This allows the mapping performed at the devices to be chosen based on a variety of methods ranging from a simple, static, network-wide configuration to a dynamic approach based on actual traffic measurements or queuing capabilities of the switches along the data path.

The SBM protocol provides the necessary mechanisms that allow boundary devices to request and receive the traffic class mapping. The ISSLL working group at IETF also recommends a default service mapping to be used at LAN switches. In the following, we describe the role of the SBM and the default service mappings.

SBM Role in Service Mapping

As discussed before, a network layer boundary device that wishes to send a PATH message on to a shared segment uses the SBM protocol and sends it to the DSBM for the shared segment. The PATH will then proceed to visit one or more DSBMs as it traverses the shared segments in the LAN until it reaches its next hop network layer node. Along this path, the downstream DSBMs will insert a new traffic class object (TCLASS object) in the PATH message that specifies the appropriate service class for the flow according to the service mapping determined at all the intervening switches. To some extent, the TCLASS object contents are treated like the ADSPEC object in the RSVP PATH messages.

The network layer device at the edge of the LAN (next hop network node) that receives the PATH message removes and stores the TCLASS object as part of its path state for the session. Later, when the same network layer device needs to forward an RSVP RESV message toward the sender of the PATH, it must include the TCLASS object in the RESV message. The RESV message will eventually arrive at the previous network layer boundary device that originally sent the PATH message over the LAN. That network layer device must then pass the user_priority value in the TCLASS object to its local packet classifier (traffic control) so that subsequent outgoing data frames corresponding to this particular RSVP flow will be marked with the user_priority value now assigned to the flow.

Default Service Mapping

Table 8.1 presents the default mapping from delay targets of individual flows to the corresponding IEEE 802.1 user_priority classes as suggested in the IETF document [802-srvc]. These mappings must be viewed only as best-guess defaults and are subject to change in the future as people get more experience with deployment of switches and SBMs. These values are likely to be held in a table inside switches and will be modifiable under management control. The mapping table also lists the target delay values that approximate the current needs of audio and video applications.

Table 8.1   Default Service Mappings for 802.1p user_priority Classes

user_priority	SERVICE
0	Default, assumed to be best effort
1	Reserved, "less than" best effort
2	Reserved
3	Reserved
4	Delay-sensitive, no bound
5	Delay-sensitive, 100-ms bound
6	Delay-sensitive, 10-ms bound
7	Network control

Example of a Switched LAN

Although an individual SBM is only intended to perform admission control for a single shared segment, a number of SBMs can cooperate over a switched link layer network. In a switched topology, individual switches are likely connected to one another and to hosts via shared segments. When two or more SBM-aware switches share the same segment, one SBM will be elected the DSBM for the segment. As always, the DSBM is the single point of control for that segment. All resource reservations affecting the segment must first go through the DSBM. Figure 8.3 shows the mapping of DSBMs to a number of switched segments. Each switch can be the DSBM for one or more segments to which it is connected. In this illustration, three switches connect seven segments, and each segment is highlighted to show its corresponding DSBM.

The interaction between DSBMs follows the same hop-by-hop model used for RSVP signaling as described earlier. PATH messages are first communicated to the DSBM for a segment. The DSBM then identifies itself to the next DSBM by replacing the RSVP_HOP and RSVP_HOP_L2 objects with its address. It will then forward the PATH message on toward the LAN_NHOP destination's segment, where it will be intercepted by the next DSBM. This process will continue, segment-by-segment, until the PATH message reaches its destination on the link layer network, the LAN_NHOP.

The LAN_NHOP may then issue a RESV message for the PATH that will travel hop-by-hop back through the DSBM chain recorded by the PATH message's journey. Each DSBM will perform admission control on behalf of the RESV to confirm that sufficient resources are available

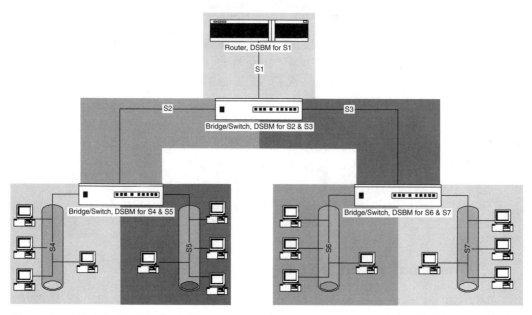

Figure 8.3 Switch DSBMs elected to serve a particular segment in a switched link layer network.

on the segment. If resources are available, the RESV will be sent on to the previous DSBM. Otherwise, an RESV Error will be directed back to the LAN_NHOP. Through this process, all affected segments can be properly provisioned using the SBM.

As with RSVP, there are plenty of legacy LAN switches that do not support SBM functionality. These devices are considered SBM-transparent switches. Networks can support both SBM-aware and SBM-transparent switches and still benefit from the SBM. In such heterogeneous networks, the SBM-aware switches will also provision the SBM-transparent switches' segments. This is possible because the SBM-transparent switches will simply broadcast all frames for the DSBMLogicalAddress and AllSBMsAddress, which are only intercepted by SBMs and DSBMs. Effectively, the SBM-transparent segments become a single shared segment that can be conservatively provisioned by a DSBM.

RSVP over ATM

ATM as a QoS networking technology was introduced before the definition of Integrated Services architecture for the Internet. Because ATM is already a QoS-aware networking architecture, it is uniquely positioned to implement the Internet's Integrated Services requirements. ATM's ability to establish point-to-point virtual circuits (VCs) with a specified QoS map directly to the Integrated Services' ability to signal end-to-end the QoS requirements of IP unicast applications. Furthermore, point-to-multipoint VCs allow leaf nodes to be added and removed from the VC dynamically, providing a way to support receiver-driven QoS for IP multicast. Overall, it is particularly attractive to utilize the QoS mechanisms and properties of ATM to implement the RSVP and Integrated Services model. Moreover, ATM technology is already employed in the Internet's WAN infrastructure for interconnecting sites and, thus, forms core areas of the Internet today.

IP's best-effort service is already implemented over ATM link layer technology using approaches known as "Classical IP over ATM" [RFC 2225] and MARS [RFC 2022]. Therefore, the key issue for mapping the Integrated Services architecture to ATM is to define a way of translating IntServ QoS over ATM QoS and methods for managing ATM VCs. In this section, we describe the way IntServ QoS is mapped using ATM service categories and service descriptors. The various ATM services we will consider are:

- CBR (constant bit rate)
- rtVBR (real-time variable bit rate)
- nrtVBR (non-real-time VBR)
- UBR (unspecified bit rate)
- ABR (available bit rate)

ATM VCs are also set up using traffic descriptors that specify the traffic characteristics of a data source. These descriptors include a peak cell rate (PCR) that specifies the maximum cell rate in each direction for a VC, a sustainable cell rate (SCR) that specifies the average cell rate over the long term, and the maximum burst size (MBS) that is similar to token bucket depth. For CBR traffic, only PCR is specified (PCR = SCR) with a nominal jitter toleration (CDVT).

Based on these service categories and traffic descriptors, Figure 8.4 shows the proposed mapping of IntServ service classes and parameters onto ATM service categories and descriptors [RFC 2381].

Guaranteed Service (GS). GS can be mapped onto ATM using either CBR or rtVBR services. The advantage of using rtVBR over CBR is that the

ATM Service Specification	RSVP Flow Specification
Average Bit Rate (SCR)	Average Bit Rate (R)
Peak Rate (PCR)	Peak Rate (P)
Emission Burst (MBS)	Burst/Bucket Size (B)
UBR/ABR	Best Effort
CBR or rtVBR	Guaranteed
nrtVBR or ABR (with min cell rate)	Controlled Load

Figure 8.4 Illustration of ATM service mappings onto the IntServ services.

former allows the network to utilize part of the allocated bandwidth that is left unused by a source. rtVBR also is more suitable for sources that are very bursty and specify large token bucket depths.

In the case of GS, remember that the source Tspec contains the peak rate p, rate r, and bucket depth parameter B. The receiver FlowSpec contains corresponding parameters (p, r, B) and an additional rate R as part of the Rspec. Typically, it is expected that the first three parameters are likely to be identical. In addition, the rate R is specified to trade delay for bandwidth.

When mapping GS onto CBR, IntServ parameters are mapped as ($p =$ PCR, MBS = CDVT). When mapping GS onto rtVBR, a simple, common mapping is ($p =$ PCR, $R =$ SCR, and $B =$ MBS). In the case of rtVBR, there are several other conditions that may lead to a range of values for the ATM traffic descriptor. These are not discussed further here; see [RFC 2381] for more details.

Controlled Load (CL) Service. The Controlled Load Service has a sender Tspec that specifies a peak rate p, a token bucket rate r, and a corresponding token bucket depth parameter b. The receiver FlowSpec values are then used to determine the amount of resource allocation for an ATM VC and the traffic descriptor is obtained by setting (PCR = p, SCR = r, and MBS = b).

When a CL flow is mapped onto an ABR VC, the rate r is used to set the minimum cell rate (MCR) parameter. There is no corresponding signaled bucket depth b parameter in ATM ABR. Therefore, the edge or boundary device at the edge of the ATM cloud should have a buffer of at least b bytes to absorb the incoming burst without loss and some additional buffer to absorb any subsequent jitter.

Differentiated Services and IP Prioritization

RSVP allows applications to signal per-flow requirements to the network and, in conjunction with IntServ parameters used for admission control at routers, provides end-to-end QoS. Nevertheless, per-flow packet classification and packet handling in intermediate routers can lead to scalability problems in backbone routers. Typically, hundreds of thousands of flows pass through routers in the heart of the Internet's backbone. If each of these routers were to classify and handle packets from each flow separately, there would be obvious limitations as to how well a backbone router could scale to handle multi-gigabit links. This leads to concerns about the scalability of RSVP for such devices. Although RSVP provides a great benefit at stub networks by enabling applications to specify their QoS requirements to the network exactly when they need QoS, many legacy applications exist that cannot be modified to express their QoS requirements. Additionally, there are applications that generate traffic corresponding to short-term transactions that cannot effectively express their QoS requirements using the IntServ model. Applications such as these can still receive better QoS through differential queuing and statically reserved bandwidth.

To facilitate immediate deployment of QoS by enabling legacy applications, as well as to address scalability concerns with RSVP, Internet Service Providers (ISPs) are developing a framework for deploying Differentiated Services (DiffServ). In contrast to RSVP's per-flow orientation, DiffServ networks classify packets into one of a small number of aggregated flows. This classification can be most simply achieved by setting bits in the TOS field (now called the DS byte according to a new standard [RFC 2474]) within each packet's IP header. The DS byte specifies the per-hop behavior for a flow aggregate at each router in terms of differential traffic class queuing and access to reserved bandwidth. Because each router can be configured to provide a certain per-hop behavior (PHB) independent of any per-flow signaling, DiffServ QoS can initially be deployed using top-down provisioning, in which a network manager may statically decide how much bandwidth is reserved for each service and then configure his or her routers accordingly.

From TOS to DS

Basically, DiffServ is revitalizing an old mechanism for providing simple, priority-based QoS on the Internet. Looking back at Chapter 2, the reader should note that the third field, and second byte, of the IPv4 header is labeled Type of Service (TOS). This field has been around for quite some time and was originally intended to provide a way of identifying the handling requirements of an IP packet. TOS could be used to give some packets precedence over others and describe their sensitivity to delay. For example, control and routing protocols are often given high precedence such that routers would be less likely to drop them in light of congestion. Obviously, if a network becomes severely congested, the control messages must still get through so that the problem can be rectified.

TOS was a nice concept, but had limited application. For one thing, the original TOS mappings are now out of date. For another, the mappings were ambiguous as to how the network would actually treat packets marked with a given precedence and delay sensitivity. Finally, there were no mechanisms defined for ensuring that traffic at each priority level was adhering to a well-defined bandwidth resource threshold. Ambiguity led to inconsistent vendor implementations and a TOS byte that left much to be desired in terms of achieving usable QoS. The IETF's DiffServ working group set out to fix such problems and ambiguities associated with the old TOS byte. Through their efforts, we now have the better-defined DS byte instead of the original TOS field.

What DiffServ really gives us is the ability to mark individual packets and act on them according to their mappings. The scalability gains are obvious from the perspective of a large backbone router handling millions of flows. There is no requirement for per-packet lookups nor is there isolation of individual micro-flows (flows-per-host application). Instead, the DS byte may simply be used to map a packet into a particular queue where it will be handled appropriately. Some default handling instructions are being laid down by the DiffServ working group and are termed *per-hop behaviors* (PHBs). As the name implies, a PHB defines how a particular device should treat a packet with the corresponding marking. Basically, then, DiffServ can be used to aggregate the QoS properties of a large number of individual micro-flows into a PHB for a conceptual macro-flow. Figure 8.5 shows the basic format of the DS byte. Two bits are left unused in support of legacy devices that

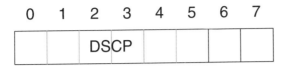

```
0   1   2   3   4   5   6   7
┌───┬───┬───────┬───┬───┬───┬───┐
│   │   │ DSCP  │   │   │   │   │
└───┴───┴───────┴───┴───┴───┴───┘
```

Figure 8.5   Illustration of the DS Byte Format.

interpret the original TOS byte, leaving six bits for identifying specific PHBs via their DiffServ Code Point (DSCP) values.

The DiffServ Architecture

From the perspective of DiffServ, all that is required to classify a packet is the one-byte DS field in the IP header. Applications or other devices must decide what the value of this byte needs to be to achieve a specific behavior from devices on the network. Fundamentally, such behavior is dependent on the kind of DiffServ traffic in question. DiffServ traffic can be considered as either quantitative or qualitative.

Quantitative Quantitative traffic is very much akin to the Integrated Services style of QoS traffic. The specific characteristics of such traffic are known ahead of time. This allows the network to accurately provision resources for the traffic and to provide some form of guarantee that it can actually support the applicable traffic's requirements with respect to network capacity and delay.

Qualitative Qualitative traffic is more appropriate for statistical multiplexing. It belongs to applications that don't have specific QoS requirements from the network other than wanting higher-priority service. The network handles qualitative traffic in a less deterministic manner than quantitative traffic. It is assumed by the law of large numbers that statistically multiplexing such traffic will typically give higher-priority qualitative traffic better QoS than ordinary best-effort traffic. As long as the qualitative traffic is never seriously overprovisioned beyond a percentage of the overall network capacity, it stands to reason that sufficient resources will be available to the higher-priority traffic wherever it takes precedence over lower-priority traffic.

As the focus of this work has been quantitative services as signaled by RSVP, we will limit our discussion on DiffServ to the quantitative only. It is enough to note that when push comes to shove, quantitatively allocated services should be given precedence over their qualitative counterparts. The reason for this is quite simple—quantitative services are deterministic and, therefore, safer to implement as high-priority traffic.

DiffServ Components: Meters, Markers, Shapers, and Droppers

DiffServ inherently achieves its scalability by supporting a hierarchy of functional components that are logically positioned in networks. The overall goal is to avoid redundancy in the functional components. Contrast this with RSVP, which, in its complete form, applies traffic control to every packet from every micro-flow individually at every RSVP-aware device. The result is that large tables may have to be maintained and searched for every outbound packet to achieve proper micro-flow behavior. Redundantly applying these same steps for all packets at all subsequent routers is probably overkill.

DiffServ is not so particular at every node. In DiffServ, individual packets from properly conditioned micro-flows can be combined into DS-marked macro-flows. This process of aggregating the fine-grain flows into coarse-grain flows is possible through the use of various traffic control components. These are classifiers, meters, markers, shapers, and droppers.

Classifiers A DiffServ classifier is a construct similar to the packet classifier used in RSVP traffic control. However, in the case of DiffServ, two different types of classifiers are defined depending on which fields in the IP header they classify. The first classifier is the Behavior Aggregate (BA) classifier. It simply classifies a packet based on its DS byte's value. The second form of classifier is the Multi-Field (MF) classifier. The MF classifier can classify packets based on a number of fields, typically including the source and destination address, source and destination port, and protocol ID (the five-tuple). The latter classifier corresponds to the type of classifier used in RSVP traffic control.

Meters A meter is a DiffServ functional component that monitors traffic based on its classification. It is the responsibility of the meter to verify that the classified traffic is conforming to its provisioned traffic characteristics. The meter can also be used to collect statistics on flows for purposes of accounting and billing.

Markers A DiffServ marker is a component that is used to set the DS-byte field in the IP header to a particular value. The marker may mark packets on behalf of a particular flow so as to provide the correct PHB for the flow. Such a marker will typically utilize an MF classifier to initially identify a packet as belonging to a particular flow that requires marking. Additionally, a marker may be used to re-mark packets, either to transform the DS-field from one value to another value mapping to the same PHB, or as a method to downgrade packets that are not conforming to their provisioned traffic limitations. Once the marker has done its job, downstream devices need only apply BA classification to their packets.

Shapers The shaper component is similar in functionality to the shapers utilized by RSVP traffic control. The role of the shaper is simply to delay packets in a queue in order to shape a traffic flow so that it conforms to its provisioned traffic specification. A shaper may take a large burst of packets, store them, and finally forward them on through the network at an acceptable rate.

Droppers The DiffServ dropper is a functional component that punishes highly nonconformant flows by dropping their excess traffic. The dropper is used to police traffic so that it is forced to conform to its provisioned traffic characteristics. Additional packets that violate their resource allotment will simply be dropped. Dropping, then, like re-marking, can be used as a form of disposition.

These building blocks can be deployed in a DiffServ network to achieve a scalable QoS infrastructure. Scalability is achieved because the edges of the network will typically deal with less traffic than the core of the network. This allows the edges to be more precise in what traffic they admit into the network. Thus, the edges of the network can employ MF classifiers that identify and meter specific micro-flows. They can then shape or drop a flow's traffic so that it conforms to some quantitative bounds. Once the micro-flow is conformant, it can be aggregated with other conformant flows by appropriately marking the DS byte of the flow's packets. The core of the network has the simplified task of performing BA classification on the marked packets belonging to the aggregated macro-flow. Once again, the core devices in the network can shape and police the aggregated traffic flows, ensuring that the macro-flows remain isolated from each other.

Ingress versus Egress Interfaces

A DiffServ network can be viewed as a cloud of devices sharing a common administrative boundary. In some sense, the entire cloud can be thought of as a single router. Data enters the cloud over one link and exits the cloud over another. The interface over which traffic enters the Diff-Serv network is called the *Ingress interface* for a given traffic flow. Correspondingly, the interface from which traffic leaves the DiffServ network is the *Egress interface*. The borders of the DiffServ network should perform the MF classification, metering, marking, and shaping on behalf of packets entering the DiffServ network on the Ingress interface. This allows the Ingress interface to ensure that traffic arriving on it is conforming to some provisioned limits. Conformant traffic may then be marked appropriately before it is admitted into the DiffServ cloud. Inside the cloud, the DiffServ network only needs to use the DS-byte value in the packet header to apply the appropriate PHB for the macro-flow. Each DiffServ-compliant device through which the traffic is forwarded will apply this PHB. Eventually, the traffic will reach the boundary of the Diff-Serv network at the Egress interface. The Egress interface may then re-mark packets before they are sent into another DiffServ network.

The Potential RSVP-DiffServ Relationship

RSVP and DiffServ can be deployed in such a way that they complement one another very nicely. RSVP can easily utilize the aggregation capabilities of DiffServ networks. Additionally, DiffServ networks can use RSVP's QoS signaling mechanism to properly provision quantitative QoS end-to-end across a network. This equates to a combination of the Integrated Services and Differentiated Services model for network resource management.

In the combined model, RSVP is still used as the way for applications to signal their QoS requirements to the network. It also provides the network with a mechanism to signal back to applications whether or not their QoS requests can be granted. In the RSVP-DiffServ model, there is the concept of RSVP-aware Integrated Services (IntServ) stub networks interacting with RSVP-unaware DiffServ transit networks. The transit networks represent service provider networks that handle large amounts of aggregated customer traffic. The stub networks represent smaller private networks that support only a relatively small number of hosts. Between these two networks sit edge routers that can be considered as half RSVP and half DiffServ devices. The RSVP side processes incoming PATH and RESV messages while the DiffServ side allocates resources on behalf of the transit network and can mark packets appropriately.

Figure 8.6 shows the interaction within the combined IntServ and Diff-Serv network. An RSVP source host will issue a PATH message for its traffic. This message will travel though the IntServ stub network and be processed at all RSVP-aware nodes it encounters. The PATH will then be sent transparently through the DiffServ transit network by the first edge router. Intermediate routers in the DiffServ transit network will not (and do not need to) process the PATH message. The receiving edge router on the other side of the DiffServ network will then receive the PATH message and process it. The PATH will then traverse the second stub network until it reaches its destination. On receipt of the PATH message, the destination host can issue a RESV message for the PATH. This message will proceed hop-by-hop though the second stub network until it reaches the edge router. The edge router will proceed to process the RESV, allocate resources on its outgoing link, and, if resources are available, forward the message transparently through the DiffServ transit network to the next hop edge router.

On receipt of the RESV message, the first edge router will proceed to verify that the DiffServ network has sufficient resources to support the reservation request. If sufficient resources are available, the RESV will be sent on through the IntServ network to the source containing information about what DSCP should be used. If sufficient resources are not available an RESV Error message will be forwarded hop-by-hop back to the destination. The methods for determining the resources available over the DiffServ network are varied. Ideally, routing information and

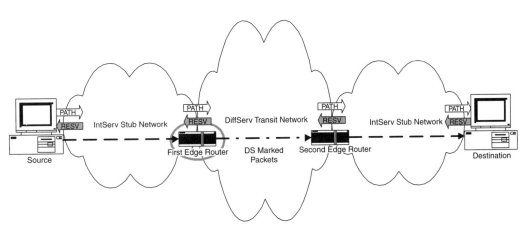

Figure 8.6 Illustration of Integrated Services stub networks interacting with a Differentiated Services transit network via RSVP.

bandwidth allocation information will be available so that the DiffServ network's currently available resources can be deterministically discovered. Additionally, the RSVP signaling process itself can be extended to interact with the DiffServ transit network and collect information related to resources available along the complete data path.

Once an RESV message makes it back to the source, the source should begin marking its conforming packets with the appropriate DS-byte value specified by the RESV. Alternatively, the edge router with the Ingress interface to the DiffServ network can mark and police packets belonging to the reserved flow on behalf of the application. These packets should then be treated appropriately within the DiffServ transit network, based solely on their DS-byte values without any consideration as to the MF classification or provisioning of a particular RSVP microflow. The result is that end-to-end QoS is achieved in a more scalable manner.

Summary

In this chapter we have described the interactions between the network layer RSVP protocol and various data link layer networking technologies. Each individual networking technology needs to be able to facilitate QoS in order for the Integrated Services architecture to provide end-to-end QoS. For simple full-duplex bidirectional links, QoS is directly achieved through RSVP and its traffic control components. For ATM networks, which natively support QoS, only a simple parameter mapping is required. For shared IEEE 802-style networks, additional support is needed in the form of a resource broker that provides a central authority for QoS admission control.

Additionally, we have presented a preview of the Differentiated Services architecture for providing QoS on the Internet. This architecture was compared with the Integrated Services architecture so that their complementary features could be determined. We then presented an example of how IntServ and DiffServ networks could work together, utilizing the best features of both.

CHAPTER 9

Policy Control and Monitoring for RSVP

R SVP provides a mechanism by which applications can request resources from the network in order to achieve better QoS for their traffic. By reserving network resources, real-time applications can be assured that their quality will not degrade as the network becomes congested. This is possible because RSVP-aware network devices will perform capacity admission control on all reservation requests, ensuring that network resources do not become overcommitted for high-priority traffic. This mechanism begs the questions, who gets to make reservations, to whom, and when? The RSVP mechanisms themselves do not include an important aspect of admission control—policy control. Network managers and service providers must be able to monitor, control, and enforce use of network resources and services based on policies. Policies need to be derived from a variety of criteria such as the identity of users and applications, traffic/bandwidth requirements, security considerations, and time of day or week. Also, if the service providers and IT administrators want to charge customers for making resource reservations, they must be able to monitor use of resources for accounting purposes.

The problems associated with the administration of network resources can be solved through policy control over RSVP. Policy represents the administratively defined rules and regulations that ensure resources are consumed in a manner acceptable to the network authority. In this chapter we will discuss some of the intricacies of policy control, describing how policies are specified, interpreted, and enforced within an administrative domain. We will also investigate models in the form of bilateral agreements for sharing policy information across administrative boundaries. Additionally, we will discuss methods by which tabs can be maintained on who makes reservations, when, and for how much bandwidth. Such information can be used by ISPs and corporate IT to bill customers for their usage of the network.

Deciding Who Gets Better QoS

Policy control for RSVP provides network administrators with the ability to control their networks' resources. Obviously, if users were allowed to make unrestricted reservations, a single user could potentially request all the available resources. This situation could result in the network refusing reservations from other users. For those with a malicious intent, the situation can even become destructive. An example of such a case would be when a malicious user floods the network with excessive amounts of QoS-protected traffic. The result could render the affected portions of the network unusable by anyone else.

In general, policies that take into account user profiles, types of applications, and other environmental factors must be applied before accepting RSVP resource reservation requests. For example, resource reservations might be allowed or disallowed based on the identity of a user (e.g., a CEO versus a junior engineer), or the group to which a user belongs (e.g., users in a finance group can reserve up to 1 Mbps of bandwidth in certain parts of the corporate network). The explosion in use of Web-based services is contributing to a significant increase in the traffic load on corporate networks. Also, the increasing availability of UDP-based audio/video streams results in additional traffic. Such real-time traffic flows have a greater potential for interfering with one another because such applications do not include TCP-like congestion avoidance mechanisms. Therefore, QoS resources may only be made available to certain types of applications. For example, traffic that belongs to Enterprise Resource Planning (ERP) transactions must always be given priority use of such resources due to the mission-critical nature of such applications. Similarly, as many customers start deploying IP telephony services over the data networks, such applications must be allowed to make QoS reservations to protect their delay-sensitive traffic from other traffic on the network. Reservations for frivolous uses of the network such as game-playing during business hours should be restricted.

In summary, there is a need for a generic policy-based control framework that allows network administrators to control use of resources in their networks.

Rules and Enforcement

Fundamentally, a network administrator would like to have the ability to create rules that regulate the use of the network. In the case of RSVP, these rules should specify who gets to make what reservations, and for how much. The RSVP devices themselves must then be able to enforce the administrative rules when determining what resource requests to accept or reject.

In general, it should be possible to specify rules in the form *who can do what*. In rules of this kind, the privileges are based on the identity of a user or type of the application that requests reservations. For example, a rule might specify that the user Russell may make reservations between the hours of 9:00 A.M. and 6:00 P.M. A rule might also specify that IP Telephony traffic can reserve network resources but only for data rates under 64 Kbps per call. Apart from considering an identity of a single user or application, it should be possible to group several such entities together and specify privileges for the entire group. Examples of groups include a user group within an NT domain, a group of machines on a subnet, or a group of applications (e.g., by protocol type, such as "all TCP streams," or by groups of transport-level port numbers, such as "all UDP applications using ports in the range of 1024–2047"). Furthermore, because network traffic conditions vary considerably depending on the time of day, it should be possible to specify policies that apply within a particular time period (e.g., 9:00 A.M. to noon on Mondays and Wednesdays). Sometimes it is desirable to allow resource usage, provided the allowed usage is within a prespecified limit. For example, it might be desirable to specify restrictions such as "up to x streams may use the resource or allow bandwidth reservations as long as the total amount reserved does not exceed 1 Mbps." Finally, it is not merely sufficient to allow specification of restrictions as described here; it should also be possible to make simple combinations of these restrictions such as "Allow John to reserve bandwidth provided it is Monday or the traffic involved comes from subnet X."

In these examples, the combination of conditions such as who and when, or what and for how much, are the rules. The actions describe what is allowed, such as the admittance of RSVP reservations. If the rules apply, the actions may be taken. Through such generic policy-description mechanisms, network administrators have the ability to express a wide variety of policies that can be tuned to their specific needs.

Prioritization and Preemption

Another aspect of the regulation of network resources concerns prioritization and preemption. These mechanisms help distribute limited network resources more effectively. *Prioritization* is the method by which the relative importance of a particular reservation can be determined. Priority is expressed as an administratively assigned value that can be associated with reservations from specific users, applications, network addresses, and so forth. *Preemption* is the mechanism by which a high-priority, or more important, reservation may take over the resources being consumed by lower-priority reservations when capacity becomes limited.

It may be perfectly acceptable to allow anyone who wants high QoS to get it, provided network resources are available. Where a simple, static policy may restrict RSVP rights to certain users or applications, a prioritization and preemption model will allow resources to be reserved by anyone, provided sufficient capacity is available. Nevertheless, the network will always operate as expected, always providing the prescribed amount of bandwidth to the high-priority reservations even if it is already committed to lower-priority users. When push comes to shove, the highest administratively assigned priority will win, taking away resources from lower-priority reservations.

Policy Data

RSVP defines a number of objects carried in its messages. Most of these objects are directly useful to RSVP-specific processing or traffic control. Some of the information in RSVP messages, such as the Session, FlowSpec, and FilterSpec, is useful for policy control in determining where a data flow is going, where it came from, and how much of the resources it is attempting to reserve. This information is contained in the appropriate objects in the RSVP message. Nevertheless, policy control may require more information than is provided by the basic RSVP objects. Thus, RSVP provides a special object specifically devoted to carrying policy information—the *RSVP Policy Data object*.

A single Policy Data object can encapsulate a number of policy attributes called *policy elements* (PE), as well as a list of RSVP-defined objects. The PEs can carry pieces of policy information. Such information can theoretically include authenticated user name information, credit card information, administratively assigned tokens, or other information useful for securely identifying the credentials of an RSVP message. Other information might be policy-specific error codes to be carried in PATH Error or RESV Error messages, priority information, or even user-defined handling instructions. RSVP objects included in the Policy Data object are useful for tying the policy processing to the underlying RSVP signaling.

RSVP PATH, RESV, PATH Error, and RESV Error messages can all carry the Policy Data object. The format of the RSVP Policy Data object is illustrated in Figure 9.1. After the common RSVP object header, the Policy Data object has two fields. The first field specifies the offset of the data portion where the PE list begins. Before the PE list there is a list of options. The Options list can provide a set of standard RSVP objects with slightly altered meanings relevant to policy.

The Options list can include FilterSpec objects for listing a set of senders associated with the Policy Data object. This object is useful for Wildcard and Shared Explicit style reservations where the policy data object can be targeted to a specific set of senders regardless of the RSVP merging process. The RSVP Hop object may also be included in the Options list to identify a neighboring policy-aware node responsible for creating the Policy Data object. If a second RSVP Hop object is included, it identifies the intended destination policy-aware node. Inclusion of the destina-

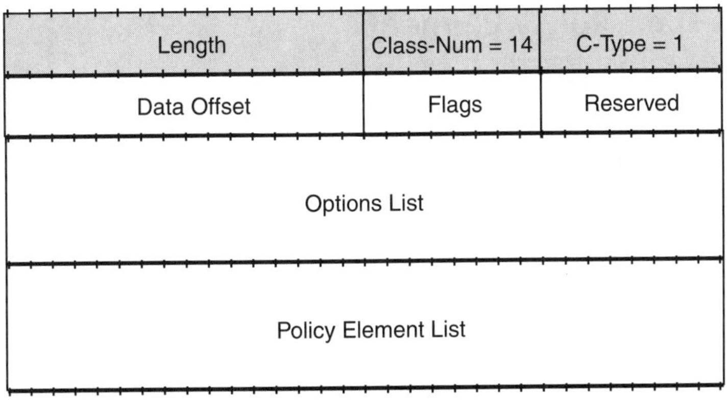

Length	Class-Num = 14	C-Type = 1
Data Offset	Flags	Reserved
Options List		
Policy Element List		

Figure 9.1 Illustration of the Policy Data object format.

tion policy-aware node ensures that the Policy Data object is delivered to a specific node, a useful capability in multicast scenarios. Additionally, when used in conjunction with the Integrity object, the destination hop information may be used to prevent replay attacks where a node maliciously reuses an observed Policy Data object in a different RSVP message. Finally, the RSVP Integrity object can be carried in the Options list to ensure that the Policy Data object was not compromised by untrusted parties. It follows the same rules specified in [MD5] for RSVP message integrity, only it is calculated over the Policy Data object. The integrity can be used to ensure that malicious third parties are not reusing valid Policy Data objects in support of other RSVP messages.

Additional options can also be specified that are not standard RSVP objects. In such cases, the RSVP NULL object is used with an appropriate C-Type value to identify the extended option. One example is the Policy Refresh Multiplier (C-Type = 1) that is used to define how often policy is to be refreshed in terms of RSVP refreshes. This information is useful when policy can deal with longer refresh periods than those prescribed by RSVP.

The PE list contained in the Policy Data object is used to identify a set of objects (PEs) that are outside of the scope of the RSVP object space. The PEs define attributes that are specifically useful to policy processing. Like RSVP objects, PEs have a 4-byte object header with a length and type field that precedes the attribute data. The type field uniquely identifies each attribute and the length determines the length of the object including the header. More details on Policy Data objects and their policy elements can be found in [RSVP-EXT].

Authentication Data Policy Element

One useful application of the Policy Data object is to securely carry authentication information that can securely (and in a verifiable way) identify a user or an application that generates an RSVP message. The key to carrying the authentication is not just to identify a user or an application, but also to verify that the user or the requesting application is legitimate and has certain privileges. In the case of RSVP, it is necessary to prove that a message was actually generated by the specified individual in order to achieve accurate policy control. It is obviously important that a message can be securely associated with the president of a company rather than with a hacker pretending to be the president.

The Authentication Policy element (called AUTH_DATA) contained in the POLICY_DATA object is used to securely carry user and application identification information. The AUTH_DATA PE is described in [IDEN-TITY]. This authentication PE is actually capable of carrying both secure authentication information and plaintext identity data. On a host, a user process or application generates an AUTH_DATA policy element and passes it to the RSVP process, which inserts AUTH_DATA into the Policy Data object that is carried in RSVP messages. Network nodes such as routers authenticate the requestor of the reservation using the credentials presented in the AUTH_DATA element and admit the request based on policy applicable to the requestor.

The AUTH_DATA policy element specifies the identity type used for authentication depending on whether the users are being identified or the type of the application. In addition, this PE carries authentication attributes that contain information specific to the authentication method to be used. Types of attributes include a *policy locator* string used to locate the admission policy (e.g., an X.500 DN in a plain or encrypted form). A *user or application credential* such as a Kerberos ticket, a digital certificate, or an application identification string may also be included. Finally, a *digital signature* attribute provides a digital signature that is used to sign all the data within the AUTH_DATA policy element (up to but not including the signature itself).

As an example, consider what happens when a QoS-aware application invokes the QoS API on a host. Assume that a system administrator has configured the RSVP service on the host to use the Kerberos authentication method to generate authentication attributes and insert an AUTH_DATA element into RSVP messages. When an RSVP session is initialized, the user application first contacts the Kerberos Distribution Center (KDC) to obtain a Kerberos ticket for the next network node (next hop router or host) and then passes it to the RSVP service for inclusion in its reservation request. When the reservation request arrives at the next network node, it uses the KDC to validate the ticket and authenticate the user or application that sent the request before admitting the request.

Priority Policy Element

Another use of the Policy Data object is to carry representative priority information on behalf of an RSVP RESV message. Routers can perform selective preemption of installed reservations based on the Priority PE.

For example, when a router's resources are completely allocated and a high-priority reservation is received, lower-priority reservations can be preempted so that the high-priority reservation can still be installed. This is also useful to support advance reservations where a user may request an advance QoS reservation for a conference call scheduled the following week. If such an advance request is admitted, it will be given higher priority and when the time for the conference call arrives, the policy may dictate that some of the accepted reservations be torn down to make room for the higher-priority reservation.

For unicast flows, it is sufficient to represent priority as simply a scalar value. Higher values represent higher priorities that are given precedence over lower values. Where the simple model of priority becomes complex is in the case of merging shared heterogeneous reservations. For instance, RSVP allows different destinations for the same multicast session to reserve different quantities of network resources. Suppose we wish to bill destinations in proportion to the size of their reservations. The use of priority in admitting requests makes this kind of billing decision more complex.

Consider a case of a multicast session where two different destinations request different amounts of reservations, R1 (16 Kbps) and R2 (32 Kbps). Further, assume that R1 has higher priority (priority value 10) than R2 (priority value 5). If these two reservations are to be merged before forwarding a single reservation (R3 at 32 Kbps), what should be the priority assigned to R3 (5, 10, or something else)? If we decide to forward R3 with the highest priority and try to establish R3 based on the merged bandwidth and largest priority, we will, in effect, allow the higher reservation to get a free ride based on the lower reservation's priority. If we choose to assign the priority value (5) corresponding to the larger reservation (R2) and it gets denied or preempted upstream based on its lower priority, we will be denying service to the higher-priority reservation (R1). If we choose to take the lowest common denominator (use the smaller reservation and lower priority), the lower-priority reservation might be cheated out of the extra bandwidth that may be available upstream. No alternative seems easily acceptable here.

More important, if we are going to bill the destinations for their reservations, how are we going to charge them? Will the charge be based on their requested priority because that determines how the reservation is treated upstream, or based on the amount of reservation they requested because that determines the resource allocation? Note that we cannot simply choose to charge them based on the largest reservation and highest priority, because neither of the destinations actually asked for both high bandwidth and priority.

The Priority PE signaling mechanism described in an IETF RSVP Admission Policy Working Group document [PRIORITY] recommends strategies for tackling this issue. In particular, it defines the contents of a preemption priority policy element (PREEMPTION_PRI) that specifies three attributes: the merging strategy to be used, a preemption priority value, and a defending priority value. Possible merging strategies are to take the priority of the highest QoS request, to take the highest priority among the merging requests, or to disallow a heterogeneous merge. Preemption priority is used to specify the priority associated with the new reservation request, whereas defending priority is used to represent the priority of a merged reservation after the merging. Thus, the preemption priority is used when a new request is to be admitted or merged with another request. Once a request is admitted and merged with other requests, its priority becomes irrelevant. In the preceding example, if each reservation request specifies that the merging strategy should be to take the priority of the highest QoS request, R3 will be forwarded with defending priority equal to 5 and the bandwidth requested equal to 32 Kbps. If another reservation request (R4 at 64 Kbps) with preemption priority 7 and similar merging strategy were to meet R3 upstream, the new, merged request will request 64 Kbps at the defending priority of 7.

Although preemption priority does raise a number of issues when it comes to heterogeneous merging of multicast reservations, the benefits of preemption are many. Preemption allows network resources to be efficiently utilized by a wide range of QoS applications. With proper design of preemption policy, network administrators can make the most effective use of their networks' QoS capabilities without overly restricting their availability. Simply put, within the preemption model, QoS privileges won't have to be limited to the company CEO.

Policy Architecture for RSVP

Already several components related to the processing and control of RSVP messages have been discussed. We will now focus on the Policy Admission Control component that provides policy awareness to network devices. Note that not all RSVP-aware nodes need to be policy aware. For example, in any administrative domain, only the routers at the edge that are responsible for forwarding traffic to and from local hosts or routers in a neighboring administrative domain need to perform policy-based admission control and will host the Policy Admission Control component. We refer to such nodes as policy-aware nodes.

The Policy Admission Control component is part of an overall policy-based admission control framework. Two main architectural elements of the framework are the Policy Enforcement Point (PEP) and the Policy Decision Point (PDP). Figure 9.2 shows a simple configuration involving these two elements. The PEP is part of a network node and is the component that always runs on the policy-aware node. It is the point at which policy decisions are actually enforced. Policy decisions are made primarily at the PDP. The PDP may not be colocated with the PEP at a network node. Instead, it will most likely reside at a central policy server that is responsible for making policy-based decisions for one or more network nodes in an administrative domain. The PDP itself may make use of other mechanisms and protocols to achieve additional functionality such as user authentication, accounting, or policy information storage. For example, the PDP is likely to use a centralized directory service for storage and retrieval of policy information. In the following pages we discuss these components and their interaction in more detail.

Policy Enforcement Point

A Policy Enforcement Point (PEP) is a network device, or a process on a network device, that is actually capable of enforcing policy. From the perspective of RSVP, a PEP is an RSVP-aware network device that is

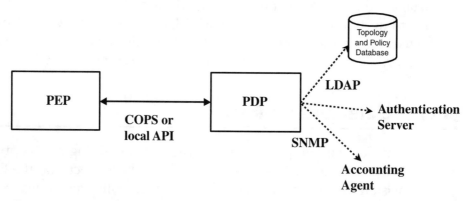

Figure 9.2 Illustration of PEP and PDP interaction.

involved in the forwarding of packets and reservation requests from a data flow. A PEP may, therefore, be the source or destination host of the data flow. It may also reside in switches or routers that comprise the data path. On a policy-aware node, the policy admission control component is called the Local Policy Module (LPM) and it interacts with the RSVP process. When the RSVP process receives and processes an RSVP message, it will contact the LPM to request a decision on how the message must be handled based on administratively specified policies. The LPM, in turn, will include the PEP that interacts with the PDP to obtain the policy decisions and then enforce them by specifying the resulting action (e.g., deny this request) to the RSVP process.

Policy Decision Point

A Policy Decision Point (PDP) is a logical entity representing the component actually responsible for making policy decisions. While the PEP simply enforces decisions, it is the responsibility of the PDP to actually interpret the policies that apply to the request and make a decision. PDPs determine who gets what QoS, when, from or to where, and so forth. The PEP must interact with a PDP so that policies can actually be enforced on the network. The interaction between a PEP and a PDP takes place as follows. When the RSVP process receives a message such as an RESV message, it contacts its local PEP to request a policy decision. The PEP then formulates a request for a policy decision and sends it to the PDP. The request for policy control from a PEP to the PDP contains one or more policy elements (encapsulated into one or more Policy Data objects) in addition to the admission control information (such as the FlowSpec) in the original message or event that triggered the policy decision request. The PDP returns the policy decision and the PEP then enforces the policy decision by appropriately accepting or denying the request from the RSVP process. The PDP may also return additional information to the PEP that includes one or more policy elements. This information need not be directly associated with the original admission control request, but may instead be used by the RSVP process to formulate an error description to be included in the outgoing RSVP message.

A PDP makes its decisions based on administratively defined policies. These policies may reside either within the PDP or in a remote database such as a directory service or a network file system. Wherever the policies are stored, the PDP must be capable of properly interpreting the policy's rules and actions such that it can render appropriate decisions in response to the PEP's queries.

The PDP process may be colocated with the PEP on a single device, or it may be a remote process running on a network server. The distinction is that of performance versus flexibility. A network device that locally enforces and interprets policy probably provides the highest performance benefit for policy control. Nevertheless, in a large and varied network with many such devices, each device may have distinct policy interpretation abilities leading to potential inconsistencies when it comes to policy deployment. Furthermore, it would be inconvenient for network administrators to have to directly configure policy on a large number of devices. To simplify problems such as these, a network administrator may want a separate policy server that can be utilized by many PEPs. This model provides greater consistency in the interpretation of policy, as there can be a single PDP for all PEPs. It is also somewhat more flexible, in that a remote PDP will probably run on a general-purpose server platform that can be upgraded with the latest and greatest software components. All that is required to support a remote PDP model is a common outsourcing protocol capable of delivering policy requests from PEPs to PDPs and then delivering policy decisions back to the PEPs. We will cover one protocol designed for this purpose in the next section. Figure 9.3 shows the various configurations that can be used in PEP- and PDP-based policy control.

Whether local to a device or remote, a PDP can take advantage of other protocols in order to make policy decisions and provide monitoring,

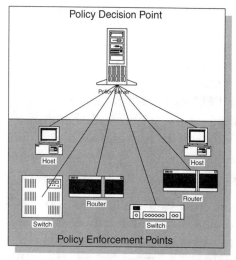

Multiple Devices Sharing a PDP

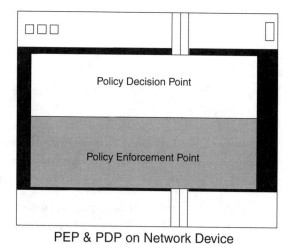

PEP & PDP on Network Device

Figure 9.3 Various PEP and PDP configurations for RSVP policy control.

accounting, and billing information. As an example, the PDP can use authentication protocols to validate the identity of a user. Additionally, as the PEP will notify its PDP of all events that require a policy decision, the PDP is a logical aggregation point for monitoring network activity. In the case of RSVP, accounting information related to who has made reservations for what amount and for how long can also be used in billing customers for their RSVP requests.

Protocols that Support Policy Control and Monitoring for RSVP

Network administrators require the ability to control and monitor their networks' activities. Such control and monitoring implies that network devices can be administratively configured, communicate with remote policy servers, and be queried about their operations. Ideally, standard mechanisms can be employed so that every device in the network does not implement a proprietary solution. This section will investigate some of the standard protocols used for policy control and monitoring of RSVP activity in a network.

COPS and COPS for RSVP

The Common Open Policy Service (COPS) Protocol can be used by a PEP to outsource its policy decision functionality to a remote PDP. COPS is a simple request/response protocol that allows a network device to query a policy server about what it should do with signaled messages [COPS].

COPS is based on a stateful model where requests from a PEP are remembered by the remote PDP until they are explicitly deleted by the PEP. This model allows the PDP to asynchronously change its decisions while a request remains valid. As an illustration of a stateful COPS exchange, suppose a message arrives at a PEP that requires a policy decision. The PEP will issue a COPS Request message to the PDP. The PDP will then process the request and return a COPS Decision message specifying what action the PEP should take. The PEP will then execute its PDP's decision, and proceed normally. After some time, the PDP can issue an unsolicited Decision message for the original PEP Request modifying its decision (say, moving from an accept decision to a reject decision). The PEP will then take the newly dictated action. Eventually, when the PEP removes its state associated with the signaled message, it will issue a COPS Delete message to the PDP. The PDP will then clean up any state associated with the deleted request and cease sending unsolicited Decision messages for it.

COPS also facilitates accounting by allowing a PEP to asynchronously send Report messages to the PDP. Report messages are associated with a specific request. They allow the PEP to provide the PDP with accounting and monitoring information regarding an existing request state.

Fundamentally, COPS distinguishes between three different types of requests. Requests can be with respect to admission control, resource allocation, or forwarding events triggered on a network device. An admission control request asks the remote PDP what to do with an incoming message received by the PEP that requires an admission control decision. The resource allocation request queries whether local resources are to be committed locally on the device and how they should be committed when necessary. Finally, where applicable, the forwarding request determines if and how a signaled message is to be forwarded out of the device. COPS also provides a configuration request that allows a PEP to be configured by its PDP.

The COPS protocol runs over TCP for reliable message transfer. Additionally, COPS provides support for fault tolerance and synchronization so PEPs can detect when they lose communication with their PDPs and gracefully recover. Security can be achieved through the use of IPSec that supports integrity verification and data encryption for the TCP stream.

As RSVP is a signaling protocol, network devices can use COPS to outsource RSVP requests to a remote PDP. When a PEP receives an RSVP message, it should notify the PDP via a COPS Request message. The type of request depends on whether the message just arrived, is about to allocate resources from the device, or is being forwarded out of the device. COPS will return the appropriate decision corresponding to the request. The decision may instruct the PEP to accept or reject an arriving RSVP message, allocate resources for a reservation request, or either forward or drop an outgoing message, depending on the request.

As RSVP messages received by a PEP result in either path or reservation states, COPS requests are maintained with respect to these states. Due to this stateful model, RSVP refresh messages do not have to be continuously re-requested to the PDP via COPS. Rather, the initial request is retained, and a new request is issued only when a new or updated RSVP message is received. When a path or reservation state is finally removed from the device due to a timeout situation or RSVP Tear message, a COPS Delete message should be sent to the remote PDP notifying it of the state's removal.

Data Replacement and Client-Specific Decisions

COPS can return more than just a simple yes or no decision to a PEP's request. COPS can also specify that specific information be replaced in a signaled message. In the case of RSVP, for example, the PDP can use COPS to command the PDP to replace the Policy Data object in a forwarded RESV message. This mechanism allows PDPs to insert information into the RSVP messaging and potentially communicate with other policy servers.

One example of Policy Data Replacement is user authentication. A border router along an ISP may receive reservations for a shared multicast session from multiple hosts within its administrative domain. These reservations may carry Policy Data objects with user authentication information. The border router is responsible for authenticating each of the reservations and then merging them before sending them to the peer router. The peer router may require reservations to carry a token or certificate that proves the ISP will pay for the high QoS. The process in this example involves a PDP that authenticates a user's reservation using the incoming Policy Data information and then producing a certificate Policy Data for the forwarded reservation. COPS simply specifies that the incoming Policy Data needs to be replaced with the new Policy Data before the RSVP message is forwarded across the administrative boundary. The Policy Data object is simply carried opaquely by RSVP messages and is interpreted only by PDPs.

COPS also allows for the PDP to issue arbitrary commands and other kinds information to the PEP. In the case of RSVP, this allows the PDP to provide the PEP with secret key information used for generating and checking RSVP message integrity. Other examples might include packet-marking commands for the data flow's packets or altered packet-handling instructions.

COPS Control over RSVP Error Messages

COPS not only interacts with RSVP PATH and RESV messages, it also interacts with the PATH Error and RESV Error messages. By interacting with the RSVP error messages, COPS allows PDPs to control error propagation or provide information back to hosts. As an example, the PDP may insert information into the error message's Policy Data object. This error information might specify details such as "policy control failed to admit a particular user's reservation because it was 10 Kbps more than administratively allowed."

COPS Unicast RSVP Illustration

As an example of a typical RSVP PEP and PDP exchange, consider the arrival of a unicast PATH message at a PEP, as illustrated in the top left hand corner of Figure 9.4. When the PEP receives the PATH message, it

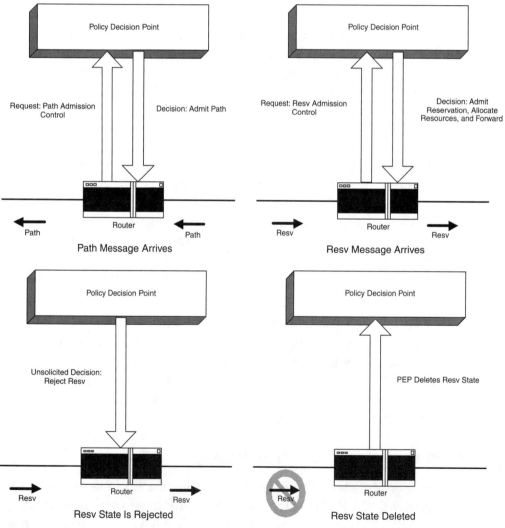

Figure 9.4   Illustration of COPS messaging for RSVP.

will issue a COPS Request to the PDP asking if the message can be admitted and forwarded toward its destination. Assuming the PATH is allowed, the PDP will return a positive decision to the PEP that will then set up a path state and forward the message downstream.

Next, suppose that an RESV message eventually arrives for this path state, as shown in Figure 9.4. Again the PEP will issue a request to the policy server asking if the RESV can be admitted, whether resources should be allocated for the RESV, and whether it should forward the message on to the previous hop. Assuming the PDP responds positively, the PEP will accept the reservation and install a corresponding reservation state, reporting to the PDP whether or not the reservation passed capacity admission control.

As COPS follows a stateful model, PDPs can update their decisions at any time. In this example, after some time the PDP may change its decision about the RESV from accept to reject. This will result in an unsolicited decision sent to the PEP specifying that the RESV is to be rejected. The PEP will then issue an RESV Error to the downstream hop, remove its reservation state, and, finally, send a Delete message to the PDP for the removed request.

COPS Multicast RSVP Illustration

COPS can exercise precise policy control over RSVP multicast signaling as well. This is due to the fact that COPS can separate admission control requests from forwarding requests. Whereas admission control requests apply to arriving RSVP messages, forwarding requests apply to messages that are about to be routed upstream. By asking the PDP once for each, COPS allows the PDP to control where messages are admitted from, and what location they are forwarded to.

A multicast flow arriving for a network device can fork into multiple forwarded flows. This situation is called *fan out*. Likewise, multiple messages can merge into a single outgoing message. This situation is called *fan in*, and in RSVP may result in the merging of RESVs for shared sessions.

A PEP is able to make separate COPS requests for each arriving message it receives and each forwarded message it sends. Through this process, the PDP can control fan in and fan out. In the case of fan in, some arriving messages for the same session can be accepted while others may not be. For RESVs this process controls what reservations are actually merged for a particular multicast session. If multiple admitted RESVs then merge into a single forwarded RESV, the PDP again has the opportunity to drop or modify the merged and forwarded reservation. Similarly, fan out can be controlled via the COPS forwarding request. Each RSVP message that is about to be forwarded can be requested independently by the PEP. This process allows the PDP to decide to drop some messages that would otherwise have been forwarded while still forwarding others for the same session.

Figure 9.5 demonstrates some examples of fan in and fan out for RSVP messages. In the fan out case, a single multicast PATH message arrives on one interface and is to be forwarded out three other interfaces. Separate COPS requests are sent to the PDP for the incoming and each of the outgoing messages, for which the PDP can then issue separate decisions. In this case, the PDP determines that the PATH should not be forwarded out the middle interface, perhaps because policies have determined that the corresponding link leads to a network that is disallowed use of RSVP for administrative reasons.

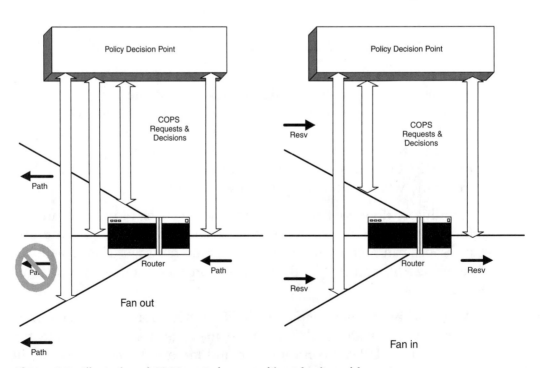

Figure 9.5 Illustration of COPS control over multicast fan in and fan out.

The fan in case simply shows RESVs for the two remaining PATHs arriving on each of the outgoing interfaces. Again, the PDP will issue separate decisions for the two arriving messages and the resulting merged message. In this example, all RESVs are admitted by the PDP but the merged RESV is modified to contain a new Policy Data object before it is forwarded. This new Policy Data object may have been used to replace user identity information in each of the incoming reservations with a single credential so that a neighboring ISP can authenticate the merged reservation.

RSVP MIB

The Simple Network Management Protocol (SNMP) is a mainstay management protocol for network administrators. This protocol is supported by most Internet routers and switches and is ideal for providing a large variety of monitoring and status information. To this end, SNMP is also a practical choice for monitoring the RSVP states established in an RSVP-aware network device.

SNMP is a query/response protocol that can be used to remotely retrieve and set information in a network device. Each piece of information that can be viewed or managed by SNMP must have a unique Object Identifier (OID). Complete sets of OIDs that together describe a functional component are called *Management Information Bases* (MIBs). An MIB is typically expressed as a tabular set of values within the hierarchical Structure of Management Information (SMI) namespace within which all OIDs must be represented. An MIB can be used to describe the operational status of a device, monitor TCP connections, describe a network interface, and so forth. The possibilities are limitless.

The RSVP MIB can be used to monitor RSVP activity on SNMP-aware network devices. The RSVP MIB records tables of information that describe a set of RSVP flows. Specifically, the MIB records information on the path and reservation states within a device using two tables, one for path and the other for reservation states. Each table has a number of rows, one for each individual state on the device. Each row is logically separated into a number of columns, where the column specifies the type of attribute. For example, the session address is an example of a column entry, which, when indexed by a particular row, specifies the session address for a particular reservation state. All the corresponding attributes found in RSVP signaling are dutifully recorded in this way.

Thus, using the RSVP MIB, a management station can observe what path and reservation states are currently active on a network device and all their relevant attributes.

LDAP

Administratively defined policies should be readily accessible by the PDPs that are to interpret them. A logical shared storage for policy data is a network directory. This is due to the fact that directory services are readily becoming widely available and may soon become ubiquitous. A directory is a form of hierarchical network database remotely accessible via a standard protocol. It provides a common place that can hold information on users, applications, and network devices. A directory can also hold the policies that regulate the usage of network services.

The Lightweight Directory Access Protocol (LDAP) is a standard protocol for accessing directory services available on the Internet. This protocol represents a common transport that can be used to search an LDAP-compliant directory for specific information. LDAP can also be used to add information to, or remove information from, the directory. A network device such as a router or switch can query the directory using LDAP to locate its policies.

LDAP assumes a hierarchically structured database. The hierarchical organization of the database allows a single name space to be used Internet-wide. The directory has a common root for the entire name space. From that, like a giant tree spouting branches everywhere, everything that exists in the Internet can be virtually represented somewhere in the directory's name space. For example, under the root, the directory may specify country information. Under a specific country, organization information can be found. Under individual organizations, specific information on users, machines, and policies may be found. A device anywhere on the Internet can find its virtual representation within the directory and gather information about what policies apply to it.

Defining Standard Schemas

Having a common storage for network policies is only a first step in achieving network-wide policy-based control. Policy-based control is necessary for exercising control over access to various network services such as QoS, IPSec-based security services, IP-multicast-based streaming, and access control at firewalls and proxy servers. A common representation for various policies is useful and necessary because many of these services will utilize common attributes such as user/application identity, source and destination subnets, and other administrative information. Currently, efforts are afoot in two industry standard-setting bodies (IETF and the Desktop Management Task Force, or DMTF) to agree upon a common representation for policy schemas for various service domains [SCHEMA]. Meanwhile, some commercial, network operating systems, and network management suites have already included LDAP-based policy schemas that allow network administrators to configure QoS admission control policies to take into account criteria such as user or application identity, source/destination addresses, and time of day.

Policy Considerations for Network Administrators

The policy control framework described in this chapter allows network administrators to achieve staged deployment of policy-based control by making routers in only certain parts of the network policy-aware. RSVP routers may differ in degree of sophistication, varying from a router that only processes RSVP messages to a router that includes both a PEP and a PDP. Moreover, policies can be designed and configured according to the needs of each administrative domain. For example, an ISP may only deploy policy-based control at edges of its administrative domain where it exchanges traffic with its peers, whereas a corporate network administrator may deploy policy-based control at a router that connects the corporate network to its ISP over a leased line—a precious resource. Figure 9.6 shows an example set of network nodes that belong to three administrative domains (ADs) where each AD may belong to a different ISP. Nodes A, B, and C belong to administrative domain AD-1, advised by PDP PS-1, while D and E belong to AD-2 and AD-3, respectively. E communicates with PDP PS-3, whereas D includes both PEP and PDP locally. In general, it is expected that there will be at least one PDP per administrative domain.

Across the Internet, when traffic flows from one source to destination, it typically traverses more than one service provider's network and ISPs typically agree to carry each other's traffic. In the absence of QoS reservations and priority-based reservations, the usage agreements between

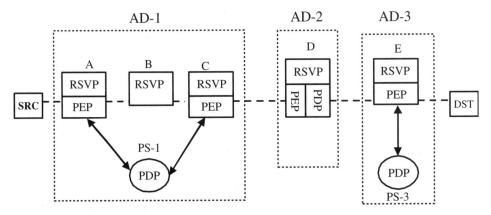

Figure 9.6 Illustration of network nodes interacting across administrative domains.

adjacent service providers for traffic crossing their border have been quite simple. For example, two ISPs may simply agree to accept all the traffic from each other, often without performing any explicit accounting for each other's traffic. However, once the QoS reservations are possible, service providers would like to protect their customers' traffic from other traffic and also charge for preferential treatment given to the QoS traffic. As a result, the ISPs need policies and mechanisms for determining how much QoS traffic to accept from each other and how to bill for resources reserved in their networks.

Such policies will be based on bilateral agreements where providers that manage a network cloud will contact their peers in the adjacent networks to agree on access control and accounting procedures. In the preceding example, provider AD-1 will establish arrangements with AD-2 (but not AD-3), and provider AD-2, in turn, will have a usage agreement with AD-3, and so on. Thus, when AD-1 forwards a reservation request to AD-2, AD-2 will charge AD-1 for use of all resources beyond AD-1's network. The information for charging will be obtained along the reservation's path by recursively applying the bilateral agreements in place between adjacent ADs until the reservation reaches the sender. To implement such a scheme, each reservation message must contain one or more policy objects. At each boundary, the router will add a policy object that will provide the authorization information, such as the identity of the provider that generated it and the equivalent of an account number where charges will be accumulated. Since agreements only hold among neighboring nodes, policy objects will have to

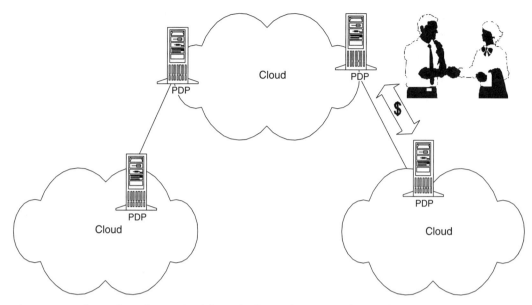

Figure 9.7 Illustration of recursive bilateral relationships for end-to-end QoS.

be rewritten as RSVP messages cross administrative boundaries. PDPs in each administrative domain must provide such information to the PEPs for inclusion in RSVP messages. Figure 9.7 presents the concept of recursive bilateral relationships across three administrative domains to achieve end-to-end QoS.

Summary

In this chapter we presented policy control and monitoring for RSVP. RSVP as a protocol does not directly support mechanisms for applying administrative policy control. Who gets to make what RSVP reservations, and when, is a problem addressed by the Policy Admission Control component for RSVP. Fundamentally, policy admission control can be logically divided into points that enforce policy (PEPs), and points that make policy decisions (PDPs). Together, these points lay the foundations for policy control in a distributed network environment. Through the use of these mechanisms and Policy Data objects carried in RSVP messages, neighboring administrative domains can form bilateral relationships and potentially provide QoS services end-to-end across the Internet.

We also briefly discussed monitoring of RSVP usage via SNMP and COPS. Monitoring provides a way for administrators to collect information on the QoS usage of their networks. Ultimately, monitoring and accounting information can be used to bill customers for QoS service. This capability represents an important shift and a potential new direction in the evolution of Internet economics.

CHAPTER 10

QoS-Aware Applications

T his chapter will investigate various aspects of QoS application development. First, QoS application design considerations will be reviewed. Next we will investigate some of the salient issues in quantifying the QoS needs of a particular application. Finally, we will examine two Application Programming Interfaces (APIs) for use with RSVP and present an example program that demonstrates use of RSVP.

Considerations for Applications

QoS-aware applications must take into account not only their own behavior, but the behavior of the network and its transport protocols as well. The transport protocol used by the application will have specific implications with respect to data transmission rates, reliability, and timely delivery. The effect of QoS on the transport protocol must be considered. QoS applications must also be able to deal with any variability the network may introduce in terms of the timely delivery of data and capacity limitations.

Transport Mechanisms

Applications will need to utilize the appropriate transport protocol to send their data. These underlying transport protocols have different delivery characteristics, depending on whether they are designed to provide reliable delivery or simply to deliver data in a timely fashion with no guarantees on delivery. Therefore, different transport protocols will interact differently with the QoS mechanisms supported in the network. This section will examine the relevant properties of the TCP and UDP transport protocols.

TCP

As described in Chapter 2, TCP provides reliable delivery of a byte stream over the Internet Protocol. TCP achieves reliable delivery by establishing a connection between two endpoints and by use of positive acknowledgments, flow control, and congestion control over the connection. Applications that use TCP for transport normally send data at will without any specific consideration of the transmitting data rate. Instead, TCP probes the capacity limitations of the data path and then transmits data at a rate that can be sustained at available capacity. During a connection's lifetime, TCP will continue to probe the capacity limits of the data path. Whenever additional capacity becomes available, TCP will increase its data rate to utilize the additional capacity. Similarly, when congestion arises along the data path, TCP will dynamically reduce its transmission rate to match the available capacity. TCP probes the available capacity by increasing its transmission rate to detect congestion along a path. Whenever it discovers loss of data via acknowledgments failing to arrive for previously sent data, TCP will back off and send at a previously sustainable rate.

A reservation can be made for a TCP connection in order to commit network resources for use by the connection. Even if congestion occurs along the data path, capacity will still be available for the TCP traffic corresponding to the reserved connection. Essentially, data from a reserved connection will not be dropped in places of congestion while it is conforming to its reserved traffic characteristics. TCP will automatically adapt to take advantage of the reserved capacity, as well as any additional capacity it discovers. So, applications utilizing TCP can make reservations in order to guarantee some lower bound on their performance.

When making reservations for TCP applications it is important to take into account the bidirectional communication requirements imposed by TCP. Even if data is being sent in only one direction, TCP will still be sending control messages in the opposite direction. These messages are the TCP acknowledgments, reporting which data bytes were successfully received by the destination.

Given the bidirectional nature of all TCP communication, it is important that RSVP reservations account for both directions. If the data gets through in one direction, but the acknowledgments are lost due to congestion in the other direction, the result is that TCP would slow down data transmission and retransmit the unacknowledged data. Under TCP, it makes no difference if the data actually is successfully received or not if this information cannot be fed back to the sender. Typically, however, the TCP acknowledgments in the reverse direction will require only a small fraction of the bandwidth required for actually transmitting the data.

UDP

UDP was described in Chapter 2 as a simple datagram delivery protocol. The purpose of UDP is to ensure error-free data using a checksum and to multiplex/demultiplex data to/from different applications using source and destination ports for identification. Everything else is left up to the application, giving the application a great deal of control over the behavior of its data transport. UDP is a good candidate transport protocol for applications such as real-time audio or videoconferencing that don't require reliability and have timing constraints on data delivery.

Of course, since UDP doesn't do much on behalf of the application, the application must provide all the necessary facilities it requires. The application must take measures to ensure that if it utilizes QoS it is in conformance with its advertised transmission rate. On the receiving side, the application must be prepared to deal with lost, delayed, or duplicated packets, even if a reservation is in place. Additionally, the network may reorder packets. This potential for lost and out-of-order delivery will likely require the application to add some form of sequence identification within each packet.

Unlike TCP, UDP does not require a reverse path from the sending direction. UDP can be strictly unidirectional, because a UDP sender does not require acknowledgments from a UDP receiver. Once a UDP packet is released into the network, there is no direct feedback that it successfully arrived at its destination. Thus, if the application is strictly unidirectional in terms of data flow, there is no need to make reservations in both directions.

RTP

The Real-Time Transport Protocol (RTP), described in RFC 1889, provides end-to-end transport functions suitable for applications that send/receive real-time data such as audio, video, or simulation data over unicast or multicast data services. RTP itself does not include mechanisms for resource reservation, nor does it guarantee Quality of Service for real-time traffic. RTP provides useful services such as identification of a particular payload type (e.g., which codec is used to generate audio/video stream and how the stream is packetized), sequence numbers, and time stamps (so that the original stream can be reconstructed at the receiver). Applications typically use RTP on top of UDP to make use of UDP's checksum and multiplexing services. In addition, RTP is augmented by a control protocol called Real-Time Control Protocol (RTCP) that allows monitoring of the data delivery at one or more participants and provides feedback on the Quality of Service received in an ongoing session.

RTP itself does not guarantee timely delivery of real-time data, relying instead on network layer services to provide Quality-of-Service guarantees. It also does not guarantee reliable delivery or prevent out-of-order delivery. However, its sequence numbers and time stamps provide information necessary for the receiver to reconstruct the original sequence or to determine the proper location of a packet within a stream without having to decode the packets in a sequence.

The RTP packet encapsulates real-time data generated by an application. The RTP packet, shown in Figure 10.1, contains a common 12-byte header that provides five fields for characterizing the encapsulated data. Three fields identify the type of data and provide timing information. These are the Payload Type, Sequence Number, and Timestamp fields. The Payload Type identifies the type of media following the RTP header as described in RFC 1889. The Sequence Number provides sequencing information such that lost and out-of-order packets can be determined. The Timestamp provides a 32-bit time stamp that describes the moment that the data was generated. The Payload Type determines the resolution of the Timestamp field in terms of clock frequency. Defined clock frequencies can vary from 8000 to 90,000 Hz.

Several RTP applications, such as audio and videoconferencing tools and multimedia presentation tools (including a distributed, shared whiteboard and multicast streaming tool), have been implemented and

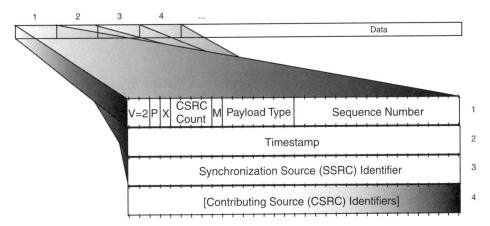

Figure 10.1 Illustration of the RTP header.

are commercially available. However, the Internet does not yet support the high bandwidth needed by a large number of video applications. To this end, RSVP provides the necessary QoS support to request reservation of dedicated services for such applications.

Dealing with Packet Switched Networks

The Internet is a collection of packet switched networks where each network may be built using a variety of link layer technologies such as Ethernet, Frame Relay, ATM, and so on. As a result, applications using the Internet encounter a wide range of performance-related characteristics, including unexpected amount of packet loss, wide variations in transmission and queuing delays, and jitter in the presence of congestion or due to the mix of different link capacities in the path. In addition, some portions of the Internet may support QoS while others may not. As a result, Internet applications that wish to use QoS mechanisms may still be designed to deal with wide variations in underlying network capabilities. Next, we discuss some of the ways applications can gracefully deal with such variations.

Application Buffering

Real-time applications operating over the Internet will have to deal with variations in packet delay. One of the most useful tools that applications can utilize to smooth out the discontinuities of network delay is a playback buffer at the receiver. Basically, if data received need not be used immediately, it can wait in a buffer until the original timing of a sequence of packets can be restored.

Buffering is a simple method to recover interpacket timing. Time-sensitive applications can take advantage of a small buffer to smooth out network-induced jitter at the receiving side. The buffer is basically a cache that holds the received data packets for some short period of time at the end host. This concept allows packets that may have been delayed by network conditions to recover their initial timing and ordering before they are used for playback.

Let's look at a detailed example of how buffers can be effectively employed. We will begin by considering the sending application. Immediately after the sending application creates a packet of data for transmission, it will stamp the packet with the current time. The time should be as precise as required by the application, perhaps down to a millisecond of precision or less, depending on the sampling rate. Each packet created by the sender is time-stamped in this way before it is transmitted to the destination, thereby recording the original timing information. The RTP protocol provides a facility to include this kind of timing and sequencing information with the data.

Meanwhile, the application at the destination will employ the buffering mechanism, which we call the *playback buffer*. The receiver chooses its playback buffer size based on the maximum delay expected for each packet. When the receiver starts receiving packets, it first waits for the playback buffer to fill before starting to play back the real-time stream. As each packet is received, the receiver looks at the time-stamp information in each packet to place it in the correct order in the playback buffer. That is, the time stamp for each packet that arrives can be compared to the time stamps of the buffered packets. Given this information, the receiving application can insert the packet into the correct location in the playback buffer. If the packet was excessively delayed—beyond the interval supported by the playback buffer—it can simply be discarded. After the playback buffer fills with enough packets such that the buffer interval is met, the receiving application can start pulling packets from the playback buffer at a rate consistent with the intervals determined by the time-stamp information. If the buffer size is large enough to account for maximum delay variation, the buffer will never go empty and the receiving application will be able to play the data back at a rate consistent with the original encoding rate. Except for the occasional lost packet that might create a gap in an otherwise continuous stream, the end user simply experiences jitter-free playback, unaware of any network-induced anomalies.

To see how such a playback buffer works, consider Figure 10.2, which shows a buffer that holds three time ticks' worth of data. Data is pulled from the buffer at each time tick. The sequence shown has packet 1 arriving in one time tick and then packet two arriving in another. As packets arrive they fill the playback buffer. Packet 3 is delayed a time tick while packet 1 is being played. Packets 3 and 5 arrive together as packet 2 is being played. Finally, packet 4 arrives and is inserted in the correct order in the playback buffer. Despite the discontinuous packet arrival times, the buffer provides consistent playback at every clock tick from the perspective of the user.

Buffering data for playback is a useful feature that can be employed by most applications. How much data can be buffered and for how long depends very much on the type of application, however. Although buffering removes jitter from a playback stream, it does induce an artificial delay that may become obvious to the user. In some cases, excessive playback delay could become an unacceptable annoyance to the user.

For unidirectional applications, such as audio and video streaming, buffers can be quite large. Several seconds to minutes of data can be first buffered, accounting not only for network delay but data retransmission delays as well. Of course, if there is no need for quick or real-time playback the complete data stream can be stored to a file for playback at any time. Streaming implies that the user is unwilling to wait for the complete media stream to be downloaded before it is played. The user is willing to wait only a short period of time for the media to be buffered so that it can be played while it continues to download. Obviously, if a user wanted to watch a film clip while on-line, the user would most likely want to watch the video while it downloads. Alternatively, if the entire film clip had to be first downloaded to the user's computer before it could be viewed, the user might end up waiting hours before being able to view the content.

Nevertheless, not all applications can afford to wait several minutes before playing the content of a media stream. Bidirectional real-time communication, such as a phone conversation, requires much tighter delay bounds than the unidirectional case. Bidirectional applications can still benefit from some amount of buffering, but perhaps only on the order of a few hundred milliseconds. Obviously, in the case of IP Telephony, if one

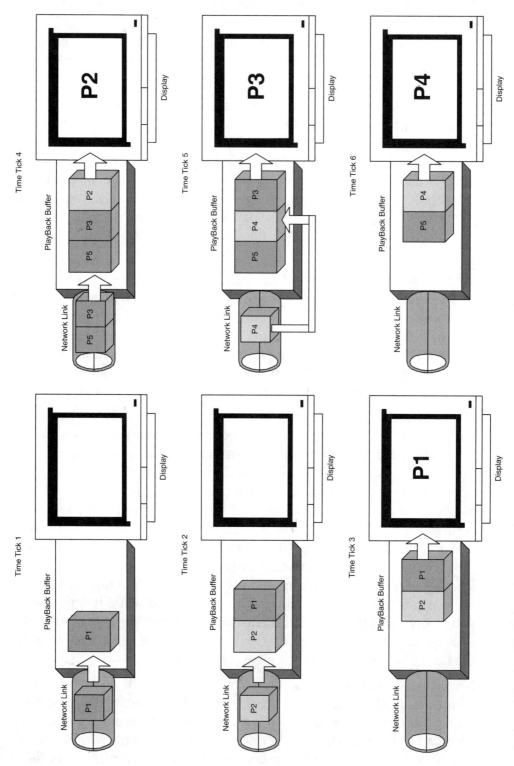

Figure 10.2 Simplified example of a playback buffer.

caller is talking and then stops and waits for the other caller to respond, long delays would become cumbersome to the conversation. Studies on voice communication have found round-trip delays of less than 250 ms are tolerable for most people. This implies that up to 250 ms of buffering, minus the round-trip time caused by the network itself, should be acceptable even for interactive voice communication.

Layering (Scalable Content)

Buffering at the receiver is one method of dealing with delay and jitter variations caused by congestion and/or capacity limitations along the data path. Nevertheless, real-time applications designed for communication over the Internet must deal with heterogeneity of many kinds, including network technologies, processing capabilities at receivers, and available link capacity. Multicast applications must deal with an additional aspect of receiver heterogeneity. For example, when a video stream is multicast to several participants, the participants may differ in their ability to receive and process the stream. Some participants on corporate networks might be receiving the stream over a high-capacity link, while others (working from home) are connected over a low-speed link. In addition, some receivers may use computers with limited processing capability that cannot decode a high-quality video stream in real time. Therefore, multimedia applications that interact over the Internet must be designed to scale to accommodate wide variations in network conditions, link capacities, and processing capabilities. Typically, an audio or video stream can be structured or segmented to scale across three dimensions, namely, time (*temporal resolution*), space (*spatial resolution*), and *content*. Let's look at each of these aspects in some detail.

Temporal Scaling

Audio and video streams are encoded at a particular sampling rate depending on the level of playback fidelity desired. For example, an audio stream may be sampled at rates varying from 4 to 128 Kbps, whereas a video stream has a playback rate in the range of a few (2 to 4) frames per second up to 30 to 60 frames per second for high fidelity. To achieve scalability, playback applications may choose to adapt their playback rate to provide the highest possible playback quality within the limitations of link and processing capacity at a receiver. For applications that use RSVP, a receiver can only reserve bandwidth proportional to the amount of capacity available on the path between the sender and itself. Therefore, the receiving application can choose a playback rate based on the accepted reservation to ensure consistent playback at a particular level of quality. Note that when a receiver reserves resources to cover only a portion of the data stream, routers on the path will not distinguish among different packets in the stream; thus, receivers cannot control which portion of the data stream will be protected from loss.

If the application uses RTP for transport, a receiver can use the RTCP protocol to provide feedback to the sender about the available capacity so that the sender can adjust its sampling rate to match the playback rate—thus avoiding sending additional, unnecessary data. However, such sender-based adaptation may not be possible if the application is multicasting the stream to multiple receivers and the receivers differ in terms of the data rates they can sustain. In that case, each receiver must adjust its own playback rate and make an appropriate QoS reservation to protect the part of the stream it wishes to receive. In addition, to avoid sending unnecessary traffic in a multicast environment, the sender can generate different streams at different temporal resolutions and advertise them to the participants using a session advertisement tool (e.g., the Session Description Protocol [RFC 2327]), and the receivers can choose to subscribe to an appropriate stream that matches its capability. These streams will use different UDP ports to distinguish themselves as belonging to different RSVP sessions so that a receiver can make reservation for the appropriate session corresponding to the stream of his or her choice.

Scaling Based on Spatial Resolution

Another method of scaling a multimedia stream to adapt to available capacity is to vary the spatial resolution of the stream by changing the frame or sample size. For example, in the case of video, the frame size can vary from a thumbnail size to a full size of 1024×768 pixels (1920×1152 in the case of very high resolution MPEG-2) with a set of choices in between, such as 320×240 or 640×480. Each of the frame sizes leads to a different bandwidth requirement and different playback quality. Out-of-band communication is necessary for the receiver to provide feedback to the sender about its capability so that the sender can adapt the resolution to match the receiver's capability. As in the case of scaling by varying temporal resolution, a sender can generate multiple, distinct streams to meet the varying demands of receivers in a multicast session.

Scaling Based on Content

Another way to achieve scalability is to vary the quality or resolution of the content itself. For example, in the case of a video stream, each video frame is made up of a two-dimensional array of pixels, where each pixel has a certain resolution to represent the image. For example, a single-bit pixel will only capture and represent a black-and-white image, whereas a 24-bit pixel will provide a high-definition, high-quality color image with a range of possibilities in between. Similarly, each audio sample can have a range of resolution for each value in the sample. Again, in the case of unicast communication, the sender can adapt the resolution to match a receiver's capability if feedback is available from the receiver through some out-of-band mechanism or an explicit control protocol such as RTCP. However, such an adaptation is not so easy in the case of multipoint communication involving sender(s) multicasting (or broadcasting) to an arbitrarily large number of receivers scattered along paths with potentially high variability in network bandwidths. Multicasting multiple streams, each with a different resolution, is not practical and may lead to suboptimal use of resources, as similar content may have to be sent multiple items over identical paths in some cases. Next, we describe another way of achieving content scalability without sacrificing efficiency.

Scaling by Layered Content

Ideally, when scalability is to be achieved by segmenting data within a particular type of media, it would be best to make the most efficient use of whatever resources are available. If, as in a previous example, a media server were to provide both black-and-white and color media streams, there is obvious redundancy. It would be better if the content of the black-and-white stream simply laid the foundation for the color video stream. The color stream would then utilize information within the black-and-white stream and thus reduce the network load overall. This can be achieved by combining a layered compression algorithm with a layered transmission scheme. In this approach, the original video or audio signal is encoded into a number of layers that can be incrementally combined to provide progressively better-quality reproduction. Each of the layers is transmitted as a separate multicast stream so that receivers need only subscribe to a subset of layers they can handle.

In addition, in the case of congestion, a router can selectively forward only those layers a link can manage, dropping the rest if necessary. For example, in a video presentation session, receivers downstream of an ISDN line may choose to receive only a subset of layers that add up to 64 Kbps, whereas receivers on a corporate network may choose to receive layers adding up to a 640-Kbps video stream.

It is possible to see how different segments could build on one another when considering the case of different video resolutions. For example, suppose that a video stream is multicast in two resolutions, one at 320×240 pixels and another at 640×480 pixels. Because the video content is the same for both streams, the 640×480 stream represents the highest resolution of the video. Instead of having one 320×240 and one 640×480 stream of the same video, two 320×240 streams could be provided: one for displaying the odd-numbered pixels and the other for displaying the even-numbered pixels. If only low-resolution video is required at the receiver, then just one of the two streams would be sufficient. If high-resolution were required, then both streams could be merged. By sharing information across the two streams, a 50 percent savings is achieved in terms of network resources.

Segmented Data Reassembly

In the preceding illustrations of media segmentation, it is still required that the destination be able to merge the associated streams. This reassembly of the complete media sequence can be achieved through the use of buffering. When related data arrives from different ports, it can be reassociated via the use of sequence numbers and time-stamp information. Obviously, when a video shows a person's mouth move, it is necessary that the corresponding sounds be in sync. The video and audio streams in such cases could be correlated using time-stamp information. If both data packets are to be played together, they could simply be stamped with the same time. The receiving application would then simply play both data packets at the same time from the playback buffer.

Traffic Characteristics

Once applications are made QoS-friendly, it is necessary to analyze the traffic requirements of these applications. That is, what are the characteristics of a data flow? On the sending side, this requires that the token bucket parameters be determined for describing the generated traffic. Additionally, the receiving application must understand what size and kind of reservation is necessary to adequately protect a data flow.

Determining Appropriate Data Rates

When using RSVP, the sender must first describe its traffic characteristics, and these traffic specifications are then carried in the PATH message's Tspec object. The sending traffic characteristics are expressed in terms of token bucket parameters. The token rate r should accurately express the average data rate generated by the source application. The peak rate p should express the maximum short-term data rate that the application will ever produce. The token bucket size b should be large enough to accommodate the largest burst the application may generate. Mathematically, this means the bucket size should be chosen such that X amount of data sent over any arbitrary time interval t does not exceed the data sent at the token rate plus the token bucket depth or $X \leq b + (r \times t)$. The maximum MTU size M and the minimum-policed size m should reflect the largest and smallest packets that the application will produce. The token bucket depth should be at least as large as M. The token bucket size is determined by the maximum potential burst size that the sending application may produce and is typically a multiple of M, or at least as large as M.

In addition to the Sender Tspec, the RSVP AdSpec object carries information that describes the properties of the data path, including the availability of specific services (CL or GS) and parameters needed by a specific service such as Guaranteed Service. On the receiving side, the destination application will receive the path information describing the traffic characteristics of the corresponding data flow. Based on this information and on the application itself, an appropriate reservation can be issued. The receiver will select the filter style, service type, and required token bucket parameters. Typically, the receiver will issue a reservation using the same parameters specified in the path and thereby protect all the delivered data. If the reservation is simply too big to pass admission control by the network, or if the receiver is unwilling to pay for the full reservation, it may opt to make a smaller reservation. In many real-time applications, having some reservation in place is better than having none.

The sender's Tspec always bounds the receiver's token bucket parameters specified in the Flow Specification object. This means that the token rate will be the minimum token bucket rate as specified in the Flow Spec and corresponding Tspec. Similarly, the receiver-specified peak rate, token bucket size, and maximum MTU size will also be bounded by their corresponding values in the sender's Tspec. The minimum-policed size is chosen from the value specified in the corresponding Tspec.

Additionally, if the destination application chooses guaranteed service, it will provide the Rspec that supplies the rate R and slack S terms that specify the desired bandwidth and delay guarantees. Chapter 7 describes how these terms are selected by an application.

For applications that send data at a constant rate the selection of variables is relatively straightforward. The peak rate and token rate should simply be set to the application's data rate. The token bucket size can remain small, just large enough to hold the maximum packet size, because the constant data rate will not exceed $(X \times t)$ for any period of time t.

For applications that send VBR (variable bit rate) traffic, the token bucket parameters must be selected carefully to reflect the bursty nature of the traffic. For example, the peak rate must be specified to match the expected maximum rate that will ever be generated for a stream (or set to infinity if it is not known). Similarly, the token rate and token bucket size should be selected based on the expected maximum burst size and average data rate for the stream. As an example, consider a video stream sent at a frame resolution of 320×240 8-bit pixels and at the rate of 10 frames per second. For such a stream, the maximum frame size can be computed (76.8K uncompressed and about 8K assuming minimum compression ratio of 10), and token rate can be computed based on the average amount of data sent over a longer interval. The next section discusses the variable or bursty nature of compressed data and its implications on specifying token bucket parameters.

Bursty Traffic

Applications will typically not produce data at a constant rate. Typically, applications will present short bursts of data to the network exceeding the average data rate. To support bursty real-time traffic, RSVP allows applications to express a token bucket description of their traffic instead of just providing a single average bit rate parameter. The token bucket is flexible in that the application need not specify overly large constant data rates to accommodate the infrequent data bursts.

Codecs (Encoder/Decoders) and Data Compression

Typically, a bursty data stream can be attributed to compression. Compression is used throughout the Internet to compress images, such as Joint Picture Experts Group (JPEG) files, sounds, and, most important, video. The benefits of compression are obvious. A 24-bit color video stream at a resolution of 352×288 pixels at 30 frames per second would yield a constant data rate of 69.6 Mbps. Most of the uncompressed video data is highly redundant, as sequential frames do not typically vary much. Frames temporally close together tend to be quite similar. Therefore, instead of sending a complete frame every 1/30 second, a source could send only the changes (or differences) between consecutive frames. If, on average, there was only a 10 percent difference between sequential frames, the required bandwidth for transmitting the video stream would be reduced substantially.

The term *codec* is used as an abbreviation for encoder/decoder. It is a term typically used to describe compression algorithms or devices that compress audio and visual data. A variety of codecs exist that will typically convert a large constant–bit rate stream into a compressed bursty data stream. The compressed streams are bursty simply because the compression depends on the original media content. In the case of video, if the frames were changing rapidly, the result would be a higher data rate, while relatively constant frames will result in a smaller data rate. For example, if you are watching a newscast, the long sequences where the anchorperson presents news have few changes and produce a stream with a relatively constant and small data rate. However, whenever the scene changes to show a shot of sports or a live event, the scene change causes a burst of data to reflect new content that has very little in common with the previous scene. As the scenes or objects within a scene change, we see a bursty sequence of data corresponding to changes in the content.

MPEG Illustration

As an example of a VBR codec, consider the MPEG-1 compression algorithm. MPEG stands for the Moving Picture Experts Group, a suite of compression techniques for audio, video, and other media. MPEG-1 is a standard for medium–bit rate video and audio compression. It is typically used to compress VHS-quality video, or picture sizes of 288×352 pixels. First, MPEG-1 compresses individual video frames spatially via a discrete cosine transform–based compression technique. Second, MPEG-1 performs temporal compression by employing motion-compensation techniques to encode sequential frames. Taken together, this spatial and temporal compression can achieve 100:1 compression ratios. Effectively the 69.6-Mbps stream discussed previously for a 288×352-pixel 30-frame-per-second image could be reduced to 1.5 Mbps or less using MPEG-1.

Looking deeper into the MPEG-1 codec, there are three distinct types of information for representing compressed video. These are called the I-frames, P-frames, and B-frames. Basically, the I-frames spatially compress a complete portion of a video frame. The I-frames can be used to accurately reconstruct a video frame. The P-frames are used to construct a new frame based on the changes from a past reference frame, which may be either the last preceding I-frame or P-frame. Finally, the B-frames represent changes from both proceeding and succeeding I-frames or P-frames.

In terms of importance, the I-frames are the most damaging to the video playback if lost. Losing an I-frame would render useless all the succeeding P-frames and B-frames that use it as their initial reference. The result would be a noticeable degradation in the playback video quality. Obviously, it would be useful in the case of MPEG-1 to select packets carrying P-frames and B-frames to be dropped if the token bucket overflows. The result of dropping an I-frame would be much more obvious to the end user. Unfortunately, RSVP does not provide a mechanism by which specific packets of a single flow can be identified as more important than others. Switches and routers along the data path may randomly drop packets from a data flow that exceeds its reservation specification in the presence of congestion. One possible work-around would be to use different ports (and, as a result, different RSVP sessions) to transmit the different kinds of information produced by the MPEG-1 codec. Ideally, the application should reserve a sufficiently large proportion of the path's bandwidth such that packet loss becomes unlikely.

I-frames are also the largest in terms of data transmitted. They consist of almost 80 percent of the data stream. The I-frames demonstrate the bursty nature of the MPEG-1 codec. Every time an I-frame has to be transmitted, a burst of data would likely result. In between the I-frames, there will be a period with only the smaller P-frames and B-frames being transmitted at a decreased data rate. When determining the peak rate and token bucket size for MPEG-1 traffic, the requirements for how quickly the I-frames should be transmitted must be considered. An application must also ensure that the data rate caused by I-frames does not violate the traffic agreements made with the network by ensuring the peak rate is not exceeded. See Figure 10.3 for an illustration of the capacity and temporal relationship between the I-frames, P-frames, and B-frames.

Traffic Measurement and Reservation Updates

RSVP allows applications to update their reservation states and path states as their requirements change. An application may want to change its existing path or reservation state for a number of reasons. A sender may have to update its traffic description to account for dynamically increasing or decreasing data rates. A receiver may want to increase its reservation if its current level of QoS is not acceptable—or to lower its

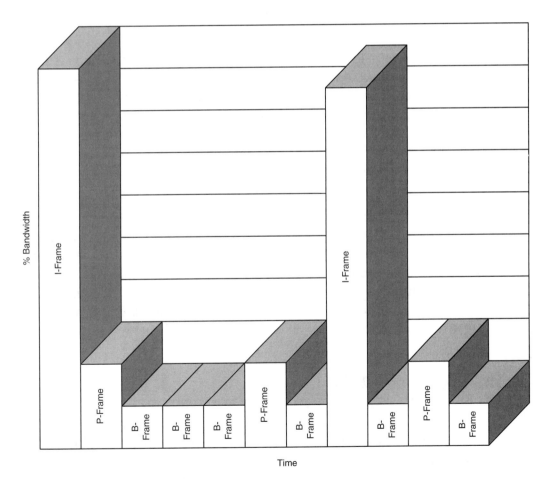

Figure 10.3 Illustration of the bursty nature of MPEG-1 data streams.

reservation rate if there is an upstream capacity admission control failure. A Fixed Filter or Shared Explicit receiver may also wish to change its sender selection list and add or remove sources.

Additionally, third-party applications can make reservations and trigger RSVP messages on behalf of another application. When applications do not know their traffic characteristics, it is possible that a third-party application can measure the application's traffic rate and send the appropriate RSVP messages.

On the sending side, the third-party application could measure the current data rate and issue a PATH message specifying the observed data characteristics. As the traffic characteristics change, updated PATH messages can notify the network and the destinations of the current data rate. By dynamically measuring the observed traffic characteristics of a flow, either the participating application or a third-party application can use the measurements to produce more timely and accurate QoS specification.

On the receiving side, a third-party application can also issue reservations based not just on the PATH message information but also on the observed data rates. In circumstances where the receiver is billed for making reservations, it may prove advantageous to issue reservations only for the amount currently being utilized by the data flow. As the data rate increases, updated reservations can be issued tracking the observed data characteristics.

Inherently, the measurement-based approach depends on the application sending traffic at a reasonably sustained rate. If the data rate changes often and in unpredictable ways, the measurement-based approach will have to resort to determining average rates and upper bounds, effectively being reduced to the establishment of a constant reservation. Alternatively, rapidly changing reservations will also potentially cause the amount of RSVP messaging to increase beyond acceptable levels. The result could cause network performance to degrade for all RSVP control messages.

GQoS and Other APIs

Now that we have reviewed some of the high-level concepts applicable to QoS applications, it is time to get into some of the details. Fortunately, applications do not have to ship with a complete RSVP stack. Several operating systems (OS) ship with a ready-made RSVP stack.

Even if the OS does not directly support RSVP, several third-party packages can be found that provide RSVP functionality. Once RSVP functionality is available on a platform, applications should have a standard API available with which they can interact with the RSVP stack. We will review two such APIs: (1) RAPI (RSVP API), which is one example of an API used to support RSVP on some UNIX platforms, and (2) GQoS, which is Microsoft's API for generalized QoS available on some Windows platforms.

RAPI

RAPI is one example of an RSVP API. RAPI is described in an IETF informational draft [RAPI] at the time of this writing and is available on some UNIX platforms. RAPI assumes that an RSVP daemon is running on the system. This daemon is responsible for the actual RSVP signaling. The RSVP daemon may also interact with a packet classifier and scheduler running in the kernel, if supported by the OS, to initialize traffic control on any reserved flows.

In a typical scenario, an application loads the RAPI library module that interfaces with the RSVP daemon. The application will then use RAPI to initialize a QoS session and provide a callback routine. The application provides sender information and/or receiver information, including traffic characterization parameters, to the RSVP daemon though RAPI. When network events occur with respect to the initialized QoS session, a callback routine will be invoked to notify the application.

Specifically, to invoke RAPI, the application will first create a QoS session via the rapi_session call:

```
unsigned int rapi_session (struct sockaddr *Dest, int Protoid, int flags,
    int (*Event_rtn) (), void *Event_arg, int *errnop );
```

The rapi_session call returns a session identifier (sid), if successful, or 0 otherwise. The Dest parameter specifies the sockaddr for the session, which includes the destination address and port. The Protoid parameter specifies the protocol identifier, either UDP or TCP. The flags field is used to specify whether virtual ports will be used and whether the IntServ or RAPI simplified traffic specification formats are to be used. The Event_rtn and Event_arg parameters specify a callback routine and a callback argument used to notify the application of QoS events and errors. The erronop is a pointer to an integer through which RAPI can return a specific error code.

Once a session is created, its sid can be used to invoke sender or receiver functionality. If the application is to send traffic, it will notify the RSVP daemon of the sender parameters via the rapi_sender call:

```
int rapi_sender(unsigned int sid, int flags, struct sockaddr *LHost,
                rapi_filter_t *SenderTemplate, rapi_tspec_t *SenderTspec,
                rapi_adspec_t *SenderAdspec, rapi_policy_t *SenderPolicy,
                int TTL );
```

The rapi_sender call will return an error code if the call fails. Otherwise, the RSVP daemon will create a path state for the sid specifying the LHost as the local host and source port. The optional SenderTemplate parameter is used to identify the source address and protocol in the PATH message. The SenderTspec parameter specifies the application's traffic characteristics via a token bucket description. The SenderAdSpec is an optional parameter for specifying an AdSpec object to be included within the PATH message. Likewise the optional SenderPolicy specifies a policy structure for including Policy Data within the PATH message. Finally, the TTL specifies the time to live for the generated IP packets in terms of a hop count for controlling the number of hops the message can travel.

If the application is to receive QoS traffic, it will notify the RSVP daemon of the appropriate reservation parameters via the rapi_reserve call:

```
int rapi_reserve ( unsigned int sid, int flags,
                struct sockaddr *RHost, int StyleID,
                rapi_stylex_t *Style_Ext, rapi_policy_t *Rcvr_Policy,
                int FilterSpecNo, rapi_filter_t *FilterSpecList,
                int FlowSpecNo, rapi_flowspec_t *FlowSpecList);
```

The rapi_reserve will return an error code if the call fails. Otherwise, the RSVP daemon will create a reservation state for the sid specifying the RHost as the local destination and port. The flags parameter can be set to RAPI_REQ_CONFIRM to request that confirmation messages be sent after the reservation is successfully installed. The StyleID parameter is used to specify the style of the reservation (Fixed Filter, Shared Explicit, or Wildcard Filter). The optional Rcvr_Policy is used to specify the Policy Data to be included in the RESV message. Depending on the style, a list of zero or more Filter Specifications can be included. For Wildcard Filters, no Filter Specification structures need to be included. For Shared Explicit and Fixed Filter reservations, one or more Filter Specification structures should be included to select the appropriate senders. Also, depending on the style, one or more Flow Specification structures may be included. In the case of Wildcard and Shared Explicit filter reservations, only one Flow Specification needs to be included. Fixed Filter reservations will match each specified Filter Specification to its corresponding Flow Specification using one-to-one matching between the lists.

The rapi_sender and rapi_reserve calls may be invoked more than once to update existing path or reservation states. The most recent call to the functions will take precedence.

To receive notification of events, the application will call rapi_getfd to get a file descriptor associated with the UNIX socket for the QoS session:

```
int rapi_getfd ( unsigned int sid );
```

This call takes the QoS session identifier as its only parameter and returns the appropriate file descriptor or –1 if there is none. The application can perform a select operation on the returned file descriptor, which will wait until a socket read event is signaled on the file descriptor. Once the file descriptor is signaled, the application should call rapi_dispatch:

```
int rapi_dispatch ( );
```

This call will cause the RSVP daemon to invoke the application's callback function when viable events have occurred. This call will synchronously return zero if successful; otherwise, it will return an appropriate error code. The viable read events that will signal the file descriptor are directly related to RSVP messaging. A RAPI_PATH_EVENT signifies that a PATH message has arrived or that the local path state has changed. A RAPI_RESV_EVENT is signaled when a RESV message arrives or when the local reservation state has changed. Similarly, RAPI_PATH_ERROR and RAPI_RESV_ERROR events signify that a PATH Error or RESV Error message arrived or that a local error occurred. Finally, the RAPI_RESV_CONFIRM event is used to notify the receiving application that a reservation confirmation has arrived for its reservation. The application's callback function provided via the rapi_session call looks like this:

```
Event_rtn (   unsigned int sid, int EventType,
         int StyleID, int ErrorCode, int ErrorValue,
         struct sockaddr *ErrorNode,
         unsigned char ErrorFlags, int FilterSpecNo,
         rapi_filter_t *FilterSpecList,
         int FlowSpecNo, rapi_spec_t *FlowSpecList,
         int AdSpecNo, rapi_adspec_t *AdSpecList, void *Event_arg );
```

The callback function specifies a large number of parameters. The provided sid is the session identifier that generated the event. The EventType specifies the RAPI event that was triggered. The remaining arguments are only to be considered relevant if their corresponding event type was triggered.

The StyleID parameter is valid only for the RAPI_RESV_EVENT or RAPI_RESV_ERROR event and specifies the style of the reservation. The ErrorCode, ErrorFlags, and ErrorValue parameters specify the appropriate RSVP error information, valid only for the RAPI_PATH_ERROR and RAPI_RESV_ERROR events. Correspondingly, the ErrorNode parameter specifies the IP address of the node that is responsible for the error message. The FilterSpecNo and FilterSpecList, FlowSpecNo and FlowSpecList, and AdSpecNo and AdSpecList all specify the number of corresponding structures and a pointer to the memory block containing the respective listings. When lists are not available, the pointer parameter will be set to NULL. What list information is available depends on the RSVP messages. See Chapters 5 and 6 for a description of the listed objects and their corresponding RSVP messages. Note that the FlowSpecList and FilterSpecList are also used to carry SenderTspec and SenderTemplate information, respectively, in the case of PATH-related events, as these structures are similar.

The Event_arg is the pointer to the argument originally provided by the application in the rapi_session call. This argument can be used by the callback function to signal back to the application the type of event once the application calls rapi_dispatch (and thus invokes this callback routine).

Finally, when the application wishes to delete a particular session it will simply call rapi_release:

```
int rapi_release ( unsigned int sid );
```

If the sid is valid, this call deletes any existing reservation state or path state information associated with the session identifier. The appropriate tear notifications will also be provided to the network at the time of this call.

This speedy overview of RAPI is intended only to demonstrate a basic RSVP API. The purpose of this discussion is to simply provide an understanding of how an application may interact with a third-party RSVP daemon. The next section will investigate another method of specifying QoS requirements within a layered sockets–based architecture.

GQoS

Generic QoS (GQoS) represents one solution for supporting QoS in general and RSVP in particular. It will be available on some Microsoft Windows platforms such as Windows 98 and Windows 2000. GQoS utilizes the generalized interface provided by WinSock 2 to interact with a QoS layered service model.

WinSock 2 and the Layered Service Model

Windows Sockets 2 (WinSock 2) is an extension to the original WinSock found on various flavors of the Windows OS. WinSock 2 is a general networking API usable by a number of networking protocol stacks. WinSock 2 was developed in order to provide a common interface to a variety of networking protocols typically used by Windows applications.

Fundamentally, WinSock 2 assumes a layered service provider model. This model allows multiple service providers to exist, accessible via the common WinSock 2 APIs. Services can also be layered one on top of another, providing additional levels of functionality, such as traffic control over a traditional TCP/IP protocol stack.

GQoS Usage of the WinSock 2 APIs

GQoS takes advantage of the standard WinSock 2 APIs. Basically, an application must first find an appropriate layered service provider that supports RSVP. Once an appropriate service provider is found, the standard WinSock 2 APIs can be invoked to create a socket and specify QoS information. The application can be notified about QoS updates by callbacks, asynchronous (Windows) messages, or events.

To invoke QoS using GQoS, an application needs to first discover if an appropriate QoS service provider is available. Once WinSock 2 has been initialized, this can be accomplished by calling:

```
int WSAEnumProtocols (LPINT lpiProtocols,
                      LPWSAPROTOCOL_INFO lpProtocolBuffer,
                      ILPDWORD lpdwBufferLength );
```

This call will return the protocol information structures for all available protocols if lpiProtocols is NULL. Otherwise, it will return protocol information structures only for the protocol indices specified in the NULL terminated lpiProtocols array. The lpProtocolBuffer parameter is a pointer to a buffer that will be filled in with a list of WSAPROTOCOL_INFO structures. These structures identify the available protocols and their capabilities. The lpdwBufferLength contains the size of the lpProtocolBuffer on input and the required size of the lpProtocolBuffer on output. The application should reallocate the buffer if it turns out to be smaller than the returned lpdwBufferLength and should again call WSAEnumProtocols. Protocols that support QoS will set the XP1_QOS_SUPPORTED flag in the WSAPROTOCOL_INFO structure's dwdeviceServiceFlags field. Additionally, the iAddressFamily field should be set to AF_INET for the Internet Protocols and the iProtocol field should be set to either IPPROTO_UDP or IPPROTO_TCP depending on the application's transport requirements.

Once an appropriate protocol information structure is found, or if the application already knows the identity of the appropriate QoS service provider, it can proceed to initialize a socket:

```
SOCKET WSASocket (  int addressFamily, int type, int protocol,
                    LPWSAPROTOCOL_INFO lpProtocolInfo, GROUP grp,
                    DWORD dwFlags );
```

This call will create a new socket via the service provider specified in the lpProtocolInfo structure if the addressFamily, type, and protocol parameters are all set to FROM_PROTOCOL_INFO. Otherwise, an appropriate protocol will be used as determined from the specified addressFamily, type, and protocol parameters. The dwFlags parameter should be set to WSA_FLAG_OVERLAPPED in support of overlapped IO, which is required by some QoS service providers. If a socket could not be created, WSASocket will return NULL. Before the socket can be used, it must be bound to a particular address and port via the bind call.

Note: Overlapped IO allows WinSock 2 calls to return immediately, without waiting for them to complete. Applications can instead register for asynchronous Windows messages, events, or callback functions to be called upon the completion of a particular call.

Once a new socket has been created, the application can communicate QoS information to the service provider though a number of standard WinSock 2 calls. Regardless of the call, the common QualityOfService (QOS) data structure is used to hold and provide the QoS data. The QOS structure is as follows:

```
typedef struct _QualityOfService
{
```

```
    FLOWSPEC           SendingFlowspec;
    FLOWSPEC           ReceivingFlowspec;
    WSABUF             ProviderSpecific;
} QOS, *LPQOS;
```

This structure contains two FLOWSPEC structures that specify the sending and receiving token bucket parameters. The optional Provider-Specific buffer can be used to carry additional structures such as RSVP AdSpec information or Policy Data. The FLOWSPEC structure is formatted as follows:

```
typedef struct _flowspec
{
    unsigned long      TokenRate;
    unsigned long      TokenBucketSize;
    unsigned long      PeakBandwidth;
    unsigned long      Latency;
    unsigned long      DelayVariation;
    SERVICETYPE        ServiceType;
    unsigned long      MaxSduSize;
    unsigned long      MinimumPolicedSize;
} FLOWSPEC;
```

The token bucket parameters described in the FLOWSPEC are the same as those defined for the Integrated Services. These are the TokenRate and PeakBandwidth parameters, which are expressed in bytes per second, and the TokenBucketSize parameter, which is expressed in bytes. Again, the MaxSduSize and MinimumPolicedSize parameters describe the possible maximum and minimum size of a packet that will still receive QoS protection. Both these parameters are expressed in terms of bytes. The Latency field is used to describe the maximum acceptable latency, in microseconds, that a packet can endure. The DelayVariation field describes the difference, in microseconds, between the maximum and minimum delay that a packet may experience. The application can use the QOS_NOT_SPECIFIED value by default for all fields except for ServiceType to instruct the QOS service provider to derive the appropriate values when possible. The ServiceType field specifies the appropriate Integrated Services defined type of service such as Best Effort, Controlled Load, or Guaranteed Service.

There are a variety of ways an application can communicate its QoS requirements for a socket to the QoS service provider. The choice depends on the type of application and whether it utilizes UDP or TCP for transport.

Both active TCP client applications and UDP peer applications can use WSAConnect to provide either sender or receiver QoS information to the service provider. The prototype for WSAConnect appears as follows:

```
int WSAConnect (SOCKET s,
                const struct sockaddr FAR * address, int addressLen,
                LPWSABUF lpCallerData, LPWSABUF lpCalleeData,
                LPQOS lpSQOS, LPQOS lpGQOS );
```

Socket s is the socket created via WSASocket. The address parameter specifies either the passive server address in the case of TCP, or the peer host's address in case of UDP. In all cases the relevant QoS information is provided via the lpSQOS parameter. Depending on whether the application is a sender or receiver, it should populate the Sending-Flowspec with its traffic characteristics, the ReceivingFlowspec with the requested traffic characteristics, or both. If WSAConnect fails, it will return SOCKET_ERROR and the corresponding error code can be recovered via WSAGetLastError.

Similarly, multicast UPD applications can utilize WSAJoinLeaf to specify their QoS requirements to the layered service provider:

```
int WSAJoinLeaf (SOCKET s,
                 const struct sockaddr FAR * address, int addressLen,
                 LPWSABUF lpCallerData, LPWSABUF lpCalleeData,
                 LPQOS lpSQOS, LPQOS lpGQOS, DWORD dwFlags );
```

WSAJoinLeaf is used to join the specified multicast session. Like in the WSAConnect call, the lpSQOS parameter should be used to provide the necessary QoS information.

If the application is acting as a passive TCP server, it can provide QoS information to the service provider for an accepted socket. Typically, a TCP server application will listen on a socket waiting for a FD_ACCEPT event to be triggered. On receipt of an FD_ACCEPT notification, the application may use the WSAAccept call to accept a socket and specify a callback function through which it can set QoS information:

```
SOCKET WSAAccept (  SOCKET s, struct sockaddr FAR * address,
                    LPINT addressLen, LPCONDITIONPROC conditionFunc,
                    DWORD dwCallbackData );
```

This function will return a handle to the newly created socket if successful or INVALID_SOCKET otherwise. Socket s is the listening socket on which an accept was triggered. The address parameter will be populated with the address of the connecting client if provided by the application. The conditionFunc is the callback routine:

```
int CALLBACK ConditionFunc (LPWSABUF lpCallerID, LPWSABUF lpCallerData,
                            LPQOS lpSQOS, LPQOS lpGQOS,
                            LPSWABUF lpCalleeID, LPWSABUF lpCalleeData,
                            GROUP FAR * grp, DWORD dwCallbackData );
```

The application can provide QoS information for the accepted socket through this callback routine via the lpSQOS parameter. The dw-CallbackData parameter corresponds to the callback data originally specified by the application in the corresponding WSAAccept call. The remaining parameters can be ignored. Once the application provides its QoS information via lpSQOS, it should return from the callback with the value of CF_ACCEPT.

Regardless of the transport protocol, the application can provide QoS information to and receive QoS information from a socket by using WSAIoctl with either the SIO_SET_QOS or SIO_GET_QOS control code:

```
int WSAIoctl (  SOCKET s, DWORD dwIoControlCode, LPVOID lpvInBuffer,
                DWORD cbInBuffer, LPVOID lpvOUTBuffer,
                DWORD cbOUTBuffer, LPDWORD lpcbBytesReturned,
                LPWSAOVERLAPPED lpOverlapped,
                LPWSAOVERLAPPED_COMPLETION_ROUTINE
                lpCompletionRoutine );
```

This routine can be used to set or get QoS information for socket s. In order to get QoS information, the dwIoControlCode should be set to SIO_GET_QOS. If successful, a QOS structure will be provided in the lpvOUTBuffer allocated by the application. To set QoS information, the dwIoControlCode should be set to SIO_SET_QOS and the application should provide its QOS structure via the lpvInBuffer parameter. In support of overlapped IO, the lpOverlapped parameter can be used by the application to specify a WSAOVERLAPPED structure that contains an event field. This event will be signaled when the function completes, or a callback function can be specified via the lpCompletionRoutine parameter that will be called on completion. WSAIoctl will return a SOCKET_ERROR if it does not complete successfully or if the call would block. In the latter case, the application should simply wait for its event to be signaled or its callback routine to be invoked.

This section has provided a basic overview of GQoS, including ways for an application to interact with a QoS service provider via WinSock 2.

The next section will actually make use of GQoS in several short example programs.

Example Applications and GQoS Sample Code

Because the best presentation of any API should rightly include examples, this section will present three programs that demonstrate the use of GQoS and WinSock 2. The first two programs are a TCP client and a TCP server. The third is a UDP peer-to-peer-style application. Two peers can be used to send packets back and forth at a constant rate.

The following samples were created to run on the command line. The programs can be compiled using Microsoft Visual C++ 6.0, and all must be linked with ws2_32.lib for WinSock 2 support.

Simple QoS Test Topology

The applications that follow are not particularly useful other than to demonstrate QoS. To acutally demonstrate QoS via RSVP, one needs an RSVP-aware network. On the hosts, the applications should be run on a WinSock 2–ready system with an appropriate RSVP service provider. Windows 98 was the platform we used to run our applications. The test network minimally should have two RSVP-aware routers with low-bandwidth interfaces connecting them.

A simple topology for experimenting with the applications is shown in Figure 10.4, where two routers are connected together. To each of these routers a host is connected. These hosts will run the application samples across the one-link network. The key is to connect the two routers via a low-bandwidth link. The low-capacity link between the routers allows the effectiveness of reservations to be assessed. By adding a third host to the network as a traffic generator, the link can be driven to congestion. If the applications correctly protect their flows by issuing reservations, the effects of the traffic generator will be minimized.

The hosts can run either the TCP client-server programs or the UDP peer-to-peer programs. The data source such as the TCP server and the traffic generator should be connected to the same router. The traffic generator itself can run the UDP peer-to-peer program, sending to the destination host on the other router. A UDP program can be configured as a traffic generator by maximizing its data rate while not sending a

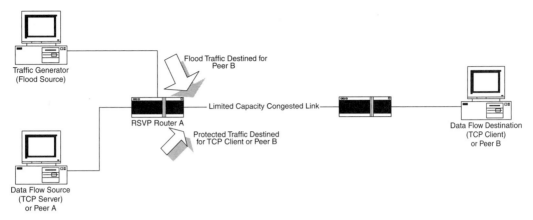

Figure 10.4 Simple network topology for testing QoS applications.

PATH or an RESV message for its traffic. If the UDP data rate is high enough, the low-bandwidth link will be forced into congestion, and something will have to give. These conditions are ideal for testing whether QoS is really being achieved.

The UDP peer-to-peer programs can also be used in this environment. Here, peer A is shown as the sending peer, while peer B is the destination peer. In reality, both peers can be senders and receivers. The only condition is that the generator's traffic cross paths with the source peer's traffic, or else QoS performance cannot be evaluated. The UDP traffic generator should also be sending to the appropriate peer (peer B), but not to the same data port used by the source (peer A). Having two sets of traffic destined for the same port will simply confuse the results.

TCP Client and Server Communication

TCP provides reliable, connection-oriented data communication over the Internet. Typically, TCP is used in the client-server model. Here, a server application sits passively and waits for clients to connect. By initiating the connection, the client is considered to be the active side of the connection. Nevertheless, in the real world, it is the server that is usually found downloading bulk data to its clients. The most familiar example of such client-server interaction is the World Wide Web, where an HTTP server sits and waits for clients, such as Web browsers, to connect. Once connected, the server will proceed to download HTML files, graphics, or other media content back to the client. Our TCP programs will simulate this kind of client-server bulk-data transfer. Additionally, these programs will attempt to trigger a WinSock 2 GQoS service provider to make a reservation on behalf of the data flow. Through this process, RSVP's interaction with TCP bulk-data transport can be evaluated.

TCP Server (Passive Sender)

We begin with the TCP server's code listing. The required include files for this project are as follows (note the definitions QOS that establish our program's defaults):

```
#include <process.h>
#include <winsock2.h>
#include <qos.h>
#include <qosname.h>
#include <stdlib.h>
#include <stdio.h>
#include <time.h>

#define SERVER_TCP_PORT     17293                   // Server's port number
#define MAX_PROTOCOLS       30                      // Maximum number of
                                                    // protocols
#define MAX_RECV_LEN        1024                     // Receive buffer
#define MAX_SEND_LEN        1024                     // Send buffer
#define WSA_WAIT_EVENT_1    WSA_WAIT_EVENT_0 + 1// Second wait event
// version of Winsock required
#define VERSION_MAJOR       2
#define VERSION_MINOR       0
```

Next is the listing for the callback function used by the main program. This function is called by WSAAccept once a new connection is attempted. The callback is used to set the QoS values for the connection supplied by the main program via the dwCallbackData parameter. The QoS parameters are simply copied into the lpSQOS pointer location. The function will then return CF_ACCEPT to accept the new connection.

```
int CALLBACK ConditionFunc( LPWSABUF lpCallerId, LPWSABUF lpCallerData,
                            LPQOS lpSQOS, LPQOS lpGQOS, LPWSABUF lpCalleeID,
                            LPWSABUF lpCalleeData, GROUP FAR * g,
                            DWORD dwCallbackData)
{
    LPFLOWSPEC              FlowSpec;      // Flowspec pointer

    fprintf(stdout,"In callback function\n");

    if(lpSQOS)
    {
        memcpy(lpSQOS,(void *)dwCallbackData,sizeof(QOS));
        FlowSpec = &lpSQOS->ReceivingFlowspec;

        fprintf(stdout,
                "Receiving QOS: TokenRate=%d, BDepth=%d, PeakRate=%d\n",
```

```
                FlowSpec->TokenRate,
                FlowSpec->TokenBucketSize,
                FlowSpec->PeakBandwidth);

        FlowSpec = &lpSQOS->SendingFlowspec;

        fprintf(stdout,
            "Sending QOS: TokenRate=%d, BDepth=%d, PeakRate=%d\n",
                FlowSpec->TokenRate,
                FlowSpec->TokenBucketSize,
                FlowSpec->PeakBandwidth);
    }

    return CF_ACCEPT;

}
```

The next listing is the main program. Its two input parameters represent the command-line arguments included by the user. The server will bring up a listing of command-line options if the user did not include any. Of course, we also have an extensive set of variables for this code snippet.

```
void main(int argc, char** argv)
{
    int                 i;
    int                 iRetVal, nErr;
    int                 numProtocols;
    unsigned long       eventVal;
    WSAPROTOCOL_INFO    ProtocolInfo[MAX_PROTOCOLS];
    WSAPROTOCOL_INFO    *qosProto;
    unsigned long       protocolInfoSize;
    SOCKET              listenS;
    SOCKET              acceptedS;
    int                 soutLen;
    struct              sockaddr_in sout;
    struct              sockaddr_in sin;
    int                 error;                  // Return value of WSAStartup
    WORD                versionRequested;       // Passed to WSAStartup
    WSADATA             wsaData;                // Receives data from
                                                // WSAStartup
    char*               argument;
    QOS                 QualityOfService;       // QOS structure, used by
                                                // WSAConnect
    QOS                 QualityOfService2;
    LPFLOWSPEC          FlowSpec;               // Flowspec pointer
    WSAEVENT            hEventObject[3];
    WSANETWORKEVENTS    events;
    BOOL                eventLoop;
    char                message[MAX_SEND_LEN];
    WSABUF              wsasendbuf;
```

```
unsigned long      bytesSent;
unsigned long      totalBytesSent;
WSAOVERLAPPED      overLapped;                 // Overlapped struct for
                                              // WSAIoctl

unsigned long      outSize;

int                duration=10;               // Default duration
time_t             currenttime, starttime;
unsigned long      buffersize=MAX_SEND_LEN;
// Flow Spec parameters
unsigned long      tokenrate=QOS_NOT_SPECIFIED;              // Bytes/sec
unsigned long      tokenbucketsize=QOS_NOT_SPECIFIED;        // Bytes
unsigned long      peakbandwidth=QOS_NOT_SPECIFIED;          // Bytes/sec
unsigned long      latency=QOS_NOT_SPECIFIED;                //
                                                            Microseconds
unsigned long      delayvariation=QOS_NOT_SPECIFIED;         //
                                                            Microseconds
SERVICETYPE        servicetype=SERVICETYPE_CONTROLLEDLOAD;
unsigned long      maxsdusize=QOS_NOT_SPECIFIED;             // Bytes
unsigned long      minimumpolicedsize=QOS_NOT_SPECIFIED;     // Bytes

if(argc < 2) // Need at least two arguments
{
    fprintf(stdout,"Usage: server D=duration \n");
    fprintf(stdout,
            "         B=buffer_size r=token_rate b=bucket_depth \n");
    fprintf(stdout,"      p=peak_rate m=min_policed_size \n");
    fprintf(stdout,"      M=max_packet_size\n");
    return;
}
```

The server requires at least one command-line argument. Acceptable arguments include values for the sending token rate, bucket size, and peak-rate traffic characterization parameters, as well as the minimum-policed size and maximum packet size. Buffer size specifies the size of the buffer used to send and not the actual packet size. Finally, the duration of the connection can be specified in seconds. The following loop simply collects the command-line arguments into their corresponding variables.

```
for(i=1; i<argc; i++)    // Get all argumented values
{
    argument = argv[i];
    if(strlen(argument) < 3)
        fprintf(stdout,"Error: Invalid Argument.\n");
    switch(argument[0])
    {
        case 'r':
            tokenrate=atol(&argument[2]);
            fprintf(stdout,"Token Rate is %d Bytes/Sec\n", tokenrate);
        break;
```

```
        case 'b':
            tokenbucketsize=atol(&argument[2]);
            fprintf(stdout,"Token Bucket Depth is %d Bytes\n",
                tokenbucketsize);
        break;
        case 'p':
            peakbandwidth=atol(&argument[2]);
            fprintf(stdout,"Peak Bandwidth is %d Bytes/Sec\n",
                peakbandwidth);
        break;
        case 'm':
            minimumpolicedsize=atol(&argument[2]);
            fprintf(stdout,"Minimum Policied Packet Size is %d Bytes\n",
                minimumpolicedsize);
        break;
        case 'M':
            maxsdusize=atol(&argument[2]);
            fprintf(stdout,"Maximum Packet Size is %d Bytes\n",
                maxsdusize);
        break;

        case 'D':
            duration=atol(&argument[2]);
            fprintf(stdout,"Duration is %d Seconds\n", duration);
        break;
        case 'B':
            buffersize=atol(&argument[2]);
            if(buffersize>MAX_SEND_LEN)
                buffersize=MAX_SEND_LEN;
            fprintf(stdout,"Buffersize is %d Bytes\n", buffersize);
        break;

        default:
            fprintf(stdout,"Error: Unknown Argument.\n");
            return;
        break;
    } // switch(aargument[0])
} // for(i=0; i<argc; i++)
```

Next, WinSock is initialized. Specifically, the version we are looking for is 2.0.

```
// Initialize the winsock library.
versionRequested = MAKEWORD(VERSION_MAJOR, VERSION_MINOR);
error = WSAStartup(versionRequested, &wsaData);
if (error)
{
    fprintf(stdout,"Old WinSock version.\n");
    return;
}
else
{
```

```
// Now confirm that the WinSock2 DLL supports the version
// reqired. If not, make sure to call WSACleanup().
if (LOBYTE(wsaData.wVersion) != VERSION_MAJOR ||
    HIBYTE(wsaData.wVersion) != VERSION_MINOR)
{
    fprintf(stdout,"Could not find the correct version of WinSock\n");
    WSACleanup();
    return;
}
}
```

This is not any ordinary sockets application, so we need to find the specific service provider that supports QoS (hopefully via RSVP). We do this by searching through all installed protocols looking for the Internet protocol suite's TCP protocol (IPPROTO_TCP) with support for QoS (XP1_QOS_SUPPORTED). The QoS flag should suggest RSVP support with respect to the TCP/IP protocol suite. We will print out the name of the corresponding service provider we find—if there is one.

```
// Enumerate available protocols looking for QoS support
protocolInfoSize=sizeof(WSAPROTOCOL_INFO)*MAX_PROTOCOLS;
numProtocols = WSAEnumProtocols(NULL, &ProtocolInfo[0], &protocolInfoSize);
if (numProtocols == SOCKET_ERROR)
{
    fprintf(stdout,"WSAEnumProtocols Failed (Error=%d).\n",
        WSAGetLastError());
    WSACleanup();
        return;
} // if
qosProto=NULL;
for(i=0;i<numProtocols;i++)
{
    if((ProtocolInfo[i].dwServiceFlags1&XP1_QOS_SUPPORTED)&&
       (!(ProtocolInfo[i].dwServiceFlags1&XP1_CONNECTIONLESS))&&
       (ProtocolInfo[i].iAddressFamily==AF_INET)&&
       (ProtocolInfo[i].iProtocol==IPPROTO_TCP))
    {
        // then we have found the protocol we are looking for
        qosProto=&ProtocolInfo[i];
        break;
    }
} // for

if (qosProto)
{
    fprintf(stdout,"Using QoS Protocol %s.\n", qosProto->szProtocol);
}
else
{
    fprintf(stdout,"Could not find connection oriented QoS protocol.\n");
```

```
    WSACleanup();
    return;
}
```

As this is a TCP server, we need to first create a socket on which we can listen for connection events. The socket is created from the service provider we just found. As most QoS service providers will receive asynchronous events, it is also necessary to set the overlapped IO flag.

```
// Open the socket
if((listenS = WSASocket(FROM_PROTOCOL_INFO, FROM_PROTOCOL_INFO,
    FROM_PROTOCOL_INFO, qosProto, 0, WSA_FLAG_OVERLAPPED)) ==
    INVALID_SOCKET)
{
    fprintf(stdout,"WSASocket(...) failed with error %d\n",
        WSAGetLastError());
    WSACleanup();
    return;
}
```

As this is a command-line program, we don't have a Windows message loop, we need to rely on events for asynchronous notification. Because the TCP server will have two sockets, a listening socket and an accepted socket, it will likewise require two events. The event is triggered on the listening socket whenever a connection is made. This event registration is handled via the WSAEventSelect call.

```
// Create two events
hEventObject[0] = WSACreateEvent();
hEventObject[1] = WSACreateEvent();
if ((hEventObject[0] == WSA_INVALID_EVENT) ||
    (hEventObject[1] == WSA_INVALID_EVENT))
{
    closesocket(listenS);
    fprintf(stdout,"WSACreateEvent(): failed with error %d.\n",
        WSAGetLastError());
    WSACleanup();
    return;
}

// Select appropriate events on the first socket
if(WSAEventSelect(listenS, hEventObject[0], FD_QOS|FD_ACCEPT|FD_CLOSE) ==
    SOCKET_ERROR)
{
    closesocket(listenS);
    fprintf(stdout,"WSAEventSelect(): failed with error %d.\n",
        WSAGetLastError());
    WSACleanup();
    return;
}
```

If all has gone well, it is time to bind the socket to a port. We will use the static SERVER_TCP_PORT just defined.

```
// Bind the socket to a port
sin.sin_family = AF_INET;
sin.sin_addr.s_addr = INADDR_ANY;
sin.sin_port = htons(SERVER_TCP_PORT);
if (bind(listenS,(LPSOCKADDR) &sin,sizeof(sin)) == SOCKET_ERROR)
{
    nErr = WSAGetLastError();
    fprintf(stdout,"bind(): failed with error %d\n", nErr);
    closesocket(listenS);
    WSACleanup();
    return;
}
```

Now that the socket has been properly initialized it is time to listen for clients. The listen call will prepare the socket such that it is notified of any connection attempts.

```
// Listen for clients attempting to connect:
if(listen( listenS, SOMAXCONN) == SOCKET_ERROR)
{
    nErr = WSAGetLastError();
    fprintf(stdout,"listen(): failed with error %d\n", nErr);
    closesocket(listenS);
    WSACleanup();
    return;

}
fprintf(stdout,"Did listen\n");
```

Following is the main event loop. The program will remain in the event loop indefinitely, waiting for connections to be made. Both the listen socket and the accepted socket are watched for events. The switch statement is used to determine which event object was signaled. This can be either the listening socket's event object or the accepted socket's event object. Once the corresponding event object has been ascertained, WSAEnumNetworkEvents is used to determine exactly what network condition has transpired.

```
bytesSent=totalBytesSent=0;
acceptedS=NULL;
eventLoop=TRUE;
while(eventLoop)
{
    eventVal=WSAWaitForMultipleEvents( 2,
        (const WSAEVENT FAR * )hEventObject, FALSE, WSA_INFINITE, FALSE);
```

```
switch(eventVal)
{
    case WSA_WAIT_TIMEOUT:

    break;
    case WSA_WAIT_EVENT_0:

        fprintf(stdout,"Event was triggered for socket listenS\n");
        iRetVal = WSAEnumNetworkEvents(listenS, hEventObject[0],
            &events);
        fprintf(stdout,"EnumNetworkEvents returned %x on socket\n",
            events.lNetworkEvents);

        if (iRetVal == SOCKET_ERROR)
        {
            fprintf(stdout,"WSAEnumNetworkEvents FAILED\n");
            return;
        }
        // ACCEPT Event
        if ((events.lNetworkEvents & FD_ACCEPT))
        {
            fprintf(stdout,"ACCEPT event\n");

            if (acceptedS)
            {
                fprintf(stdout,"Only one connection at a time.\n");
                continue;
            }
            if (events.iErrorCode[FD_ACCEPT_BIT] == WSAENETDOWN)
            {
                fprintf(stdout,"ACCEPT WSAENETDOWN\n");
                return;
            }

            // Accept the client
```

Now that it has been determined to be the accept event, it is necessary to set up the QoS structure with the user-defined values given via the command-line arguments. As the server is also the data sender, the sending FlowSpec field of the QoS structure should be set. These values correspond to the data carried in the PATH message's Tspec object. The receiving FlowSpec fields can also be set such that the reverse direction can be reserved for TCP acknowledgments. Note that only a small fraction of the sending traffic rate need be reserved in the reverse path because the client is not actively sending data.

```
// Set up quality of service info.
// No provider specific info.
QualityOfService.ProviderSpecific.len = 0;
```

```
QualityOfService.ProviderSpecific.buf = NULL;
FlowSpec = &QualityOfService.SendingFlowspec;
FlowSpec->TokenRate = tokenrate;
FlowSpec->TokenBucketSize = tokenbucketsize;
FlowSpec->PeakBandwidth = peakbandwidth;
FlowSpec->Latency = latency;
FlowSpec->DelayVariation = delayvariation;
FlowSpec->ServiceType = servicetype;
FlowSpec->MaxSduSize = maxsdusize;
FlowSpec->MinimumPolicedSize = minimumpolicedsize;

FlowSpec = &QualityOfService.ReceivingFlowspec;
FlowSpec->TokenRate = tokenrate/2;
FlowSpec->TokenBucketSize = tokenbucketsize/2;
FlowSpec->PeakBandwidth = peakbandwidth/2;
FlowSpec->Latency = QOS_NOT_SPECIFIED;
FlowSpec->DelayVariation = QOS_NOT_SPECIFIED;
FlowSpec->ServiceType = servicetype;
FlowSpec->MaxSduSize = maxsdusize/2;
FlowSpec->MinimumPolicedSize = minimumpolicedsize;
```

The WSAAccept function does not actually take the QoS information as a parameter. Rather it is the responsibility of the callback function to set the QoS for the accepted socket. The QoS structure provided as the last parameter is passed directly to the ConditionFunc callback routine defined at the beginning of the program. We will also select the appropriate events for the socket once it is accepted.

```
soutLen=sizeof(sout);
if((acceptedS = WSAAccept(listenS, (sockaddr *)&sout,
    &soutLen, ConditionFunc,
    (unsigned long) &QualityOfService)) == INVALID_SOCKET)
{
    nErr = WSAGetLastError();
    fprintf(stdout,"WSAAccept(): failed with error %d\n",
        nErr);
    closesocket(acceptedS);
    WSACleanup();
    return;
}
else
{
    fprintf(stdout,"WSAAccept(): Accepted socket for %s\n",
        inet_ntoa(sout.sin_addr));
}
// Select appropriate events
if(WSAEventSelect(acceptedS, hEventObject[1],
    FD_QOS|FD_WRITE|FD_CLOSE ) == SOCKET_ERROR)
{
    fprintf(stdout,
        "WSAEventSelect(): failed with error %d.\n",
```

```
            WSAGetLastError());
        closesocket(acceptedS);
        acceptedS=NULL;
    }

    time(&starttime); // Get the starting time
```

Alternatively, the QoS information can be set on the accepted socket at any time by using the WSAIoctl SIO_SET_QOS call.

```
// Set the QoS
overLapped.hEvent=hEventObject[1]; // Associate with event
outSize=0;
if(WSAIoctl(acceptedS, SIO_SET_QOS,
    (LPVOID) &QualityOfService,
    sizeof(QualityOfService),
    NULL, 0, &outSize, &overLapped, NULL) == SOCKET_ERROR)
{
    fprintf(stdout,"WSAIoctl(): failed with error %d.\n",
        WSAGetLastError());
    closesocket(acceptedS);
    acceptedS=NULL;
}

}
break; // case WSA_WAIT_EVENT_0
```

Once a connection has been accepted, the second event object will be triggered on events for the accepted socket.

```
case WSA_WAIT_EVENT_1:
    fprintf(stdout,"Event was triggered for socket acceptedS\n");

    if(!acceptedS)
        continue;

    iRetVal = WSAEnumNetworkEvents(acceptedS, hEventObject[1],
        &events);
    fprintf(stdout,"EnumNetworkEvents returned %x on socket\n",
        events.lNetworkEvents);

    if (iRetVal == SOCKET_ERROR)
    {
        fprintf(stdout,"WSAEnumNetworkEvents FAILED\n");
        return;
    }
```

The QoS event will be triggered by receipt of a new or modified PATH or RESV message from the client. The application will be notified of changes in the current QoS via this event. WSAIoctl SIO_GET_QOS can then be used to retrieve the updated QoS information. Note that the loop is used to collect all the QoS structures that may be available.

```
// Check for QOS Event
if (events.lNetworkEvents & FD_QOS)
{
    fprintf(stdout,"QoS event\n");
    overLapped.hEvent=hEventObject[1]; // Associate with event

    while(WSAIoctl(acceptedS, SIO_GET_QOS,
        NULL, 0, (LPVOID) &QualityOfService2,
        sizeof(QualityOfService2),
        &outSize, NULL, NULL) != SOCKET_ERROR)
    {
        FlowSpec = &QualityOfService2.ReceivingFlowspec;

        fprintf(stdout,
            "Receiving QOS: TknRate=%d, BDepth=%d, PeakR=%d\n",
            FlowSpec->TokenRate,
            FlowSpec->TokenBucketSize,
            FlowSpec->PeakBandwidth);

        FlowSpec = &QualityOfService2.SendingFlowspec;

        fprintf(stdout,
            "Sending QOS: TknRate=%d, BDepth=%d, PeakR=%d\n",
            FlowSpec->TokenRate,
            FlowSpec->TokenBucketSize,
            FlowSpec->PeakBandwidth);

    }
    fprintf(stdout, "WSAIoctl(GETQOS) failed with error %d.\n",
        WSAGetLastError());

    WSASetEvent(hEventObject[1]); // Fire event again for write
}
```

Write events are used to notify the application that the socket is available for writing. We trigger this event such that the server can send as fast as TCP allows. This sort of bulk-rate transfer is typical of TCP applications.

```
// Check for WRITE Event
if ((events.lNetworkEvents & FD_WRITE)||
    (events.lNetworkEvents == 0))
{
    fprintf(stdout,"Write event\n");

    if(acceptedS)
    {
        time(&currenttime);
        if(currenttime>=starttime+duration)
        {
            closesocket(acceptedS);
            acceptedS=NULL;
            fprintf(stdout,"Time Is Up!\n");
            continue;
        }
```

```
            fprintf(stdout,"Sent %d bytes since last WSASend.\n",
                bytesSent);
            totalBytesSent+=bytesSent;

            overLapped.hEvent=hEventObject[1];
            wsasendbuf.len=buffersize;
            wsasendbuf.buf=message;
            if(WSASend ( acceptedS, &wsasendbuf, 1, &bytesSent, 0,
                &overLapped,NULL)==SOCKET_ERROR)
            {
                fprintf(stdout,"WSASend(): failed, error %d.\n",
                    WSAGetLastError());
            }
            else
            {
                totalBytesSent+=bytesSent;
                fprintf(stdout,"Sent %d bytes to client.\n",
                    bytesSent);
            }

        }
    }
    // Check for CLOSE Event
    if (events.lNetworkEvents & FD_CLOSE)
    {
        fprintf(stdout,"CLOSE event\n");
        closesocket(acceptedS);
        acceptedS=NULL;

    }

    break; // case WSA_WAIT_EVENT_1

    default:

    break;
    }
  }
}
```

And that's it. The server application will send as fast as it can over the accepted socket for the duration specified by the user. The server will then continue to run, waiting for additional clients to connect so that the process may be repeated.

TCP Client (Active Receiver)

Next we examine the TCP client. This client application takes the server's IP address as a parameter. Based on this address, the client will connect to the server. The client also takes command-line arguments used for issuing a reservation for the server's traffic. These parameters correspond to the server's traffic characteristic parameters and are expressed in terms of the token bucket. Once the client connects to a server, it should begin to receive the bulk data that the server provides under the QoS constraints specified by the user.

Note that these programs post information to standard output (stdout). This allows the user to collect the screen output in a log file. The client program will post the time, in milliseconds, that each packet arrived. This time stamp can be used to plot the performance of the network over a period of time. The log file can collect all the relevant packet-arrival timing information from this mechanism.

The TCP client program looks quite similar to the TCP server. Our listing begins with the necessary include files and definitions. Again, the main program specifies a plethora of relevant variables for our program:

```c
#include <process.h>
#include <winsock2.h>
#include <qos.h>
#include <qosname.h>
#include <stdlib.h>
#include <stdio.h>
#include <time.h>

#define SERVER_TCP_PORT    17293     // Server's port number
#define MAX_PROTOCOLS      30        // Maximum number of protocols
#define MAX_RECV_LEN       1024      // Receive buffer
// version of Winsock required
#define VERSION_MAJOR      2
#define VERSION_MINOR      0

void main(int argc, char** argv)
{
    int                 i;
    int                 iRetVal, nErr;
    int                 numProtocols;
    unsigned long       eventVal;
    WSAPROTOCOL_INFO    ProtocolInfo[MAX_PROTOCOLS];
    WSAPROTOCOL_INFO    *qosProto;
    unsigned long       protocolInfoSize;
    SOCKET              s;
    struct              sockaddr_in sout;
    struct              sockaddr_in sin;
    unsigned long       laddr;
    PHOSTENT            pHostEntry;
    int                 error;                // Return value
    WORD                versionRequested;     // Passed to WSAStartup
    WSADATA             wsaData;              // Receives data from WSAStartup
```

```
char*                    argument;
QOS                      QualityOfService;    // QOS structure, used by
                                              // WSAConnect

QOS                      QualityOfService2;
LPFLOWSPEC               FlowSpec;            // Flowspec pointer
WSAEVENT                 hEventObject;
WSANETWORKEVENTS         events;
BOOL                     eventLoop;
BYTE                     message[MAX_RECV_LEN];
int                      bytesRecvd;
unsigned long            totalbytes=0;
unsigned long            buffersize=MAX_RECV_LEN;
WSAOVERLAPPED            overLapped;              // Overlapped struct for
                                                 // WSAIoctl

unsigned long            outSize;

double                   fstarttime, fendtime, fbytespersecond;
clock_t                  startclock, curclock;

// Flow Spec parameters
unsigned long            tokenrate=QOS_NOT_SPECIFIED; // Bytes/sec
unsigned long            tokenbucketsize=QOS_NOT_SPECIFIED; // Bytes
unsigned long            peakbandwidth=QOS_NOT_SPECIFIED; // Bytes/sec
unsigned long            latency=QOS_NOT_SPECIFIED; // Microseconds
unsigned long            delayvariation=QOS_NOT_SPECIFIED; // Microseconds
SERVICETYPE              servicetype=SERVICETYPE_CONTROLLEDLOAD;
unsigned long            maxsdusize=QOS_NOT_SPECIFIED; // Bytes
unsigned long            minimumpolicedsize=QOS_NOT_SPECIFIED; // Bytes

if(argc < 2) // Need at least two arguments
{
    fprintf(stdout,"Usage: client a=server_address r=token_rate \n");
    fprintf(stdout,"       b=bucket_depth p=peak_rate \n");
    fprintf(stdout,"       m=min_policed_size M=max_packet_size\n");
    fprintf(stdout,"       B=buffer_size \n" );
    return;
}
```

Like the server, the client requires at least one command-line argument. This argument should be the server's IP Address. Other acceptable arguments include values for the reserving token rate, bucket size, and peak-rate QoS parameters, as well as the minimum-policed size and maximum packet size. The buffer size is used to specify the size of the buffer used to receive the data stream. The following loop simply collects the command-line arguments into their corresponding variables.

```
for(i=1; i<argc; i++)  // Get all argument values
{
    argument = argv[i];
```

```
if(strlen(argument) < 3)
    fprintf(stdout,"Error: Invalid Argument.\n");
switch(argument[0])
{
    case 'a': // Server's address
        sout.sin_family = AF_INET;
        if((laddr = inet_addr(&argument[2])) == INADDR_NONE)
        {
            pHostEntry = gethostbyname(&argument[2]);
            if (pHostEntry == NULL) {
                fprintf(stdout,
                    "Error: Server name %s is unknown.\n",
                    &argument[2]);
                return;
            }
            else
                memcpy(&laddr, pHostEntry->h_addr, 4);
        }
        sout.sin_addr.s_addr = laddr;
        sout.sin_port = htons(SERVER_TCP_PORT);
    break;
    case 'r':
        tokenrate=atol(&argument[2]);
        fprintf(stdout,"Token Rate is %d\n", tokenrate);
    break;
    case 'b':
        tokenbucketsize=atol(&argument[2]);
        fprintf(stdout,"Token Bucket Depth is %d\n",
            tokenbucketsize);
    break;
    case 'p':
        peakbandwidth=atol(&argument[2]);
        fprintf(stdout,"Peak Bandwidth is %d\n", peakbandwidth);
    break;
    case 'm':
        minimumpolicedsize=atol(&argument[2]);
        fprintf(stdout,"Minimum Policed Packet Size is %d\n",
            minimumpolicedsize);
    break;
    case 'M':
        maxsdusize=atol(&argument[2]);
        fprintf(stdout,"Maximum Packet Size is %d\n", maxsdusize);
    break;

    case 'B':
        buffersize=atol(&argument[2]);
        if(buffersize>MAX_RECV_LEN)
            buffersize=MAX_RECV_LEN;
        fprintf(stdout,"Receiving Buffer Size is %d\n",
            buffersize);
    break;
```

```
                default:
                    fprintf(stdout,"Error: Unknown Argument.\n");
                    return;
                break;
        } // switch(aargument[0])
    } // for(i=0; i<argc; i++)
```

The client has the same requirements as the server for WinSock 2. By the same process specified in the first sample we will find the appropriate service provider for both TCP and QoS.

```
// Initialize the winsock library.
versionRequested = MAKEWORD(VERSION_MAJOR, VERSION_MINOR);
error = WSAStartup(versionRequested, &wsaData);
if (error)
{
    fprintf(stdout,"Old WinSock version.\n");
    return;
}
else
{
    // Now confirm that the WinSock2 DLL supports the version
    // reqired. If not, make sure to call WSACleanup().
    if ((LOBYTE(wsaData.wVersion) != VERSION_MAJOR) ||
        (HIBYTE(wsaData.wVersion) != VERSION_MINOR))
    {
        fprintf(stdout,
            "Could not find the correct version of WinSock\n");
        WSACleanup();
        return;
    }
}

// Enumerate available protocols looking for QoS support
protocolInfoSize=sizeof(WSAPROTOCOL_INFO)*MAX_PROTOCOLS;
numProtocols = WSAEnumProtocols(NULL, &ProtocolInfo[0],
    &protocolInfoSize);
if (numProtocols == SOCKET_ERROR)
{
    fprintf(stdout,"WSAEnumProtocols Failed (Error=%d).\n",
        WSAGetLastError());
    WSACleanup();
        return;
} // if
qosProto=NULL;
for(i=0;i<numProtocols;i++)
{
    if((ProtocolInfo[i].dwServiceFlags1&XP1_QOS_SUPPORTED)&&
        (!(ProtocolInfo[i].dwServiceFlags1&XP1_CONNECTIONLESS))&&
        (ProtocolInfo[i].iAddressFamily==AF_INET)&&
        (ProtocolInfo[i].iProtocol==IPPROTO_TCP))
```

```
        {
            // ... Then we have found the protocol we are looking for
            qosProto=&ProtocolInfo[i];
            break;
        }
    } // for

    if (qosProto)
    {
        fprintf(stdout,"Using QoS Protocol %s.\n", qosProto->szProtocol);
    }
    else
    {
        fprintf(stdout,
            "Could not find connection oriented QoS protocol.\n");
        WSACleanup();
        return;
    }
```

Once a usable service provider is located, we will create a socket from it. The client program requires only one socket that is connected to the server and then simply reads data. One socket implies we require only one event object as well. The event object should register for the appropriate events, namely the QoS, Connect, Read, and Close events.

```
// Open the socket
if((s = WSASocket(FROM_PROTOCOL_INFO, FROM_PROTOCOL_INFO,
    FROM_PROTOCOL_INFO, qosProto, 0, WSA_FLAG_OVERLAPPED)) ==
    INVALID_SOCKET)
{
    fprintf(stdout,"WSASocket(...) failed with error %d.\n",
        WSAGetLastError());
    WSACleanup();
    return;
}

// Create an event
hEventObject = WSACreateEvent();
if (hEventObject == WSA_INVALID_EVENT)
{
    closesocket(s);
    fprintf(stdout,"WSACreateEvent(): failed with error %d.\n",
        WSAGetLastError());
    WSACleanup();
    return;
}

// Select appropriate events
if(WSAEventSelect
    (s, hEventObject, FD_QOS|FD_CONNECT|FD_READ|FD_CLOSE) ==
    SOCKET_ERROR)
{
```

```
        fprintf(stdout,"WSAEventSelect(): failed with error %d.\n",
            WSAGetLastError());
        return;
    }
```

Again, the client program must bind to a port. In this case we have no requirements for the port since this is the active connecting program. Any available port number will do.

```
    // Bind the socket to a port
    sin.sin_family = AF_INET;
    sin.sin_addr.s_addr = INADDR_ANY;
    sin.sin_port = 0;

    if (bind(s,(LPSOCKADDR) &sin,sizeof(sin)) == SOCKET_ERROR)
    {
        nErr = WSAGetLastError();
        fprintf(stdout,"bind(): failed with error %d\n", nErr);
        closesocket(s);
        WSACleanup();
        return;
    }
```

The next step for the TCP client is to actually connect to the server. As noted before, the WSAConnect call accepts a QoS structure. Thus, we can simply provide the user-specified QoS parameters at connect time. As this is a TCP socket, we will also provide sender information for the reverse direction such that the TCP acknowledgments sent by the client can receive protection as well. Note that the reverse direction comprises only a fraction of the server's sending rate.

```
    // Connect to the server

    // Set up quality of service info.
    // No provider specific info.
    QualityOfService.ProviderSpecific.len = 0;
    QualityOfService.ProviderSpecific.buf = NULL;

    FlowSpec = &QualityOfService.ReceivingFlowspec;
    FlowSpec->TokenRate = tokenrate;
    FlowSpec->TokenBucketSize = tokenbucketsize;
    FlowSpec->PeakBandwidth = peakbandwidth;
    FlowSpec->Latency = latency;
    FlowSpec->DelayVariation = delayvariation;
    FlowSpec->ServiceType = servicetype;
    FlowSpec->MaxSduSize = maxsdusize;
    FlowSpec->MinimumPolicedSize = minimumpolicedsize;

    FlowSpec = &QualityOfService.SendingFlowspec;
    FlowSpec->TokenRate = tokenrate/2;
    FlowSpec->TokenBucketSize = tokenbucketsize/2;
```

```
FlowSpec->PeakBandwidth = peakbandwidth/2;
FlowSpec->Latency = QOS_NOT_SPECIFIED;
FlowSpec->DelayVariation = QOS_NOT_SPECIFIED;
FlowSpec->ServiceType = servicetype;
FlowSpec->MaxSduSize = maxsdusize/2;
FlowSpec->MinimumPolicedSize = minimumpolicedsize;

if((iRetVal = WSAConnect(s, (sockaddr *)&sout, sizeof(sout),
    NULL, NULL, &QualityOfService, NULL)) ==
    SOCKET_ERROR)
{
    nErr = WSAGetLastError();
    if(nErr!=WSAEWOULDBLOCK)
    {
        fprintf(stdout,"WSAConnect(): failed with error %d\n", nErr);
        closesocket(s);
        WSACleanup();
        return;
    }
}
```

The client's event loop watches for Connect events, QoS events, and
Read events. The Connect event will be triggered when the client successfully connects to its server. The QoS event will signal that a Path or
Resv message has been received. The Read events are triggered whenever there is data ready to be read. Each time data is successfully
retrieved, a message will be printed to the standard output, specifying
the time in milliseconds. Finally, the Close event will signal that the
server has closed its connection after the duration has expired.

```
eventLoop=TRUE;
while(eventLoop)
{
    eventVal=WSAWaitForMultipleEvents( 1,
        (const WSAEVENT FAR * )&hEventObject, FALSE, WSA_INFINITE,
        FALSE);

    switch(eventVal)
    {
    case WSA_WAIT_TIMEOUT:
        fprintf(stdout,"Event timedout.\n");
        break;

    case WSA_WAIT_EVENT_0:

        fprintf(stdout,"Event was triggered\n");
        iRetVal = WSAEnumNetworkEvents(s, hEventObject, &events);
        fprintf(stdout,"EnumNetworkEvents returned %x on socket\n",
            events.lNetworkEvents);

        if (iRetVal == SOCKET_ERROR)
```

```
{
    fprintf(stdout,"WSAEnumNetworkEvents FAILED\n");
    return;
}

// Check for CONNECT event
if (events.lNetworkEvents & FD_CONNECT)
{
    fprintf(stdout,"Connected to Server\n");

    // Start the timer
    startclock=clock();

}
// Check for QoS event
if (events.lNetworkEvents & FD_QOS)
{
    fprintf(stdout,"QOS event\n");

    // Get the QoS
    overLapped.hEvent=hEventObject; // Associate with event

    while(WSAIoctl(s, SIO_GET_QOS,
        NULL, 0, (LPVOID) &QualityOfService2,
        sizeof(QualityOfService2),
        &outSize, NULL, NULL) != SOCKET_ERROR)
    {
        FlowSpec = &QualityOfService2.ReceivingFlowspec;
        fprintf(stdout,
            "ReceivingQOS:TknRate=%d,BDepth=%d,PeakR=%d\n",
            FlowSpec->TokenRate,
            FlowSpec->TokenBucketSize,
            FlowSpec->PeakBandwidth);

        FlowSpec = &QualityOfService2.SendingFlowspec;

        fprintf(stdout,
            "SendingQOS:TknRate=%d,BDepth=%d,PeakR=%d\n",
            FlowSpec->TokenRate,
            FlowSpec->TokenBucketSize,
            FlowSpec->PeakBandwidth);
    }
    fprintf(stdout,
        "WSAIoctl(GETQOS) failed with error %d.\n",
        WSAGetLastError());

}
// Check for READ event
if (events.lNetworkEvents & FD_READ)
{
    fprintf(stdout,"READ event\n");

    if (events.iErrorCode[FD_READ_BIT] == WSAENETDOWN)
    {
```

```
                    fprintf(stdout,"READ WSAENETDOWN\n");
                    return;
                }
                bytesRecvd = recv(s, (char *)message, buffersize, 0);
                if (bytesRecvd != SOCKET_ERROR)
                {
                    // Note current time.
                    curclock=clock();
                    fprintf(stdout,"Received %d bytes at time %d.\n",
                        bytesRecvd,curclock);
                }
                // Total number of bytes received.
                totalbytes+=bytesRecvd;
            }
            // Check for CLOSE event
            if (events.lNetworkEvents & FD_CLOSE)
            {
                fprintf(stdout,"CLOSE event\n");

                // Millisecond resolution duration calculation
                fstarttime=(startclock);
                fendtime=(curclock);

                fbytespersecond=(totalbytes/(fendtime-fstarttime))*
                    CLOCKS_PER_SEC;

                fprintf(stdout,"Received %f Bytes/Sec\n",
                    fbytespersecond);
                closesocket(s);
                return;
            }

        break; // case WSA_WAIT_EVENT_0

        default:

            fprintf(stdout,"Unknown event\n");

        break;

    } // switch(eventVal)
  } // while(eventLoop)

}
```

And that completes the TCP client code walk-through. The average observed data rate will be printed for the session before the client exists due to a Close event.

UDP Peer-to-Peer Communication

TCP is valuable for a wide range of applications that require reliable data transport. Nevertheless, many real-time multimedia applications don't require reliability. Instead, they require timeliness of their data transport. For such applications, never getting a piece of data is just as good as getting the data late. Protocols layered on top of UDP present a better alternative for these kinds of applications. UDP provides connectionless, packet-by-packet delivery of data. It also works for multicast as well as unicast data transfer.

Given UDP's uses, we have also provided a simple program for peer-to-peer UDP communication. This sample can be used to simulate real multimedia applications running over the Internet. Two peers simply run the program simultaneously and use it to send traffic to one another.

The UDP program is designed to communicate with a single peer running on another host. Two hosts simultaneously run the program and select each other to be their peers. The programs will then send packets at a constant rate to one another across the network for some duration. The results of the sending and receiving packet arrival times will be recorded to the standard output.

Like the TCP programs, the UDP program accepts a number of command-line arguments. These can be used to specify port information, the peer's IP address, data rates, and traffic-characterization parameters. Instead of sending at the fastest rate possible, the user can specify a sending rate at which the program will send its data.

What follows is the listing for the UDP peer program. We begin as before with the necessary include files and definitions for the default parameters. (*Note:* The local port and peer port numbers can be the same if running on separate systems.)

```
#include <process.h>
#include <winsock2.h>
#include <qos.h>
#include <qosname.h>
#include <stdlib.h>
#include <stdio.h>
#include <time.h>

#define THIS_UDP_PORT       17294    // This host's default port number
#define PEER_UDP_PORT       17295    // Peer's default port number
#define MAX_PROTOCOLS       30       // Maximum number of protocols
#define MAX_PACKET_LEN      512      // Receive buffer
// version of Winsock required
#define VERSION_MAJOR       2
#define VERSION_MINOR       0
```

```
void main(int argc, char** argv)
{
    int                     i;
    int                     iRetVal, nErr;
    int                     numProtocols;
    unsigned long           eventVal;
    WSAPROTOCOL_INFO        ProtocolInfo[MAX_PROTOCOLS];
    WSAPROTOCOL_INFO *      qosProto;
    unsigned long           protocolInfoSize;
    SOCKET                  s;
    struct sockaddr_in      sout;
    struct sockaddr_in      sin;
    struct sockaddr_in      srecv;
    char                    thisHostName[256];
    int                     srecvlen;
    unsigned long           laddr;
    PHOSTENT                pHostEntry;
    int                     error;              // Return value of WSAStartup
    WORD                    versionRequested;   // passed to WSAStartup
    WSADATA                 wsaData;            // Receives data from
                                                // WSAStartup

    char*                   argument;
    QOS                     QualityOfService;   // QOS structure
    QOS                     QualityOfService2;
    LPFLOWSPEC              FlowSpec;           // Flowspec pointer
    WSAEVENT                hEventObject;
    WSANETWORKEVENTS        events;
    BOOL                    eventLoop;
    char                    packetbuf[MAX_PACKET_LEN];
    char                    recvpacketbuf[MAX_PACKET_LEN];
    int                     bytesRecvd;
    unsigned long           bytessent;
    unsigned long           totalbytes=0;
    unsigned long           packetbufsize=MAX_PACKET_LEN;
    unsigned long           recvpacketsize=MAX_PACKET_LEN;
    WSAOVERLAPPED           overLapped;         // Overlapped struct for
                                                // WSAIoctl
    unsigned long           outSize;
    unsigned long           totalBytesSent=0;
    unsigned short          peerport=PEER_UDP_PORT;
    unsigned short          thisport=THIS_UDP_PORT;
    WSABUF                  wsasendbuf;
    DWORD                   recvflags=0;

    double                  fstarttime, fendtime, fbytespersecond;
    clock_t                 thisclock, lastsendclock, startclock, recvclock;
    int                     thisinterval, nextinterval;

    int                     interval=0;         // Wakeup interval
    int                     duration=10;        // 10 second duration
    unsigned long           datarate=1000;      // Data rate in bytes/second
```

```
time_t                   currenttime, starttime;

// Flow Spec parameters
unsigned long        tokenrate=QOS_NOT_SPECIFIED; // Bytes/ sec
unsigned long        tokenbucketsize=QOS_NOT_SPECIFIED; // Bytes
unsigned long        peakbandwidth=QOS_NOT_SPECIFIED; // Bytes/ sec
unsigned long        latency=QOS_NOT_SPECIFIED; // Micro-seconds
unsigned long        delayvariation=QOS_NOT_SPECIFIED; // Micro-seconds
SERVICETYPE          servicetype=SERVICETYPE_CONTROLLEDLOAD;
unsigned long        maxsdusize=QOS_NOT_SPECIFIED; // Bytes
unsigned long        minimumpolicedsize=QOS_NOT_SPECIFIED; // Bytes

if(argc < 2) // Need at least two arguments
{
    fprintf(stdout,"Usage: client a=peer_address r=token_rate \n");
    fprintf(stdout,"          b=bucket_depth p=peak_rate \n");
    fprintf(stdout,"          m=min_policed_size \n");
    fprintf(stdout,"          M=max_packet_size B=buffer_size\n" );
    fprintf(stdout,"          R=send_data_rate D=duration \n");
    fprintf(stdout,"          P=peer_port T=this_port\n" );
    return;
}
```

The UDP peer program takes a considerably longer list of possible parameters. One required parameter is the IP address of the remote peer.
The traffic-description parameters are the same as in the previous programs, only they now apply to both the sending and receiving directions. The buffer-size parameter specifies the data portion of the UDP
packets. The program's sending data rate can be specified as an argument. This is the rate at which the application will actually send data in
buffer-sized chunks. The duration parameter specifies how long the
application will actually send data before it quits. Finally, the two port
parameters can be used to specify the local port and the remote peer's
port at runtime.

```
for(i=1; i<argc; i++)    // Get all argumented values
{
    argument = argv[i];
    if(strlen(argument) < 3)
        fprintf(stdout,"Error: Invalid Argument.\n");
    switch(argument[0])
    {
        case 'a':            // Server's address
            sout.sin_family = AF_INET;
            if((laddr = inet_addr(&argument[2])) == INADDR_NONE)
            {
                pHostEntry = gethostbyname(&argument[2]);
                if (pHostEntry == NULL) {
```

```
                fprintf(stdout,
                    "Error: Remote address %s is unknown.\n",
                    &argument[2]);
                return;
            }
            else
                memcpy(&laddr, pHostEntry->h_addr, 4);
        }
        sout.sin_addr.s_addr = laddr;
        sout.sin_port = htons(peerport);
    break;
    case 'r':
        tokenrate=atol(&argument[2]);
        fprintf(stdout,"Token Rate is %d\n", tokenrate);
    break;
    case 'b':
        tokenbucketsize=atol(&argument[2]);
        fprintf(stdout,"Token Bucket Depth is %d\n",
            tokenbucketsize);
    break;
    case 'p':
        peakbandwidth=atol(&argument[2]);
        fprintf(stdout,"Peak Bandwidth is %d\n", peakbandwidth);
    break;
    case 'm':
        minimumpolicedsize=atol(&argument[2]);
        fprintf(stdout,"Minimum Policied Packet Size is %d\n",
            minimumpolicedsize);
    break;
    case 'M':
        maxsdusize=atol(&argument[2]);
        fprintf(stdout,"Maximum Packet Size is %d\n", maxsdusize);
    break;

    case 'R':
        datarate=atol(&argument[2]);
        fprintf(stdout,"Application Data Rate is %d Bytes/Sec\n",
            datarate);
    break;
    case 'D':
        duration=atol(&argument[2]);
        fprintf(stdout,"Duration is %d Seconds\n", duration);
    break;
    case 'B':
        packetbufsize=atol(&argument[2]);
        if(packetbufsize>MAX_PACKET_LEN)
            packetbufsize=MAX_PACKET_LEN;
        if(packetbufsize<sizeof(clock_t) )
            packetbufsize=sizeof(clock_t);
        recvpacketsize=packetbufsize;
```

```
                    fprintf(stdout,"Packet Buffer Size is %d\n",
                        packetbufsize);
                break;
                case 'P':
                    peerport=(unsigned short)atoi(&argument[2]);
                    sout.sin_port = htons(peerport);
                    fprintf(stdout,"Peer's Port is %d\n",peerport);
                break;
                case 'T':
                    thisport=(unsigned short)atoi(&argument[2]);
                    fprintf(stdout,"This host's Port is %d\n",thisport);
                break;
                default:
                    fprintf(stdout,"Error: Unknown Argument.\n");
                    return;
                break;
        } // switch(aargument[0])
    } // for(i=0; i<argc; i++)

    // Initialize the winsock library.
    versionRequested = MAKEWORD(VERSION_MAJOR, VERSION_MINOR);
    error = WSAStartup(versionRequested, &wsaData);
    if (error)
    {
        fprintf(stdout,"Old WinSock version.\n");
        return;
    }
    else
    {
        // Confirm that the WinSock2 DLL supports the version
        // reqired. If not, make sure to call WSACleanup().
        if (LOBYTE(wsaData.wVersion) != VERSION_MAJOR ||
            HIBYTE(wsaData.wVersion) != VERSION_MINOR)
        {
            fprintf(stdout,
                "Could not find the correct version of WinSock\n");
            WSACleanup();
            return;
        }
    }
```

Once WinSock is successfully initialized, we begin the process of searching though the service providers. Our application is specifically interested in UDP support with QoS. Remember that UDP is connectionless.

```
    // Enumerate available protocols looking for QoS support
    protocolInfoSize=sizeof(WSAPROTOCOL_INFO)*MAX_PROTOCOLS;
    numProtocols = WSAEnumProtocols(NULL, &ProtocolInfo[0],
        &protocolInfoSize);
```

```
if (numProtocols == SOCKET_ERROR)
{
    fprintf(stdout,"WSAEnumProtocols Failed (Error=%d).\n",
        WSAGetLastError());
    WSACleanup();
        return;
} // if
qosProto=NULL;
for(i=0;i<numProtocols;i++)
{
    if((ProtocolInfo[i].dwServiceFlags1&XP1_QOS_SUPPORTED)&&
        (ProtocolInfo[i].dwServiceFlags1&XP1_CONNECTIONLESS)&&
        (ProtocolInfo[i].iAddressFamily==AF_INET)&&
        (ProtocolInfo[i].iProtocol==IPPROTO_UDP))
    {
        // then we have found the protocol we are looking for
        qosProto=&ProtocolInfo[i];
        break;
    }
} // for
if (qosProto)
{
    fprintf(stdout,"Using QoS Protocol %s.\n", qosProto->szProtocol);
}
else
{
    fprintf(stdout,
        "Could not find connectionless QoS aware protocol.\n");
    WSACleanup();
    return;
}
```

Once we locate the appropriate service provider, it is time to create a socket using the given provider. Again, the overlapped parameter is required such that overlapped IO can be enabled. Once the socket is created, we create an event object for it. The event object is then registered to receive QoS, Read, and Close Events.

```
// Open the socket
if((s = WSASocket(FROM_PROTOCOL_INFO , FROM_PROTOCOL_INFO ,
    FROM_PROTOCOL_INFO ,qosProto, 0, WSA_FLAG_OVERLAPPED)) ==
    INVALID_SOCKET)
{
    fprintf(stdout,"WSASocket(...) failed with error %d\n",
        WSAGetLastError());
    WSACleanup();
    return;
}

// Create an event
hEventObject = WSACreateEvent();
```

```
if (hEventObject == WSA_INVALID_EVENT)
{
    fprintf(stdout,"WSACreateEvent(): failed with error %d.\n",
        WSAGetLastError());
    closesocket(s);
    WSACleanup();
    return;
}

// Select appropriate events
if(WSAEventSelect(s, hEventObject,
    FD_QOS|FD_READ|FD_CLOSE) == SOCKET_ERROR)
{

    fprintf(stdout,"WSAEventSelect(): failed with error %d.\n",
        WSAGetLastError());
    closesocket(s);
    return;
}
```

Again, the socket must be bound to a port. This is a bit trickier with UDP utilizing QoS. The service provider may require that the port be explicitly bound to the local machine's address. We can find the local machine name via the gethostname() call. Running the hostname through gethostbyname() should then provide the local IP address. The bind port is set to the given local port.

```
// Bind the socket to a port and the local address
sin.sin_family = AF_INET;

if(gethostname(thisHostName, 50) == SOCKET_ERROR)
{
    fprintf(stdout,"gethostname(): failed\n");
    closesocket(s);
    return ;
}
pHostEntry = gethostbyname(thisHostName);
if (pHostEntry == NULL)
{
    fprintf(stdout,"gethostbyname(): failed to get local host name\n");
    closesocket(s);
    return;
}

memcpy(&sin.sin_addr.s_addr, pHostEntry->h_addr, 4);
sin.sin_port = htons(thisport);

fprintf(stdout,"Binding socket to addr=%s port=%d.\n",
    inet_ntoa(sin.sin_addr),thisport);

if (bind(s,(LPSOCKADDR) &sin,sizeof(sin)) == SOCKET_ERROR)
{
    nErr = WSAGetLastError();
```

```
        fprintf(stdout,"bind(): failed with error %d\n", nErr);
        closesocket(s);
        WSACleanup();
        return;
    }
```

Even though this is a UDP socket, we can still take advantage of WSAConnect() to provide our QoS information to the service provider. The socket is never really connected, but the service provider will use the connect call to gather the QoS data and send a PATH message to the peer and an RESV message whenever the peer's PATH arrives. This is simply the most direct way for the service provider to determine the peer's address.

We will use the provided token bucket parameters as both the sending and receiving parameters. The peers can then achieve bidirectional QoS communication.

```
// Connect to the peer address

// Set up quality of service info.
// No provider specific info.
QualityOfService.ProviderSpecific.len = 0;
QualityOfService.ProviderSpecific.buf = NULL;

FlowSpec = &QualityOfService.ReceivingFlowspec;
FlowSpec->TokenRate = tokenrate;
FlowSpec->TokenBucketSize = tokenbucketsize;
FlowSpec->PeakBandwidth = peakbandwidth;
FlowSpec->Latency = latency;
FlowSpec->DelayVariation = delayvariation;
FlowSpec->ServiceType = servicetype;
FlowSpec->MaxSduSize = maxsdusize;
FlowSpec->MinimumPolicedSize = minimumpolicedsize;
FlowSpec = &QualityOfService.SendingFlowspec;
FlowSpec->TokenRate = tokenrate;
FlowSpec->TokenBucketSize = tokenbucketsize;
FlowSpec->PeakBandwidth = peakbandwidth;
FlowSpec->Latency = latency;
FlowSpec->DelayVariation = delayvariation;
FlowSpec->ServiceType = servicetype;
FlowSpec->MaxSduSize = maxsdusize;
FlowSpec->MinimumPolicedSize = minimumpolicedsize;

if((iRetVal = WSAConnect(s, (sockaddr *)&sout, sizeof(sout),
NULL, NULL, &QualityOfService, NULL))
== SOCKET_ERROR)
{
    nErr = WSAGetLastError();
    if(nErr!=WSAEWOULDBLOCK)
    {
```

```
        fprintf(stdout,"connect(): failed with error %d\n", nErr);
        closesocket(s);
        WSACleanup();
        return;
    }
}
```

Keep in mind that the application can still modify its QoS parameters at any time via the WSAIoctl(SIO_SET_QOS) call, as follows:

```
// Set the QoS
overLapped.hEvent=hEventObject;
if(WSAIoctl(s, SIO_SET_QOS,
    (LPVOID) &QualityOfService,
    sizeof(QualityOfService),
    NULL, 0, &outSize, &overLapped, NULL) == SOCKET_ERROR)
{
    fprintf(stdout,"WSAIoctl(): failed with error %d.\n",
        WSAGetLastError());
    closesocket(s);
    WSACleanup();
    return;

}
```

Given the timing considerations for this program, we must make a few calculations before entering the event loop. First we must calculate the timer interval for the WSAWaitForMultipleEvents() call, given the specified data rate and packet size. The seconds start time and milliseconds start clock are then initialized. The event loop can then be entered as we wait for events during the given time interval.

```
// Calculate the appropriate timeout interval
interval=packetbufsize/datarate*1000;

// Get the starting time
starttime=time(NULL);
startclock=clock();

// Get current time in ms to initialize last send time
lastsendclock=clock();

// Start sending data by seting the timeout interval
// Initialize interval
nextinterval=interval;

eventLoop=TRUE;
while(eventLoop)
{
    eventVal=WSAWaitForMultipleEvents( 1,
        (const WSAEVENT FAR * )&hEventObject, FALSE, nextinterval,
        FALSE);
```

```
switch(eventVal)
{
```

The WSA_WAIT_TIMEOUT is triggered whenever the next interval time has expired. This is the mechanism we use to send to the peer at a regular rate. Each time the timer expires we send a packet and then reset the time interval until the program's duration is exceeded. Each sent packet holds the local process clock time, in milliseconds, that it was sent. This allows the initial timing for the packet to be known at the receiving peer.

```
case WSA_WAIT_TIMEOUT:
    fprintf(stdout,"Event timedout.\n");
    // Get current time in ms to record last send time
    lastsendclock=clock();

    currenttime=time(NULL);
    if(currenttime>=starttime+duration)
    {
        closesocket(s);
        fprintf(stdout,"Time Is Up!\n");
        fstarttime=(startclock);
        fendtime=(recvclock);
        fbytespersecond=(totalbytes/(fendtime-fstarttime))*
            CLOCKS_PER_SEC;

        fprintf(stdout,"Received %f Bytes/Sec\n",
            fbytespersecond);

        return;
    }

    // Prepare the packet with the send time in network byte
    // order
    ((clock_t*)packetbuf)[0]=htonl(lastsendclock);

    // Send to peer
    wsasendbuf.len=packetbufsize;
    wsasendbuf.buf=packetbuf;
    if(WSASendTo ( s, &wsasendbuf, 1, &bytessent, 0,
        NULL /*(struct sockaddr *)&sout*/, 0 /*sizeof(sout)*/,
        NULL,NULL)==SOCKET_ERROR)
    {
        fprintf(stdout,"WSASendTo(): failed with error %d.\n",
            WSAGetLastError());
    }
    else
    {
        totalBytesSent+=bytessent;
        fprintf(stdout,"Sent %d bytes to client.\n",
            bytessent);
    }
```

```
                  // Recalculate the timer accounting for any skew

          break; // case WSA_TIMEOUT:
```

The next snippet is the case statement for the event object. When the event object is triggered we determine what event transpired. If it is a QoS event we use WSAIoctl(SIO_GET_QOS) to retrieve the QoS information. If the event was a read event, a data packet is read, and the time it arrived is printed to standard output. The packet's time stamp as provided by the sender is also printed for comparison.

```
          case WSA_WAIT_EVENT_0:

              fprintf(stdout,"Event was triggered\n");
              iRetVal = WSAEnumNetworkEvents(s, hEventObject, &events);
              fprintf(stdout,"EnumNetworkEvents returned %x on socket\n",
                  events.lNetworkEvents);
              if (iRetVal == SOCKET_ERROR)
              {
                  fprintf(stdout,"WSAEnumNetworkEvents FAILED\n");
                  return;
              }

              // Check for QOS Event
              if (events.lNetworkEvents & FD_QOS)
              {
                  fprintf(stdout,"QOS event\n");

                  // Get the QoS
                  overLapped.hEvent=hEventObject; // Associate with event
                  WSAResetEvent( hEventObject );

                  while(WSAIoctl(s, SIO_GET_QOS,
                      NULL,
                      0,
                      (LPVOID) &QualityOfService2,
                      sizeof(QualityOfService2),
                      &outSize, NULL, NULL) != SOCKET_ERROR)
                  {
                      FlowSpec = &QualityOfService2.ReceivingFlowspec;
                      fprintf(stdout,
                          "ReceivingQOS:TknRate=%d,BDepth=%d,PeakR=%d\n",
                          FlowSpec->TokenRate,
                          FlowSpec->TokenBucketSize,
                          FlowSpec->PeakBandwidth);

                      FlowSpec = &QualityOfService2.SendingFlowspec;

                      fprintf(stdout,
                          "SendingQOS:TknRate=%d,BDepth=%d,PeakR=%d\n",
                          FlowSpec->TokenRate,
                          FlowSpec->TokenBucketSize,
```

```
                            FlowSpec->PeakBandwidth);
                }
                fprintf(stdout,
                    "WSAIoctl() SIO_GET_QOS failed with error %d.\n",
                    WSAGetLastError());
        }
        // Check for READ Event
        if (events.lNetworkEvents & FD_READ)
        {
            fprintf(stdout,"READ event\n");

            if (events.iErrorCode[FD_READ_BIT] == WSAENETDOWN)
            {
                fprintf(stdout,"READ WSAENETDOWN\n");
                return;
            }

            // Receive from peer
            srecvlen=sizeof(srecv);
            bytesRecvd = recvfrom ( s, (char *) recvpacketbuf,
            recvpacketsize, 0, (struct sockaddr *) &srecv,
            &srecvlen);

        if (bytesRecvd != SOCKET_ERROR)
        {
            // Note current time.
            recvclock=clock();
            fprintf(stdout,
                "Received %d bytes at %d sent at %d\n",
                bytesRecvd,recvclock,
                ntohl(((clock_t *)recvpacketbuf)[0]));
        }
        else
        {
            fprintf(stdout,
                "recvfrom(): failed with error %d.\n",
                WSAGetLastError());
        }
        // Total number of bytes received.
        totalbytes+=bytesRecvd;
    }
    // Check for CLOSE Event
    if (events.lNetworkEvents & FD_CLOSE)
    {
        fprintf(stdout,"CLOSE event\n");

        return;
    }

break; // case WSA_WAIT_EVENT_0

default:

break;

}
```

Before the event loop repeats, we must also make sure that our interval timers are correct. If an event was triggered, it is necessary to recover the proper next-send-time period to account for the event's interruption.

```
// Reset the interval to account for event processing

thisclock=clock();
thisinterval=(int)(thisclock-lastsendclock);
if(thisinterval>=interval)
    nextinterval=0;
else if(thisinterval<interval)
    nextinterval=interval-thisinterval;

    }

}
```

That completes our presentation of the UDP peer program's code. This simple program can be used to simulate the functionality of real-time applications. It can also be used as a simple traffic generator. This is a useful feature for testing the effects of congestion on other QoS-protected and non-QoS-protected traffic alike.

Compiling and Running the Programs

The preceding programs can be compiled using the Microsoft Visual C++ 6.0 command-line compiler cl.exe. The programs also need to be linked with the WinSock 2 library, ws2_32.lib. The complication command should look something like this:

cl programsourcefile.cpp ws2_32.lib

The programs can then be run from the DOS command line. Just type the name of the compiled program and supply the required arguments. For example, if you are running the peer programs on two hosts (A and B), the command line might appear as follows:

Host A: peer a=HostB

Host B: peer a=HostA

The program's output can be redirected to a file for later viewing and analysis. This is accomplished by redirecting standard output via the ">" character as follows:

peer a=HostB > logfile.txt

The "logfile" will then contain the output of the peer program.

Summary

This chapter examined QoS application development. Applications need to be developed with reliability and scalability in mind. As the Internet is not a single network technology, applications must be prepared to adapt and make the best of whatever the network can provide. Playback buffering provides a mechanism by which applications can restore ordering and timing to a media stream. Layering provides applications with scalable content, usable over a range of network capacities. Finally, we investigated some of the API's valuable for developing QoS-aware applications and showed three example programs.

RFCs (Request for Comments) are typically Internet standards or documents accepted for informational purposes.

Note on Internet Drafts: Internet Drafts are Internet Engineering Task Force (IETF) documents that are works in progress and not (yet) standards. Such documents are updated or refreshed every six months (or sooner), and each iteration of a draft receives an incremental index. Updated versions of a draft will typically have the same title but a different index. The titles and dates for the Internet Drafts listed here are accurate as of November 1998.

[ATM] *ATM Theory and Application,* David E. McDysan, Darren L. Spohn, New York: McGraw-Hill, 1994.

[Comer-TCPIP] *Internetworking with TCP/IP,* D. Comer, Upper Saddle River, NJ: Prentice Hall, 1995.

[COPS] "The Common Open Policy Service (COPS) Protocol," J. Boyle, R. Cohen, D. Durham, S. Herzog, R. Rajan, A. Sastry, Internet Draft, draft-ietf-rap-cops-04.txt, December 1998.

[COPS-RSVP] "COPS Usage for RSVP," J. Boyle, R. Cohen, D. Durham, S. Herzog, R. Rajan, A. Sastry, Internet Draft, draft-ietf-rap-cops-rsvp-01.txt, November 1998.

[Digital-Systems] *Digital Control System Analysis and Design,* Charles L. Phillips, H. Troy Nagel, Upper Saddle River, NJ: Prentice Hall, 1990.

[Efficient-Fair] "Efficient Fair Queuing Using Deficit Round Robin," M. Shreedhar, G. Varghese, *Proc. SIGCOMM '95,* Boston, August 1995.

[Fair-Queuing] "Analysis and Simulation of a Fair Queuing Algorithm," A. Demers, S. Keshav, S. Shenker, *Journal of Internetworking: Research and Experience,* 1, pp. 3–26, 1990.

[Gigabit] *Gigabit Networking,* C. Partridge, Reading, MA: Addison-Wesley, 1994.

[GPS] "A Generalized Processor Sharing Approach to Flow Control in Integrated Services Networks," A. K. J. Parekh, MIT Laboratory for Information and Decision Systems, Report LIDS-TH-2089, February 1992.

[IDENTITY] "Identity Representation for RSVP," S. Yadav, R. Yavatkar, R. Pabbati, P. Ford, T. Moore, S. Herzog, Internet Draft, draft-ietf-rap-rsvp-identity-01.txt, January 1999.

[ISSLL-802] "A Framework for Providing Integrated Services Over Shared and Switched IEEE 802 LAN Technologies," A. Ghanwani, J. Wayne Pace, V. Srinivasan, A. Smith, M. Seaman, Internet Draft draft-ietf-issll-is802-framework-05.txt, May 1998.

[LDAP] *LDAP: Programming Directory-Enabled Applications with Light-weight Directory Access Protocol,* T. Howes, M. Smith, Indianapolis, IN: Macmillan Technical Publishing, 1997.

[Leaky-Bucket] "New Directions in Communications (or Which Way to the Information Age?)," J. Turner, *Proc. Zurich Seminar on Digital Communication,* March 1986, pp. 25–32.

[L4Lookup] "Fast and Scalable Layer Four Switching," V. Srinivasan, G. Varghese, S. Suri, M. Waldvogel, *Computer Communication Review Proc. ACM SIGCOMM '98,* vol. 28, no. 4, October 1998.

[LinkSharing] "Link-Sharing and Resource Management Models for Packet Networks," S. Floyd, V. Jacobson, *IEEE ACM Transactions on Networking,* vol. 3, no. 4, August 1995.

[Multicast] *IP Multicasting,* Dave Kosiur, New York: John Wiley & Sons, 1998.

[MD5] "RSVP Cryptographic Authentication," Internet Draft, Fred Baker, Bob Lindall, Mohit Talwar, February 1999.

[Networking] *An Engineering Approach to Computer Networking, ATM Networks, the Internet, and the Telephone Network,* S. Keshav, Reading MA: Addison-Wesley, 1997.

[PRIORITY] "Preemption Priority Policy Element," S. Herzog, Internet Draft, draft-ietf-rap-signaled-priority-00.txt, November 1998.

[QoS] *Quality of Service: Delivering QoS on the Internet and in Corporate Networks,* Paul Ferguson, Geoff Huston, New York: John Wiley & Sons, 1998.

[RAP Framework] "A Framework for Policy-Based Admission Control," R. Yavatkar, D. Pendarakis, R. Guerin, Internet Draft, draft-ietf-rap-framework-01.txt, November 1998.

[RAPI] "An RSVP Application Programming Interface," R. Braden, D. Hoffman, draft-ietf-rsvp-rapi-01.ps, February 1998.

[RealApps] "Supporting Real-Time Applications in an Integrated Services Packet Architecture and Mechanism," D. Clark, S. Shenker, L. Zhang, *Proc. SIGCOMM '92*, Baltimore, MD, August 1992.

RFC 768, "User Datagram Protocol," J. Postel, August 1980.

RFC 791, "Internet Protocol," ISI, September 1981.

RFC 793, "Transmission Control Protocol," ISI, September 1981.

RFC 950, "Internet Standard Subnetting Procedure," J. Mogul, J. Postel, August 1985.

RFC 1075, "Distance Vector Multicast Routing Protocol," D. Waitzman, C. Partridge, S. E. Deering, November 1998.

RFC 1363, "A Proposed Flow Specification," Network Working Group, C. Partridge, September 1992.

RFC 1458, "Requirements for Multicast Protocols," R. Braudes, S. Zabele, May 1993.

RFC 1584, "Multicast Extensions to OSPF," J. Moy, March 1994.

RFC 1889, "RTP: A Transport Protocol for Real-Time Applications," Audio-Video Transport Working Group, H. Schulzrinne, S. Casner, R. Frederick, V. Jacobson, January 1996.

RFC 1890, "RTP Profile for Audio and Video Conferences with Minimal Control." Audio-Video Transport Working Group, H. Schulzrinne, January 1996.

RFC 2022, "Support for Multicast over UNI 3.0/3.1 Based ATM Networks," G. Armitage, November 1996.

RFC 2117, "Protocol Independent Multicast-Sparse Mode (PIM-SM): Protocol Specification," D. Estrin, D. Farinacci, A. Helmy, D. Thaler, S. Deering, M. Handley, V. Jacobson, C. Liu, P. Sharma, L. Wei, June 1997.

RFC 2201, "Core Based Trees (CBT) Multicast Routing Architecture," A. Ballardie, September 1997.

RFC 2205, "Resource reSerVation Protocol—Version 1 Functional Specification," R. Braden, L. Zhang, S. Berson, S. Herzog, S. Jamin.

RFC 2206, "RSVP Management Information Base Using SMIv2," F. Baker, J. Krawczyk, A. Sastry, Standards Track, September 1997.

RFC 2209, "Resource reSerVation Protocol (RSVP)—Version 1 Message Processing Rules," R. Braden, L. Zhang, September 1997.

RFC 2210, "The Use of RSVP with IETF Integrated Services," J. Wroclawski, September 1997.

RFC 2211, "Specification of the Controlled-Load Network Element Service," J. Wroclawski, September 1997.

RFC 2212, "Specification of Guaranteed Quality of Service," S. Shenker, C. Partridge, R. Guerin, September 1997.

RFC 2215, "General Characterization Parameters for Integrated Service Network Elements," S. Shenker, J. Wroclawski, September 1997.

RFC 2225, "Classical IP and ARP over ATM," M. Laubach, J. Halpern, April 1998.

RFC 2327 "SDP: Session Description Protocol," M. Handley, V. Jacobson, April 1998.

RFC 2379, "RSVP over ATM Implementation Guidelines," L. Berger, August 1998.

RFC 2380, "RSVP over ATM Implementation Requirements," L. Berger, August 1998.

RFC 2381, "Interoperation of Controlled-Load Service and Guaranteed Service with ATM," M. Garrett, M. Borden, August 1998.

RFC 2382, "A Framework for Integrated Services and RSVP over ATM," E. Crawley, et al., August 1998.

RFC 2474, "Definition of the Differentiated Services Field (DS Field) in the IPv4 and IPv6 Headers," K. Nichols, S. Blake, F. Baker, D. Black, December 1998.

RFC 2475, "An Architecture for Differentiated Services," S. Blake, D. Black, M. Carlson, E. Davies, Z. Wang, W. Weiss, December 1998.

[Routing] *Routing in the Internet,* Christian Huitema, Upper Saddle River, NJ: Prentice Hall, 1995.

[RSVP-DiffServ] "A Framework for Use of RSVP with Diff-serv Networks," Y. Bernet, R. Yavatkar, P. Ford, F. Baker, L. Zhang, K. Nichols, M. Speer, Internet Draft, draft-ietf-diffserv-rsvp-01.txt, November 1998.

[RSVP-EXT] "RSVP Extensions for Policy Control," S. Herzog, Internet Draft, draft-ietf-rap-rsvp-ext-01.txt, November 1998.

[SBM] "SBM (Subnet Bandwidth Manager)," R. Yavatkar, D. Hoffman, Y. Bernet, F. Baker, M. Speer, Internet Draft, draft-ietf-issll-is802-sbm-07.txt, November 1998.

[Scalable] "Scalable High Speed IP Routing Lookups," M. Waldvogel, G. Varghese, J. Turner, B. Plattner, *Proc. SIGCOMM '97*, October 1997.

[SCHEMA] "Policy Framework Core Information Model," J. Strassner, E. Ellesson, Internet Draft, draft-ietf-policy-core-schema-00.txt, November 1998.

[Small] "Small Forwarding Tables for Fast Routing Lookups," M. Degermark, A. Brodnik, S. Carlsson, S. Pink, *Proc. ACM SIGCOM '97*, October 1997.

[TCP-Illustrated] *TCP/IP Illustrated*, vol. 1, Richard W. Stevens, Reading, MA: Addison-Wesley, 1994.

[802-srvc] "Integrated Service Mappings on IEEE 802 Networks," M. Seaman, A. Smith, E. Crawley, J. Wroclawski, Internet Draft, draft-ietf-issll-is802-svc-mapping-03.txt, November 1998.

[802.1D] "Information technology—Telecommunications and information exchange between systems—Local and metropolitan area networks—Common specifications—Part 3: Media Access Control (MAC) Bridges: Revision (Incorporating IEEE P802.1p: Traffic Class Expediting and Dynamic Multicast Filtering)," ISO/IEC Final CD 15802-3 IEEE P802.1D/D16, March 1998.

[802.1Q] "IEEE Standards for Local and Metropolitan Area Networks: For Virtual Bridged Local Area Networks," IEEE Draft Standard P802.1Q/D11, July 1998.

Address   A unique identifier used to identify the source or destination of a datagram.

Administrative domain   A portion of the Internet or an intranet that is controlled by a single authoritative organization. Implements its own policies and ultimately controls all traffic that passes though its domain.

Aggregation   The process of multiplexing a number of separate flows or connections over a single physical or logical communications medium.

API (application programming interface)   A software interface that applications can use to interact with the specific operating system facilities or other system daemons.

ARP (Address Resolution Protocol)   Protocol used to discover the MAC address that corresponds to a particular IP address on a LAN.

AS (autonomous system)   An independently administrated portion of the Internet that has its own routing policies and external connectivity advertisements.

ATM (Asynchronous Transfer Mode)   An asynchronous switched network technology characterized by 53-byte cells operating with respect to virtual circuits. Developed to integrate voice and data services onto a common medium.

Authentication   A method to determine securely and unambiguously the identity of a user, application, or other logical entity.

Best-effort   A service level of datagram delivery that unpredictably degrades as congestion increases because it provides no bandwidth or delay guarantees.

BGP (Border Gateway Protocol)   An Internet router advertisement protocol used to provide connectivity information across autonomous system borders. Provides reachability information, not network topology information.

Blockade state A temporary state setup in RSVP routers that prevents the continuous merging of a reservation that causes a capacity admission control failure in an upstream node.

Border router A router that sits on the border of an autonomous system or administrative domain. Such nodes typically must enforce border security, bandwidth, and routing policies between different organizations.

Broadcast The process of sending information to all reachable destinations simultaneously.

Capacity admission control An RSVP component that manages capacity resources so such resources are never overallocated in order to support QoS.

CBQ (class-based queuing) A queuing methodology where traffic is associated with a particular class. Traffic is queued with respect to its class such that certain classes can achieve higher QoS.

CBT (core-based trees) A method for multicast routing that utilizes a core node. The core node is equivalent to the root of a spanning tree. The root is the designated distribution point for a multicast session.

Circuit switching The concept of connecting a physical or logical circuit between a source and a destination.

Class A address IP address space segment that provides for 128 networks with 16,777,216 possible hosts per network. The first bit of the IPv4 address is set to zero for Class A addresses.

Class B address IP address space segment that provides for 16,384 networks with 65,536 possible hosts per network. The second bit of the IPv4 address is set to zero for Class B addresses (first bit is set to 1 in this case).

Class C address IP address space segment that provides for 4,194,304 networks with 256 possible hosts per network. The third bit of the IPv4 address is set to zero for Class C addresses (first two bits are set to 1).

Class D address IP address space segment reserved for multicast addresses. The fourth bit of the IPv4 address is set to zero for Class D addresses (first three bits are set to 1).

Codec (coder-decoder) The hardware or software that compresses or decompresses a specific digital media type.

Connectionless   A communication methodology that does not require establishment of a path through the network or advance negotiation between two end points before packetized data may be sent.

Connection-oriented   A communications methodology that requires a physical or logical connection to be established before data transfer may begin.

Controlled Load Service   An Integrated Services service type that provides a QoS equivalent to an unloaded network with the specified amount of bandwidth.

COPS (Common Open Policy Service) Protocol   A stateful request-response protocol that can be used by a network device to communicate with a remote decision point to get policy decisions or configuration information. The COPS protocol runs over TCP.

CRC (cyclic redundancy check)   An error-detection algorithm typically used to verify that a packet's header or its data was not corrupted along the data path.

Datagram   A network addressed packet of data that can be routed independently of any other similarly addressed packets. An IP packet is a datagram.

Data path   The path a data packet travels along a network from its source to its destination.

Delay   The variable amount of time it takes a packet to traverse a network, depending on the path taken or the level of congestion.

Dense-mode multicast routing   Routing algorithms that assume the network is densely populated with multicast group members interested in a particular session. Algorithms that broadcast multicast packets throughout the network generally assume this kind of density.

DiffServ (Differentiated Services)   A simplified QoS architecture based on categorizing IP packets by their DS bytes (previously known as the Type of Service field of the IP header) in order to determine an appropriate PHB.

Distance vector   A routing technique that discovers the shortest path though a network utilizing distance information provided by neighbors of a network node.

Downstream   In the direction that is toward the destination. The same direction a data flow travels through a network.

DSBM (Designated SBM)   The one SBM elected to manage bandwidth on a shared link.

DS byte (Differentiated Services Byte)   The byte in the IP header that specifies the handling characteristics of the corresponding packet. Used to be the Legacy TOS and IP Precedence fields of the IP header.

DVMRP (Distance-Vector Multicast Routing Protocol)   A multicast routing protocol based on reverse path forwarding that uses distance vectors to determine the multicast distribution tree.

Encapsulation   The process of enclosing one transport protocol message within the data portion of another.

Ethernet   Traditionally, a type of shared link network technology typically used in LANs. Recent innovations have led to Switched Ethernet, which more closely resembles a point-to-point network technology.

FF (Fixed Filter)   An RSVP sender selection style that provides explicit sender selection and devoted QoS protection per flow.

FIFO (first-in, first-out)   A simple form of queuing where the first packet into a queue is the first packet out of the queue, and all subsequent packets are delivered in the order in which they arrived.

Flow   A sequence of data packets following the same path through a network from the same source host and port to the same destination address and port.

Fragmentation   In the context of IP, fragmentation refers to the process of breaking large packets into smaller packet fragments for the transmission over packet-size restricted links.

Full duplex   Bidirectional communication over bidirectional media. For example, two sources connected by a full-duplex link can send to one another simultaneously.

GQoS (generic QoS)   A generalized extension to the WinSock 2 APIs that provides QoS information to the appropriate service provider.

Guaranteed service   A type of QoS service that provides mathematically provable guarantees on both bandwidth and delay.

Half duplex   Bidirectional communication over a shared medium. That is, all sending directions broadcast over the shared medium. Only one source on the shared medium can successfully send at a time.

Header Protocol-specific information contained in a packet that typically precedes application data carried in the packet.

Hop A node (a host system, router, switch, etc.) constituting a network or the path of a data flow.

Host Typically an end station connected to a network capable of sending and receiving datagrams.

HTTP (HyperText Transfer Protocol) A protocol for transferring information based on a URL between Web servers and clients. Runs over TCP for connection-oriented data delivery.

ICMP (Internet Control Message Protocol) A control protocol that runs over IP and provides information related to IP packet handling, such as dropped packets, echo replies, and so forth.

I-D (Internet Draft) An IETF document that is still in the open development process. Drafts are not standards and are likely to change. Eventually, a draft can be standardized to become an RFC or simply an information document.

IETF (Internet Engineering Task Force) A standards organization devoted to the development and standardization of new Internet protocols and technologies.

IGMP (Internet Group Management Protocol) A protocol used by end hosts to advertise to routers their interest in a particular multicast group.

Incoming interface The RSVP-aware interface on which a QoS protected data flow arrives.

Integrated Services A standard set of specifications developed by the Integrated Services Working Group of the IETF that formalized QoS characterization requirements, resource sharing, packet-dropping allowances, usage feedback, and a resource reservation model for Internet devices.

Integrity object RSVP object used to verify that no unknown party has tampered with the contents of an RSVP message since the last integrity-aware hop.

Interface The termination point for a physical or logical link within a network device.

IP (Internet Protocol)   A ubiquitous network layer protocol that is used for all datagram communication in the Internet.

IP address   In the Internet, an IP address is a 32- or 128-bit value that is used to uniquely identify a host or a device connected to the network.

IPv4   The traditional version of the Internet Protocol limited to a 32-bit address space. Allows for packet fragmentation and reconstruction.

IPv6   The next-generation version of the Internet Protocol, which uses a huge 128-bit address space. IPv6 has also somewhat simplified the original IP, removing little-used features such as packet fragmentation.

ISP (Internet service provider)   A company or other organization that provides Internet access and Internet-related services to end users and/or corporate customers.

ISSLL (Integrated Services over Specific Link Layers)   A Working Group of the IETF chartered to map the Integrated Services architecture to a variety of link layer technologies such as Ethernet, ATM, point-to-point links, and so forth.

Jitter   The difference between the minimal and maximal delay in delivering a stream of related datagrams. To an end user, jitter would appear as annoying interruptions in a real-time interaction due to the application having to wait for delayed datagrams.

KR (killer reservations)   A problem that arises when a destination continuously attempts to make too large of a reservation that prevents the establishment of smaller reservations for the same session.

LAN (local area network)   A computer data network that is intended to support a relatively small number of hosts within a single physical networking technology.

Latency   Synonym for *delay* in the context of QoS.

Leaky bucket   A traffic-shaping algorithm where bursty input traffic can be buffered and then released at a constant rate.

LPDP (Local Policy Decision Point)   A module that exists on a policy enforcement point that can locally make policy decisions in the absence of a remote PDP.

LPM (local policy module)   A policy component that resides on a router or switch that can make policy decisions or interact with a remote policy decision point.

Merge point   The RSVP-aware network device that merges two or more shared-filter-style reservations for the same multicast session.

Merging   In the context of RSVP, the act of combining multiple reservations for the same multicast session or flow such that a single representative (maximum) reservation is forwarded upstream.

MIB (management information base)   A simple form of management database that can be supported by network devices such that their current operating state can be accessed though a common namespace model.

MOSPF (Multicast Open Shortest Path First)   An extension to the OSPF protocol for support of multicast routing.

MTU (maximum transmission unit)   The largest-size packet that can be successfully forwarded over a network.

Multicast   A form of multipoint communications where the same information can be simultaneously sent to a select number of destinations.

Next hop   The next downstream RSVP-aware hop for a particular flow.

Node   A generic term for a network forwarding device, host, or other system comprising part of a network.

Object   In the context of RSVP, a variable-size chunk of data identified by a type value and bounded by a length value used to comprise RSVP messages.

OPWA (One Pass With Advertising)   A reservation model where the source sends a PATH message that collects delay and capacity information as it passes though each downstream hop. The collected information can be used by the destinations to predict the end-to-end service from the data path.

OSI (Open Systems Interconnection) Reference Model   A useful watermark for logically segmenting a network protocol stack into its operational layers.

OSPF (Open Shortest Path First)   A routing protocol that provides topological information to all routing devices. The routing devices use this information to generate network maps from which they can generate shortest-path routing tables.

Outgoing interface   The RSVP-aware interface from which a QoS protected data flow is forwarded.

Packet   Another term for *datagram* often used in the Internet.

Packet classifier   A traffic control module that can classify a packet based on its source, destination, and port information for purposes of applying QoS protection.

Packet scheduler   A traffic control module that schedules packets for delivery based on their QoS requirements and conformance to any provisioned traffic agreements.

Packet switching   The concept of independently switching or routing individual network addressed packets from their source to their destination.

Path message (PATH)   An RSVP message generated by the data source that describes a particular flow's traffic characteristics and provides delay and capacity information about the data path.

Path state   The state in a network device that holds information related to RSVP PATH messages.

PDP (Policy Decision Point)   The local or remote entity that is capable of making a policy decision.

Peers   Hosts on a network that communicate with each other as equals.

PEP (Policy Enforcement Point)   A switch, router, or other networked component that is capable of actually enforcing policy decisions. In the case of RSVP, a PEP can be an RSVP-aware device that resides along the data path and can either allow or deny reservations.

PHB (per-hop behavior)   A DiffServ concept that specifies how specifically marked packets are to be treated by network devices.

Policing   The act of ensuring that a flow is adhering to agreed-upon QoS traffic characteristics.

Policy control   The ability to control access to network resources based on administratively assigned policies categorized by who, when, where.

Port   A logical assignment on an end station that can be used to identify particular source/destination applications or multiplex multiple flows from or to a particular host. Also used to describe a physical interface on a network device.

Previous hop The next upstream RSVP-aware hop along the data path from the perspective of a particular flow.

Processing delay Delay associated with routing, classification, and scheduling of a packet by a network device.

Propagation delay Delay caused by the time it takes to transmit a datagram over a physical link.

QoS (quality of service) The ability of a network to support a variety of services with different delay and bandwidth requirements.

QoSR (quality of service routing) The ability of a routing algorithm to choose best routes through a network based on the QoS requirements of the routed traffic.

RAPI (RSVP API) An API used on some UNIX platforms. It allows applications to communicate QoS requests and information to an RSVP daemon.

Real-time intolerant Used to describe applications that have tight packet delay and network capacity requirements.

Real-time tolerant Used to describe real-time applications that can utilize techniques such as buffering, which reduce the need for tight bounds on packet delay.

RED (random early detection) A network congestion control technique intended to work with TCP's congestion avoidance algorithm. RED attempts to detect onset of congestion and randomly selects packets for discard from a forwarding device's queue before it becomes congested. This serves as an implicit notification to TCP stacks to throttle back their sending data rates, thus avoiding congestion collapse.

Reservation message (RESV) The RSVP message generated by destinations that carries a QoS request hop-by-hop back to the sender or first merge point.

Reservation state The state in a network device that holds information related to RSVP RESV messages.

RIP (Routing Information Protocol) A simple and popular distance-vector routing protocol used widely in the Internet for routing within an autonomous system.

Route pinning The act of setting state in network devices such that they can remember the route associated with a particular flow.

Router A network device responsible for forwarding packets from their source toward their destination.

Routing table A table containing the next hop information for routing a packet over the shortest path from its source to its destination.

RSVP (Resource ReSerVation Protocol) The Integrated Services–defined resource reservation protocol used to reserve resources for purposes of achieving QoS over the Internet. It is based on a data source sending PATH messages describing a flow's traffic characteristics and destinations sending RESV messages to actually reserve resources for the said flows.

RTCP (Real-Time Control Protocol) A control protocol used in conjunction with RTP for providing feedback on measured delay, jitter, and packet loss in real-time flow.

RTP (Real-Time Transport Protocol) A protocol carried over UDP and used for providing timing and sequencing information for real-time data flows.

RTT (round-trip time) The time it takes a packet to be echoed from its source to its destination and back.

SBM (Subnet Bandwidth Manager) An extension to the RSVP protocol that allows resource reservations and mapping of integrated services within IEEE-802 style networks such as Ethernet.

SE (shared explicit filter) A shared reservation style that allows for explicit sender selection.

Shaping The act of forcing a traffic flow into compliance with its agreed-upon traffic characteristics.

Simplex Unidirectional (one-way) communication. RSVP reserves resources from the network for a simplex flow.

Soft state Concept of a self-administrating state that will eventually time-out and be removed if not regularly refreshed.

Spanning tree The logical reduction of a network topology into a simple hierarchy such that redundant paths are eliminated.

Streaming A method for downloading an audio and/or visual file while simultaneously playing it for the user.

Subnetwork   A logical portion of a larger network class used to make Internet addressing more scalable.

Switch   A device functionally similar to a router that typically supports cut-through forwarding and can potentially forward datagrams within a layer 2 network.

TCP (Transmission Control Protocol)   A transport protocol in the TCP/IP protocol suite that provides reliable connection-oriented data stream delivery. TCP also provides mechanisms for congestion control.

TDM (time-division multiplexing)   A simple mechanism for digital data transport where a number of sessions can utilize the same physical link by being segmented into repeating time slots.

Token bucket   A flexible characterization and shaping model for traffic control that accommodates bursty data flows. It works because the token bucket may transmit data at a peak data rate so long as it has credits available. Credits are applied to the token bucket up to the bucket's capacity. In the token bucket model, a burst can be serviced at its peak rate up to the number of credits available.

Traffic control   A set of packet classification, packet scheduling, and capacity admission control modules that provide QoS functionality on an RSVP-aware network device.

TTL (Time to Live)   A field in the IP header that controls how long a packet can exist in the Internet. The field can specify 0 to 255 seconds but is often used as a hop count and is decremented by each router through which an IP packet passes.

Tunneling   The ability to logically aggregate a number of RSVP sessions through a DiffServ network.

UDP (User Datagram Protocol)   A simple form of connectionless transport that runs over IP. UDP has provisions for application port identification and can detect data corruption.

Unicast   Communication between just two hosts.

Upstream   In the direction of a data source. This is the reverse direction of a data flow.

WAN (wide area network)   A large-scale network that connects a large number of potentially distant hosts.

WF (wildcard filter)   A shared reservation style that automatically selects all available sources.

WFQ (weighted fair queuing)   The combination of fair queuing, where each data flow has a devoted traffic queue to ensure each flow gets a fair share of available bandwidth, and a relative queue weight that causes some queues to gain a higher share of link time than others. Used to support QoS.

WRED (weighted random early detection)   A form of RED where the threshold for randomly selecting packets for discard is dependent on the packets' relative priority. Higher-priority packets will have a larger drop threshold (which means lower probability of discard).